PERSPECTIVES ON AMERICAN POLITICAL MEDIA

Gary C. Woodward
Trenton State College

Allyn and Bacon
Boston • London • Toronto • Sydney • Tokyo • Singapore

Vice-President, Editor-in-Chief, Humanities: Joseph Opiela
Editorial Assistant: Kate Tolini
Editorial-Production Administrator: Joe Sweeney
Editorial-Production Service: Walsh Associates
Composition Buyer: Linda Cox
Manufacturing Buyer: Megan Cochran
Cover Administrator: Suzanne Harbison

Library of Congress Cataloging-in-Publication Data

Woodward, Gary C.
    Perspectives on American political media/Gary C. Woodward.
        p. cm.
    Includes bibliographical references and index.
    ISBN 0-205-26250-3
    1. Mass media—Political aspects—United States. 2. United States—Politics and government—1989- I. Title.
    P95.82.U6W66 1996
    302.23'0973—dc20   96-8864
                                                         CIP
Printed in the United States of America

10 9 8 7 6 5 4 3   00 99

BRSE
11/00

For Jan,
and the
citizens of Pennsylvania

CONTENTS

PREFACE

Books that talk about politics and the mass media tend to fall into several categories. The most popular are usually instant replays of moments from the current presidency or the last election. They are often written by insiders—journalists, aides, and even former first ladies—and usually seek to "correct" mistaken impressions left by the daily press. Their best feature is the chance they offer the reader to see the political process as it looks in the details of a specific moment. Another collection of books, nominally more "academic," see the political process as the product of the political and media organizations that bring its rhetoric and drama into the homes of Americans. In these sometimes lively studies, television is usually the scene of the action. And those who construct or manipulate its stories tend to be the major players. The best of these take a longer view, offering the important reminder that the features of contemporary political discourse are evolutionary rather than revolutionary.

Still another set of texts examines current institutions like Congress, the presidency, or the press. These studies rightly assume that the major institutions of politics and the media are partly reflections of their audiences. And they usually equate disturbingly low levels of political interest and awareness with the practices of these bodies. Most books in the last group are pessimistic, noting the need for a serious overhaul of the institutions that are supposed to sustain our political culture. The best also address the failings of an increasingly distracted American public, whose knowledge of political affairs paradoxically lags far behind dramatic advances in media resources.

This book intentionally mixes these approaches, not out of a desire to be all things to all readers (perhaps the ultimate political instinct!), but to offer a variety of perspectives that represent the variegated nature of American political culture. Like the society it comes from, political discourse in the United

States is not easily reduced to one or two dimensions. It cannot be adequately represented in sets of facts or simple theories. The result here is a conscious choice to mix theory with critical analysis, and abstract description with extended examples and case studies.

There is an inevitable price to be paid for a selectivity of approaches that combines theory with criticism, "dense description" of a interesting political moment with a broad summary of national trend. But this blend offers a look at the varied textures of our political life that a more uniform approach can easily miss.

In these choices certain emphases will be apparent. *Perspectives on American Political Media* pays more attention to the presidency than to local politics, and devotes more space to television as a carrier of political information than to magazines and newspapers. This study also attempts to identify some defining features of the national polity, features that directly or indirectly effect media content. This emphasis sometimes takes us to the work of cultural observers who are sometimes not included in politics texts, such as Richard Sennett, Joshua Meyrowitz, Thomas Szasz, Kenneth Burke, Christopher Lasch, and Robert Hughes. And these pages generally treat political discourse targeted to the public as inherently electoral in style, a view that lends itself to considering campaign techniques in most of the chapters of the book, rather than just one.

Thanks are due to the Trenton State College Faculty and Instructional Research Committee for a series of summer grants that provided the time and incentive to write. Over the last few years I have also benefited from briefings and seminars provided by C-SPAN, the National Endowment for the Humanities, the International Radio and Television Society, and CBS. In addition, countless colleagues and students have contributed suggestions, ideas, or support. John Pollock, Hal Hogstrom, Mary Adamson-King, Paul Frye, Justinc Gustainis, Ann Tilson, Carol and Neil Rowe, Bruce Bryski, Jennette Kenner Muir, and Amy Toth are some who have offered helpful information or advice. I am also indebted to Praeger Publishers for permission to quote at length from my earlier work on the Persian Gulf War; and to Joseph Opiela and Susannah Davidson of Allyn and Bacon, whose help was crucial to completing this project.

I would also like to thank the following reviewers: Ed Bassett, University of Washington; Kari Whittenberger-Keith, University of Louisville; Daniel W. Fleitas, University of North Carolina at Charlotte; J. Ronald Milavsky, University of Connecticut; Edmond Constantini, University of California/Davis; Silvo Lenart, Purdue University; Robert Sahr, Oregon State University; Bruce G. Bryski, Buffalo State College; and Steven Livingston, The George Washington University.

For Jan Robbins, my wife and best friend, no simple thank you can express my debt. Her eternal good cheer was effective inoculation against the frustrations that come when energies and time run low.

INTRODUCTION: POLITICS, MEDIA, AND DEMOCRACY

> *"The job is much tougher than I realized," Clinton said. "I did not realize the importance of communications and the overriding importance of what is on the evening news. If I am not on, or there with a message, someone else is, with their message."*[1]

The relationship that exists between the political world and the mass media often seems like an unusual form of courtship. Each needs the other, but the bonds of attraction are based more on suspicion than affection. Participants representing each side have clearly learned all the right moves, and the names for them. They plan their steps carefully, using a familiar language that signifies their caution in pursuing the relationship. On any given day the courtship strategy of those managing the presidency often includes a message of the day designed to set the media's and the nation's agenda of concerns. The setting for the message is usually designed as a photo opportunity to draw in television coverage. Aides or surrogates amplify the points in soundbites or lines that reinforce the message. Their goal is to avoid negative coverage that would require time-consuming damage control by other members of the administration.

Wary of being taken as a partner that is too compliant, the White House press corps responds cautiously, careful to keep some distance and make it clear to their audiences that they have not been seduced by the spin of handlers or experts in fax attacks. They know that they are in a business that is reactive, sharing the agenda-setting and gatekeeping functions of the media with political leaders. They also know their reporting must relay the words and actions of these leaders, but they have their own independence to protect. In this courtship ritual each side needs the other. But unlike most others, each ultimately uses the other to please someone else: the American public.

In the pages that follow we will examine how political figures use the press to communicate their views, and how the press—and ultimately the public—responds. We will look at how the American mass media are organized and funded, and how political figures utilize the constraints and opportunities of these structures to their own ends.

Ultimately, the book focuses on three blocks of power: major political figures or institutions, the great print and broadcast media corporations that filter their messages, and the American public. The greatest space in this text is devoted to the structures and relationships of the first two. Using a wide variety of cases and examples, we look especially at the operating systems in place that connect political figures to the media from whom they seek exposure. And we note the kinds of messages and effects these systems tend to favor.

It is more difficult to describe the impact of political media on the third block, the American public, largely because it is so heavily fragmented, and because the methods of the social sciences are limited in yielding insights on how Americans respond to the mass media. There is no shortage of useful models for assessing how individuals and groups respond to media content, and the most important are cited in these pages. But even in the age of the instant poll, we are a long way from accurately assessing the efficiency and effectiveness of many common political–public relations techniques.

The goal of this introduction is to explore some of the broad features of the politics–media courtship. We begin with some preliminary observations about the connections that link the American public to the mass media, and to the political events they portray.

THE MEDIA MIX IN AMERICAN LIFE

There is no other nation in the world with so large a supply of media outlets, and so insatiable an appetite for information and entertainment. Japanese citizens may watch slightly more television than their American counterparts, and Russian citizens may be more avid readers and book collectors. But the sheer volume of media content produced and consumed in the United States is staggering.

According to one study, the average adult American spends almost 1500 hours a year watching television, with cable programming getting an increasing percentage of these hours. Radio was estimated to consume 1100 hours, recorded music 235 hours, and newspapers 175 hours.[2] In some studies, newspaper and newsmagazine readers demonstrate a higher level of retention and knowledge about general news topics.[3] And newspaper consumption is much higher than the norm for political and media decision makers—such as television producers—who shape the news agenda for the rest of us. But television remains the venue of choice for most consumers of news and information.[4]

Television

Just how much of a television-dominated society we are is suggested by some basic estimates. The average household consumes the output of cable and broadcast suppliers for nearly seven hours a day, up from four and half hours in 1950.[5] One study estimates that the average American man will have spent the equivalant of nine years in front of the television set by the time he reaches the age of sixty-five.[6] And television viewing in the United States is surprisingly uniform across many demographic

TIME SPENT USING MEDIA

Medium	Hours per person Per Year		Difference	Percent Change
	1985	1990		
Television	1,530	1,470	−60	3.9%
Network-Affiliated Stations	985	780	−205	−20.8
Independent Stations*	335	340	5	1.5
Basic Cable Programs	120	260	140	116.7
Pay Cable Programs	90	90	0	0.0
Radio	1,190	1,135	−55	−4.6
Recorded Music	185	235	50	27.0
Newspapers	185	175	−10	−5.4
Consumer Magazines	110	90	−20	−8.2
Consumer Books	80†	95‡	15	18.8
Home Video§	15	50	35	233.3
Movies	12	12	0	0.0
Total	3,307	3,262	−45	−1.4

Source: Veronis, Suhier & Associates, A. C. Nielsen, RADAR, Newspaper Advertising Bureau. Magazine Publishers Association, Gallup, Motion Picture Association of America, Television Bureau of Advertising, Leo Shapiro and Associates, Wilkofsky Gruen Associates
* Includes Fox programming
† 1983
‡ 1988
§ Playback of prerecorded tapes only. Data is per household.
Note: Estimates of time spent were derived using rating data for television and radio, survey research data for recorded music, newspapers, magazines, books, and home video and admissions for movies. Adults 18 and older were the basis for estimates, except for recorded music and movies, where estimates inlcuded persons 12 and older.

categories. Heavy television consumption is found among women and men, the old and the young, the rich and the poor, even though most ad content is aimed at audiences under forty, and at women more than men. Selling to these vast audiences are advertisers with products available in every media market. In 1994 General Motors alone spent more than $1.4 billion to advertise its automobiles.[7]

Feeding this insatiable viewer appetite are over 3000 broadcast television stations across the nation, some in larger media markets like New York and Los Angeles devoting as much as three hours a day to news.[8] Many of these stations are affiliated with one of the major broadcast networks (CBS, NBC, ABC, and Fox). But they are all increasingly in competition with cable television systems, which now reach 66 percent of all American households.

In many ways the networks still dominate programming and news. But the rapid growth of cable television makes generalizations more difficult. Cable obviously gives viewers new options they did not have just a few years ago, with channels devoted to courtroom trials, food, comedy, sports, music, home shopping, news, and more. But much of the most popular programming carried on services like the USA network or CNN replicates rather than transforms the program or news formulas of the traditional broadcast networks.[9]

Radio

In most estimates of the time Americans spend with various media, radio ranks second behind television. One reason is because radio is a common companion to the millions who spend significant amounts of time in their automobiles. Another is that the United States is awash in local radio stations. Nearly 12,000 stations fill the airwaves with an endless blanket of sound. The medium is dominated by music programming virtually given to it by the record industry.[10] Country and western music claims the largest number of stations. But perhaps as many as 1200 devote significant periods of time to discussion, news, and talk.

Many cities are lucky enough to have an all-news station or a National Public Radio affiliate. Both are expensive to operate, but they serve as important audio windows on regional affairs and politics. The largest growth, however, has been in talk radio in all of its respectable and more questionable varieties, including political, religious, sports, and sex talk.

Publishing

Magazines and books continue to flood Americans with content designed for specialized interests. There are about 11,000 periodicals in circulation, ranging from *Southern Hog Farmer* to *Time*.[11] Beyond the many trade and profes-

Politics and Talk Radio

Perhaps as many as a thousand radio stations in the United States specialize in talk-show formats. Most—though not all—feature conservative hosts railing against "liberal" policies and policy makers. Homosexuals in the military, affirmative action programs, feminism, environmentalism, and liberal presidential appointments are favorite targets.[1] The most popular show in 1995 was Rush Limbaugh's, with an estimated audience of 20 million listeners.[2]

The dramatic rise in the number of shows is often attributed to the 1992 election, which gave listeners suspicious of government a solid roster of Democratic leaders in the Congress and White House to rally against. Former New York governor Mario Cuomo—who has been doing his own talk show for more than twelve years—believes that the current popularity of talk radio is due in part to deep feelings of discontent. These frustrations are particularly evident among poorer white Americans who have seen historically disadvantaged groups such as women and racial minorities gain economic and political power while their own wages and living standards have eroded. This "cultural corrosion over the last 20 years," he notes, has created "a lot of unhappy people. Those are the people in the middle. And the ones in the middle are the ones who are calling up."[3]

Some conservatives believe that these shows have been instrumental in derailing presidential or congressional actions. And some hosts, including Limbaugh, encourage listeners to flood the phone banks in Congress and at the White House. Others who work in the industry are more cautious in attributing extensive power to these sources of grass-roots anger, noting that regular callers rarely represent more than a few percent of the audience.

[1]Howard Fineman, "The Power of Talk," *Newsweek*, February 8, 1993, pp. 24–28.
[2]Donna Petrozzello, "Conservative Talk Shows Drown Out Liberal Voice," *Broadcasting and Cable*, June 19, 1995, p. 22.
[3]"'Plain Talk' from Mario Cuomo," *Broadcasting and Cable*, June 19, 1995, p. 19.

sional journals, as well as sports, leisure, and lifestyle publications, perhaps a few hundred regularly offer political news and opinion. Many, like the *New Republic, National Review, Foreign Affairs, Atlantic Monthly*, the *New Yorker*, and the *New York Review of Books*, represent important venues for the discussion of politics and public policy. Although the circulation numbers for these periodicals are relatively modest, the fact that they are often read by so-called "elites" in business, media, and government means that they have enlarged powers to influence decision makers.

Recent articles about Japanese culture and economics by *Atlantic Monthly*'s James Fallows, for example, have undoubtedly had impact on opinion leaders in the United States. Like many great journalists before him—including Walter Lippmann and I. F. Stone—Fallows has become an unofficial one-person think tank capable of influencing elite opinion.[12]

As for books, Bowker's standard library catalog of publishers lists an incredible 25,000 publishers and subsidiaries, even though most of the nearly 50,000 new titles published annually in the United States come from a much smaller pool of large houses. The high numbers conceal the fact that politics and meaningful political analysis is relatively rare in the important trade-book category.[13] Of the fifteen top-selling nonfiction books listed in the benchmark *New York Times* best-sellers list in a representative week in 1995, for example, only one—an assessment of Vietnam War policy by former Defense Secretary Robert McNamara—dealt with what could be called a serious public question. And that book reviewed and criticized decisions made by him and members of the Johnson administration during the Vietnam era over thirty years ago.[14] Most others in this typical week were by or about celebrities, ranging from Kathie Lee Gifford to Katharine Hepburn.

Even so, books are the prime medium for exploring the effects and consequences of policy, largely because—along with detailed analysis and reporting in some political periodicals—they are the only media forms where ideas can be fully deliberated rather than simply summarized.[15] Books provide the luxury of space to explore ideas.

Vice Presidential candidate Al Gore's substantial 1992 book on the environment, *Earth in the Balance*, was the focus of widespread commentary and debate in the presidential campaign of the same year.[16] Among other things, the book offered proposals for a comprehensive national policy on energy and environmental issues. For his part, President Bush dismissed Gore as the "Ozone Man" and a "Bozo," perhaps misjudging the growing popularity of "mainstream" environmentalism, and providing an unintentional reminder of the relatively impoverished language of political campaigns.

The Daily Press

Newspapers have often provided the most thorough reporting of the nation's political affairs, traditionally serving as a vital link connecting citizens with their communities and regions. They have undergone a tumultuous history since they first flourished as the news medium of choice in the 1920s. Although readership is down modestly for many large-city papers,[17] about 63 million copies are sold daily, produced by 1600 publishers spread throughout every region and city.[18] Unlike many foreign countries, most metropolitan centers in the United States are served by at least one quality newspaper, offering local, national, and international news, as well as opinion and entertainment.

By tradition, the newspaper business has been friendlier to political content than its newer competitor of television. In the Colonial and Civil War

The Book as a Vehicle for Public Policy Debate: The Case of *Silent Spring*

Books dealing with social issues or public policy have proven to be one of the significant forces in generating interest in social change. The dramatic awakening of the population to an issue can sometimes be identified with the cautionary warnings of a book-length jeremiad, ranging from Harriet Beecher Stow's antislavery novel, *Uncle Tom's Cabin*, to the landmark social criticism in Michael Harrington's *The Other America* and Betty Friedan's *The Feminine Mystique*.

Rachel Carson's landmark *Silent Spring*, published in 1962, remains one of the finest examples of a publication that energized public interest in a significant social issue.[1] Trained as a biologist, Carson had produced several popular books on the oceans and the natural environment. But when she signed a contract with her Boston editor to begin work on *Silent Spring*, she already knew that the book would thrust her into a storm of controversy.

The book documented the extensive ecological harm that indiscriminate use of pesticides had created on the natural world. DDT was often the pest-control chemical of choice in this era, and had powerful backers in the chemical and food industries, in addition to the U.S. Department of Agriculture and its counterparts at the state level. Many attempted to discredit her, even before the book was published. But Carson provided detailed evidence suggesting that residual levels of these chemicals remained in the food chain, sometimes devistating local populations of birds and other wildlife. Drawing on numerous government and business studies collected in over three years of research, *Silent Spring* served as an articulate warning to Americans who had believed that their food and their future health was not at risk. It also helped trigger a flood of reforms in state and federal rules on the use of chemical pesticides.[2]

[1]Rachel Carson, *Silent Spring* (Boston: Houghton Mifflin, 1962).
[2]Frank Graham Jr., *Since Silent Spring* (Boston: Houghton Mifflin, 1970).

periods in the United States papers variously fought against and sometimes represented the dominant political blocks of the day. Their vital role as vehicles of debate and discussion is a natural outgrowth of their use by early political pamphleteers.[19] That tradition survives in most good papers through their editorials, analysis columns, and occasional aggressive reporting.

By reporting and editorializing on important issues, the daily press still forms the core of a community's informational infrastructure. Without newspapers, political and civic activity would have almost no coverage in many regions and cities. Portions of the northeast would be in a virtual local news blackout without access to the print media.[20] The citizens of

New Jersey, for example, are generally poorly served by the television news that originates mostly from New York City and Philadelphia.[21] None of the major networks have affiliates in the state; instead, its nearly eight million citizens learn about the region's civic and political activities from its better daily newspapers.

POLITICS, INFORMATION, AND ENTERTAINMENT

The diversity of media in the United States suggests a need to cast our net broadly in exploring the sources of political discourse. It is tempting to limit the study of the political world to those media that cover political professionals and their institutions, for example, newspaper reports on new forms of lobbying on Capitol Hill, "serious" television news programs, the congressional action covered by C-SPAN, or the guests and topics that show up on NBC's "This Week with David Brinkley." But it is probably a mistake to limit the idea of political discussion to the people and events that form what is sometimes called the "civic culture" of the United States. Presidents, members of legislatures, and voters expressing opinions about the great issues of the day clearly fit into this culture. But Hollywood films, the prime-time schedules of the major networks, and the "soft" news and entertainment of much of the rest of the media is usually excluded. The last chapter of the book argues in detail that these nominally "nonpolitical" arenas need to be explored. We need only consider several reasons here for favoring an expanded view of political media.

The Common Thread of Storytelling

The most basic argument for an expanded outlook is that news and entertainment share the common thread of storytelling. And storytelling—as narration about the human condition—is frequently political discussion. Support for this view comes from the history of news, which clearly suggests the common origins of popular entertainment and information giving.[22] In his exhaustive history, Mitchell Stephens traces print journalism to the gossips, dramatists, and minstrels of fifteenth-century Europe.[23] Stories of fires, plagues, and court intrigues were often sung or spoken, with successive versions heightened to increase their effects. Information carried by these sources had their own rewards as entertainment, even as they communicated only modest amounts of public information. As printing evolved in the sixteenth-century, crude written accounts of murders, hangings, and the romantic exploits of England's royal family appeared in the newsbooks of the time. A pattern that survives today was clearly established.

While far newer, television shares with print a history that evolved directly from storytelling. Most of the early television news crews did not come from people well-grounded in journalism, but from disbanded newsreel units of the major Hollywood studios.[24] These units had supplied theaters with diverting news pictures of presidents, film stars, and heroes sufficient to occupy the attention of patrons waiting for a second feature to begin. It was only a short jump from these eight-minute reels for the theater to the first fifteen-minute network newscasts bringing beauty contests, auto shows, and presidential appearances into the home. These early and tentative attempts at news could hardly match the richness of reporting in the many large dailies that existed at the time. But they shared with newspapers the use of "good stories" to attract audiences and advertisers.

News must therefore compete for its audiences against other forms of popular storytelling. This fact has created a long and unending debate that raises questions about the nature and limits of journalism. Can "serious" political discourse and reporting coexist in media environments such as commercial television, where audiences are built on the understanding that they will be entertained? Can significant public discussion find an audience when it needs not only the support of readers and viewers, but advertisers as well?

The trend toward "tabloid" TV news, with a style that owes more to the storytelling of prime-time than political discourse, is the inevitable case study. Staged reenactments; "checkbook journalism," where gossips are paid for news; and "ambush" interviews that feature dramatic confrontations are only some of the tabloid format's more obvious features. At times the use of these narrative techniques has erupted into bitter and protracted feuds at organizations like NBC and CBS, where the line between "serious" and "superficial" journalism is easily crossed.[25]

An Expanded View of the Political: Two Arguments

A related reason to argue for an expanded view of the "political" involves the choices and judgments made by the media. Politics is about more than formal political institutions, such as Congress or the presidency. It also includes decisions that broadly effect the standing of individuals and groups in society. And some of those decisions are made by opinion leaders in the media as well as in government.

For several reasons it is a mistake to cling to the somewhat artificial line that divides entertainment from political reporting or policy discourse. First, the presence of any media content displaces other potential media content. And that displacement can have political and social significance, even if we cannot always measure it. The thoughtful student of news, for example, needs to go beyond the obvious first question, "How was an event reported?" to an important second question: "What might have been reported, but was not?"

The decision of the president of CBS News to resign because of his network's decision to carry "I Love Lucy" in place of Senate Hearings on a rapidly escalating Vietnam War was motivated by this awareness. Fred Friendly knew that the American public had been starved of any significant debate about Vietnam policy, largely because of the war's undeclared status. He viewed the hearings as a chance to increase public awareness about the high-stakes military policy undertaken by the administration of Lyndon Johnson.[26] Friendly felt that he could not remain in charge of a news division at a network that made such choices about what not to carry. Because they have so much to choose from and so little time, television producers, editors, and reporters are intimately aware of the fact that *omission* is an editorial option with enormous consequences.[27]

Second, content that at first appearance appears "nonpolitical" can sometimes carry a message that affirms or withholds social approval. *Politics is not just about politicians and their constituents; it is also about the communication of socially significant information that confers or denies power.* The enormous output of writers documenting the exploitation of women in television, film, and music in the last few years has offered a useful reminder that political content can reside in unlikely corners of our media, including popular music and film.

The feminist author Naomi Wolf, for example, has made compelling if sometimes selective arguments about how patterns of omission in hiring practices within the American media have played out in terms of the portrayal of women, and the discussion of important issues effecting them.[28] Wolf notes that in the recent past, gender-sensitive issues—when treated by the media at all—tended to surface in places other than traditional news forums, like television's "Oprah" or Hearst's *Cosmopolitan* magazine.[29] Similarly, she observes, too few women have worked in leadership positions in Hollywood; only a handful are members of the powerful Producers Guild of America.[30]

Whether or not one completely accepts her analysis, it would be difficult to challenge her assumption that the fantasies underwritten by the magazine or film industies are collectively an important kind of social discourse. Status is always communicated in the stories we tell each other, as well as in the stories that never get told.

In this book we therefore look at an extended range of content categories. The largest portion of this study is devoted to familiar political processes and institutions: the Congress, the courts, major federal agencies, and the presidency. But we will also look at media that have real but imprecise consequences on the American consciousness, among them sensationalistic trials, television and radio talk shows, feature films, art and music, prime-time entertainment, and crime news. What we lose in precision about the effects of such content on public opinion, we gain back in the awareness of how rich and varied the sources of political attitudes can be.

POLITICAL INFORMATION
AS MEDIATED REALITY

We frequently talk about events that occur across the culture as if we were eyewitnesses. We talk about what we have "seen" or "heard," sharing our judgments about a feud between members of the Congress and the president, the latest revelations in a court case, or a popular official who has run afoul of the law. But it is important to remember that the immediacy of news (and especially television) coverage conceals our true distance from events.

In terms of where we devote our attention and mental energies, we are profoundly different people than even our recent ancestors of the nineteenth century. We now live in two worlds; they tended to live in only one. The world we share with them is the one grounded in relations defined by our own geography: home, work, church, and the actual places and people that populate our lives. Though time changes societies, our ancestors would understand the pressures and obligations we respond to as we move through the face to face relationships that fill our days.

What Americans from the preelectric past would find puzzling is our increasing preoccupation with a second world of *mediated realities*: events and people we "know" only through television, radio, and print.[31] As time spent with various media increases as a percentage of our waking hours, there is a shift from interactions in face to face relationships to events "brought to us" by others.

For hundreds of years print sources have offered partial and selective accounts of events that were beyond the abilities of readers to witness firsthand. But the electronic media and our enormous attention to it have heightened the extent to which we "live" in a mediated environment outside of our own physical world. We may know about the death of a celebrity or leader sooner than the death of a neighbor on our own street. And we may feel a greater sense of loss in the celebrity's death. Such is the shift in where we now invest our time that our cognative energies may be spent more in response to mediated events than the simpler occurrences in our own lives.

The aftermath of the bombing and destruction of Oklahoma City's federal building in the spring of 1995, for example, was "brought to us" by CNN, other television news networks, and countless articles in the print media. In the days after the enormous explosion, television viewers became electronic bystanders, staring at the ninth-story building with its facade ripped away and hundreds of dead and wounded inside. They came to "know" the mayor of the city, the anguished faces and families of some of the children who were among the victims, and several of the heroic rescue and medical staff that attempted to locate victims in the nearly collapsed building. What we "knew" about the grisly bombing—and what we talked about to others in the days that followed—was a collection of impressions relayed to us through the filter of the news media.

After the event, two strangers from different corners of the country could share the same "experience" of Oklahoma City. And the mediated reality that shaped the national consciousness undoubtedly played out attitudes that were both accurate and inaccurate: in negative public opinion about the Arab militants or religious fanatics incorrectly associated with the act, and in positive assessments of the responses of local emergency units and federal investigators.

The phrase, *mediated reality* is thus an important part of the vocabulary of political communication. It speaks to the idea that the media regularly deliver us to distant events we more or less presume to know, events that have been reconstructed through the processes of selection, editing, and narration.

DEMOCRACY AND COMMUNITY IN THE MEDIA AGE

If the media increasingly exist as arbiters of awareness, providing selective and necessarily sporadic glimpses of our national life, what meaningful citizenship responsibilities are left to members of the society? Are citizens in the media age "participants" in democracy in any meaningful sense, or has participation been replaced by a kind of endless spectatorship?

The Dominance of Spectatorship and Partisanship

It is sobering to see how greatly restricted our popular conceptions of government and citizenship have become. We often see ourselves as observers of gladiatorial exercises carried out by professionals: elected officials, lobbyists, entrenched bureaucrats. They often seem to be our proxies as they seek power and advantage over competitors representing different constituencies we fear or endorse.

It wasn't always so. The flowering of democracy in ancient Greece provided a far more active model of participation. Life in democratic Athens involved at most a few thousand citizens who could be addressed in one place at one time. Participation in voting, debate, and policy discussion was direct and face to face.[32] Only our most local levels of government (i.e., borough, village, or township politics) allow for the same kinds of immediate interaction today.

Moreover, older concepts of democracy tend to emphasize community over conflict, the public good over private gain; the reverse of views perpetuated in today's atmosphere of intense partisanship. The framers of the constitution, for example, had little sense of how political parties would later emerge to dominate the politics of the Congress and the presidency.

The institutionalized conflict reflected in contemporary reporting is not what the original shapers of American government nor democratic philosophers envisioned. The framers of the Constitution sought to avoid the "dangers of faction" by minimizing the roles of formal political parties or direct participation.[33] Writing in the first half of this century, influential observers like Walter Lippmann and John Dewey similarly talked about the ideal of a great democratic society that could act like a community conscious of its common needs and interests. In our age we surely have the technology to create a national consciousness, but we may not have the will. Such a great community, they believed, requires an active, educated, and involved citizenry.[34]

Dewey and Lippmann still have their followers today among them Robert Bellah and his colleagues, who note in *The Good Society* that politics needs to be reclaimed from its modern emphasis on interest-group conflict. We must replace adversary models, they note, with the idea of "a discursive community capable of thinking about the common good."

Often our politicians and political parties debase the public by playing on its desires and fears: desire for private benefits at the expense of public pro-

---

Fragmented Media and the Polis

In ancient Greece and Sicily the polis was understood as the general public united by a common consciousness and shared interests. In the ancient city-states of this region these pockets of democracy nurtured a civic life that emphasized similarity rather than difference, inclusion rather than partisanship. A single leader might speak for the whole, or most of it. Does anything or any experience similarity unite Americans?

Even in comparison to the tumultuous 1960s—when Americans grappled with issues such as the Vietnam War, civil rights, and the decay of the nation's urban areas—public discourse in the 1990s seems to reflect a diminished sense of national unity. In the '60s most Americans were watching the same television news shows and reading similar news magazines. The infrastructure for news and political information was more centralized. If President John Kennedy called a news conference in 1962, all three major networks carried it live, leaving viewers in those precable days with few other viewing options. When NBC carried

Continued

Continued

one of its "White Paper" documentaries, or CBS broadcast one of its hour-long "CBS Reports" programs, millions of viewers became witnesses to problems dealing with everything from the blight of migrant workers in the United States to a distant war in Angola.[1] However imperfect sources of news and information were at the time, they nonetheless helped create a national consciousness, a common set of experiences for the polis. Anchormen Walter Cronkite at CBS and David Brinkley and Chet Huntley at NBC became reliable narrators of the national scene.

Today we still share the experience of political and social traumas. But we are less likely to witness the same moments of civil discourse about these events. In 1968 about 85 percent of those watching television in the early evening watched one of the three major network newscasts.[2] By 1991, only 54 percent watched a news show.[3] Syndicated entertainment and talk shows now sometimes outdraw audiences for network news. The presidency is similarly diminished. Networks are less likely to clear time in their schedules for a presidential press conference or major presidential address. And most now bypass the quadrennial ritual of the national nominating conventions.

Audiences for television have fragmented into increasingly separate worlds, largely because of the growth of cable television and its greater

range of choices. At the same time, the dominance of news magazines as interpreters of our national life has declined in favor of "niche" publishing targeting more specialized audiences. And advances in computer technology have made it possible to bypass public forums altogether, using the internet and the "web" as anonymous backchannels to reach other like-minded individuals.

In an age when such media fragmentation is accompanied with increasing political fragmentation, it may be even more difficult to achieve the ideal of a national polis bound by common experiences and a national discourse. Signs of strain in the political realm are easy to find: in the heavily partisan Congress, in rhetoric that seeks to annihilate rather than refute political opponents, and in the rise of *identity politics*, which—by definition—gives priority to groups pushing ethnic, class, and "lifestyle" perspectives on national issues. The widely reported not guilty verdict rendered in the 1995 trial of football star O. J. Simpson, for example, demonstrated what appeared to be nearly unbridgable split in the polis. Many outlets and hundreds of commentators offered assessments of the trial and the strategies of the prosecution and defense. But no source—not even the president—was able to command a forum for interpreting the outcome, the first step in creating a national consensus.

[1] Erick Barnow, *Tube of Plenty* (New York: Oxford, 1975), pp. 284–287.
[2] Marvin Barrett, *The Politics of Broadcasting, 1971–72* (New York: Crowell, 1973), p. 6.
[3] Ken Auletta, *Three Blind Mice: How the TV Networks Lost Their Way.* (New York: Random House, 1991), p. 563.

vision; fear of just those most in need of public provision. What we need is
precisely the opposite: a vision of how we are indeed dependent on and
jointly responsible for a common life.[35]

The ideal of the discursive community includes citizens committed to a collective search for solutions, and a rhetoric of inclusion (as opposed to division) that would allow that to happen.

Such an inclusive approach comes easily to presidents, who are quick to
see the limits of partisanship as a tool for governing. But conflict and division
drives the politics of state and federal representatives elected in two-year cycles, as well as journalism that uses contentiousnss to attract audiences. In
this sense, House of Representatives Speaker Newt Gingrich and programs
like CNN's "Crossfire" are representative products of their time.

Even so, in at least a few important ways we have improved on older
models of the democratic state. We have a far more universal franchise than
the Greeks, who limited participation in the civil life of the state to landown-
ers; and the founders of the American federalism, who left slaves, women,
and the poor unempowered.

We also have the genius of the First Amendment, the vital Constitutional
clause that offers significant if incomplete protections of citizens against governmental interference with freedom of speech and of the press.[36] One of the
features of the First Amendment that makes it so important a protection is
that it contains the only mention anywhere in the Constitution of a specific
professional activity: publishing. As interpreted by the courts, the Amendment is rather explicit in its protections of political thought, whether spoken,
written, or distributed electronically. As is documented in Chapter 1, access
to the media may be restricted as ownership of the major outlets falls under
the control of fewer corporations. With that important exception, it still remains true that Americans have generally escaped the misery of direct governmental censorship that still dominates civil life in countries such as Iran,
Iraq, and China.[37]

The Apathetic Public

A paradox raised by any discussion of the First Amendment in contemporary American life is how a nation generally unencumbered by official governmental censorship can at the same time be so apathetic about the exercise
of the franchise to engage in political discussion and dissent. The United
States is one of the world's great open societies. But it is also a nation with
relatively low levels of political interest and participation. We declare "land-
slides" when fewer than 30 percent of eligible voters bother to cast their bal-
lots. And party identification and activism is at an all-time low, replaced in
part by a segmentation of voters into groups like the Christian Coalition and

The First Amendment

The first Amendment to the Constitution of the United States was adopted in 1791. It would be difficult to locate another statement of human rights in the Western world that has been as influential as these few lines.

> *Amendment 1: Congress shall make no law respecting an establishment of religion, or prohibiting the free exercise thereof; or abridging the freedom of speech, or of the press; or the right of the people peaceably to assemble, and to petition their government for redress grievances.*

The Amendment has four important clauses promising freedom to practice or not practice any religion, freedom of journalists to write and criticize without governmental interference, similar rights of expression for all others, and access to governmental representatives for the purposes of registering complaints. All of these clauses have important and complex applications. And it is important to note that none have been interpreted by the courts to grant absolute freedom in all cases. But taken together, they represent a remarkably progressive statement of the rights of citizens to worship, meet, communicate, and lobby elected officials without governmental interference.

Initial work on the amendment was done by James Madison, and modified by congressional committees as they incorporated the Bill of Rights into the Constitution. It is dangerous to interpret the original intent of the amendment. But it is clear from events at the time that the founders of the nation had little interest in continuing the British tendency to prosecute speakers and printers for sedition, or antigovernment remarks. After all, as proponents of independence from the Crown, they were possible targets for sedition arrests. Moreover, there was little interest in a state-sanctioned church, especially one headed by a monarch, as Britain's Church of England remains today.

the American Family Association on the ideological right, both of whom have much narrower agendas than the GOP.

Answers to account for this paradox are numerous. The most frequently heard is that Americans feel unimpowered. With politics a distant mediated reality, many citizens seem to feel like spectators curtained behind a class wall. They see themselves as witnesses but not active participants in the give and take of direct democracy. By defining politics as conflict between parties, professional politicians, and "special interests," we have seemingly stripped away a popular sense of direct membership in a larger community. E. J. Dionne speaks of this distrust of politics borne of our removal from active participation.

*Over the last three decades, the faith of the American people in their demo-
cratic institutions has declined, and Americans have begun to doubt their
ability to improve the world through politics. At a time when the people of
Poland, Hungary, and Czechoslovakia are experiencing the excitement of
self government, Americans view politics with boredom and detach-
ment. . . . Election campaigns generate less excitement than ever and are
dominated by television commercials, direct mail, polling, and other approaches that treat individual voters not as citizens deciding their nation's
fate, but as mere collections of impulses to be stroked and soothed.*[38]

We are also cynical, for a variety of reasons. Increasingly rapid cycles of
governmental activism and inaction, accompanied by accompanying
rhetorics of hope and despair, have left many Americans with doubts about
the abilities of civil institutions in general and the federal government in particular to deal with national problems. Jimmy Carter campaigned in 1976 on
the hopeful theme that he would produce a "government as good as its people." Ronald Reagan defeated him four years later by noting that government itself was the problem.[39] In some ways, politics in the 1980s and '90s
looks like the politics of the 1780s. Two hundred years later, and led by a
resurgent Republican Party, we have again revisited the debates of the
founders of the nation about the limits and uses of federalism.[40]

Part of what fuels the current distrust is nearly universal agreement in
the idea that organizational units—ranging from governments to corporations—are fundamentally flawed. It is an article of faith in the 1990s that
organizations in postindustrial society are usually inadequate to the task
of addressing problems that are subtle and complex.[41] Exceptions are made
for innovators and groups that have managed to buck the tide: the Federal
government's Head Start program for young children, or the computer industry's pace-setting Microsoft Corporation. But few Americans are willing to be counted as defenders of organizational life, even while all
probably recognize its necessity. As a concept, the bureaucracy has been
analyzed, deconstructed, and dismissed as a necessary but imperfect ves-
tige of advanced societies. Stories regularly filter through the media about
government contractors who have managed to bill taxpayers for $100
screws, and Defense Department staffers who accept them as part of $25
million airplanes. Never mind that many of these stories appeal more to
enduring fantasies than realities.[42] The antigovernmental bias of our age is
its own reality, and a corrosive environment that eats at the credibility of
most political discourse.

There are no easy remedies for the decline of confidence in American
political institutions. As these pages document, a number of patterns that
contribute to public suspicions are firmly entrenched, including the deep
partisanship of the Congress, an emphasis on image sometimes at the ex-

pense of substance, and a tendency by the press to report messages in terms of their strategic objectives rather than their substance. Perhaps the most hopeful interpretation that can be gleaned from these pages is that Americans are increasingly saavy about the nature of the political processes. And though the media–politics connection is imperfect, it still manages to accomodate productive change. The specific communication modes have been altered by the rapid growth in telecommunications capabilities (satellites, faxes, computer networks, and the like) but they are still what they always have been: amoral techniques that can be used for good or ill.

The example of President Lyndon Johnson is instructive. With the possible exception of Richard Nixon, no president worked harder to manipulate the mass media and, by implication, American public opinion. Johnson was not beyond using intimidation, sometimes even asking editors to fire unfriendly reporters. His administration was also capable of witholding or badly distorting information.[43] At virtually the same time, however, he orchestrated public and congressional support to win passage of remarkably effective pieces of legislation, particularly the Civil Rights Acts of 1964 and 1965. These acts dramatically accelerated the political enfranchisement of blacks in the South, and gave powerful weapons to the courts to end "legal" discrimination in employment, housing, and other settings.[44] Like those in political power today, Johnson's objectives—whether noble or dark—were served by the same political and media-management skills.

WHAT SHOULD WE STUDY: CONTENT, STRUCTURE, OR PROCESS?

One of the difficulties in taking on the study of political communication is that there are so many avenues that can be explored. Should an analyst study the verbal and legislative record of political figures, or their reconstruction in the political media? It is somewhat out of fashion to focus on original texts of messages in the media, but meaningful dicussion of public policy is obviously impossible without such a content orientation. Would it be more useful to examine the political, financial, or social structures that shape the institutions that generate or control such content? Or is time more profitably spent on processes, what individuals or organizations actually do to produce specific effects?

One *content* orientation involves looking at the nature of messages common to certain settings, such as the Congress or the presidency. There is no shortage of such studies, and they are often productive. For example, presidents undoubtedly have certain generic requirements that must be met when addressing the nation in an inaugural, or in explaining a national crisis.[45] Useful formulaic categories exist for assessing content, and some—such as stock media storylines and character types—are used in this text.[46]

A *structure* orientation begins with the assumption that organizations have unique characteristics that ultimately explain most of their significant outcomes. Congress lends itself particularly well to this approach. The Senate, for example, has a well-documented "club" atmosphere that gives its minorities more power than their counterparts in the House. This collegial structure plays out in the way legislation is treated and debated. The sharp partisan rhetoric of leaders in the larger body is not as frequently replicated by their counterparts in the Senate.

Both the content and structure orientations are used in various segments of this book. Chapter 1 focuses on organizational structures, and Chapter 7 looks closely at messages. But most of the remainder of this study is based on the *process* assumption that the politics–press connection is most clearly understood by examining what parties in this relationship actually do. It is the virtue of good historical/descriptive research (and of good journalism or history) that one can learn a great deal from "thick description" of the professional activities of others.[47] One of the primary goals of the book is to allow readers to "observe" the routines that the press, political institutions, and media consumers undertake to communicate with each other.[48]

ORGANIZATION OF THE BOOK

The title of this book is meant to suggest its necessarily selective approach. Political communication is too vast to represent adequately in one or even several books. Each of the following seven chapters offers a perspective on communication patterns in the American political scene, not a synopsis. Even so, the seven perspectives developed in each chapter provide an overview of important issues and topics. Each uses a number of cases and examples from our recent past, as well as a number of useful theories and models that account for their effects.

Chapter 1 explores a number of the factors that shape major news and information businesses in the United States. It provides a number of examples and observations about how these organizations survive as they search for audiences, investors, and stability against their competition. Chapter 2 focuses on two essential models of mass media power: agenda setting and gatekeeping. These are described and illustrated primarily with reference to television journalism, the most common source of political information for most Americans. Chapter 3 is the first of several devoted to traditional settings for political discourse in the United States. It describes Congress, with an accent on how members use media outlets to further their publicity goals. Chapter 4 offers a look at the presidency and the mass media. Traditional media prerogatives of the president—such as the use of television to define and interpret events—are augmented by an analysis of the campaign model as a way to understand the publicity requirements of the modern presidency. Where Chapters 3 and 4 focus on domestic policy, Chapter 5 departs with a look at foreign policy, and on government–press relations in times of international crisis. After an overview of how foreign events are typically offered in mainstream American news sources, this section dwells on war reporting, and the uneasy relationship that now exists between the Pentagon and the press. The overview of routine settings for political communication is completed in Chapter 6, a survey of patterns of press coverage in the nation's courts, and the increasingly important place of television in court reporting. This chapter has two main goals: to describe how the media covers criminal and civil litigation, and to account for the heightened public fascination with crime reporting. Finally, Chapter 7 concludes the book with an exploration of the ties that exist between the political and entertainment worlds. It argues for an enlarged view of what constitutes political discourse, and attempts to define the ways in which art is "political." It also departs from the other chapters in proposing some methodological suggestions for discovering political meaning in nonpolitical settings.

The first chapter is intended to provide background for all of the rest. And each of those that follow offer some useful commentary on the contents of the others. But as the title suggests, each of the chapters advance self-contained perspectives that can be productively explored in any sequence.

NOTES

1. Bill Clinton, quoted in Bob Woodward, *The Agenda: Inside the Clinton White House* (New York: Simon and Schuster, 1994), p. 313.

2. *The Veronis, Suhler and Associates Communications Industry Forecast* (Privately printed, 1991), p. 55.

3. See, for example, Doris A. Graber, *Processing the News: How People Tame the Information Tide* (New York: Longman, 1984) p. 214.

4. For a useful review of research on patterns of media use, see John P. Robinson, "Long Term Information and Media Usage," in John P. Robinson and Mark R. Levy, *The Main Source* (Beverly Hills, Calif.: Sage, 1986), pp. 57–86.

5. "By the Numbers," *Broadcasting*, March 2, 1992, p. 60.

6. Nicholas Johnson, *How to Talk Back to Your Television Set* (New York: Bantam, 1970), p. 11.

7. "Top 10 Companies by 1994 Ad Spending," *Advertising Age*, May 1, 1995, p. 33.

8. "By the Numbers," *Broadcasting*, May 8, 1995, p. 105. Approximately 1,500 are full-power television stations. The rest are smaller, low-power stations with more limited coverage.

9. Cable services, of course, offer fragmented programming that is typically more specialized than the broadcast networks. Even so, ratings for top cable shows show a consistent tendency toward content that is also common to network television. These shows usually include sports events, such as the NBA playoffs or a major league baseball game, and a hit drama series, like USA's off-network reruns of CBS's "Murder She Wrote." See "People's Choice: Top Cable Shows," *Broadcasting*, May 8, 1995, p. 51.

10. Stations playing music are assessed fees by music licensing agencies such as ASCAP and BMI. These fees are then distributed to those who hold the ownership rights to the music. But these fees are relatively modest, representing only a small percent of the station's revenues.

11. Melvin L. DeFleur and Everette E. Dennis, *Understanding Mass Communication*, 5th ed. (Boston: Houghton Mifflin, 1994), p. 131.

12. Lippmann is perhaps the most honored journalist-thinker who commanded the attention of political and business leaders through the first half of this century. See Ronald Steel, *Walter Lippmann and the American Century* (New York: Vintage, 1981).

13. Trade books can be contrasted with textbooks, professional books, and other publications that would have very limited audiences. Books published for trade are judged to be popular enough to be sold in ordinary bookstores, with sales usually in excess of 10,000 copies.

14. Robert S. McNamara, *In Retrospect* (New York: Times Books/Random House, 1995).

15. President Kennedy, for example, was said to be enormously influenced by Michael Harrington's 1962 book on the effects of poverty, *The Other America*, and John Kenneth Galbraith's *The Affluent Society*. See Arthur Schlesinger Jr., *A Thousand Days* (Boston: Houghton Mifflin, 1965), p. 1010.

16. Albert Gore, Jr. *Earth in the Balance: Ecology and the Human Spirit* (Boston: Houghton Mifflin, 1992).

17. Mark Fitzgerald, "Newspaper Circulation Report," *Editor and Publisher*, May 6, 1995, pp. 12–13.

18. Defluer and Dennis, *Understanding Mass Communication*, p. 92.

19. Ibid., p. 88–99.

20. The political boundaries of some states do not easily correspond with the physics and geography of broadcast television signals. States like Delaware, New Jersey, New Hampshire, Vermont, Maine, and Rhode Island all have some television stations, but their citizens also receive signals from surrounding states. Under FCC rules, a station is primarily obligated to serve its city of license, not an entire region.

21. Andy Newman, "No News, Most of the Time," *New York Times*, June 4, 1995, Sec. 13, pp. 1–10.

22. See, for example, Walter R. Fisher, *Human Communication as Narration: Toward a Philosophy of Reason, Value, and Action* (Columbia: University of South Carolina, 1987), p. xi.

23. Mitchell Stephens, *A History of News: From the Drum to the Satellite* (New York, Viking, 1988) pp. 100–131.

24. Erik Barnouw, *Tube of Plenty: The Evolution of American Television* (New York: Oxford, 1979), pp. 168–169.

25. See, for example, Peter J. Boyer, *Who Killed CBS? The Undoing of America's Number 1 News Network* (New York: Random House, 1988).

26. Fred Friendly, *Due to Circumstances Beyond Our Control* (New York: Vintage, 1967), pp. 213–234.

27. One of the useful objectives served by so-called "alternative media" is an ongoing critique of issues allegedly slighted by more mainstream media. The popular *Utne Reader*, which is a kind of Reader's Digest of articles from smaller magazines, publishes an annual list of "News the mainstream press overlooked or suppressed." Among the neglected stories of 1994, they cited hazardous materials in the workplace, political power of the radical right, "corporate welfare" for military contractors, and the return of tuberculosis. "Presswatch: The Top 10 Censored Stories," *Utne Reader*, May–June, 1995, pp. 33–35

28. Naomi Wolf, *Fire with Fire* (New York: Random House, 1993), pp. 89.

29. Ibid, p. 88.

30. Ibid, p. 85.

31. Joshua Meyrowitz, *No Sense of Place* (New York: Oxford, 1985), pp. 115–125

32. Stanley I. Benn, "Democracy," in *The Encyclopedia of Philosophy*, vols. 1 and 2 (New York: Macmillan and Free Press, 1967), pp. 338–339.

33. James Madison was especially clear on this point in paper number ten of *The Federalist Papers* (New York: Mentor, 1961), pp. 77–84.

34. John Dewey, *The Public and Its Problems* (Chicago: Swallow Press, 1954), pp. 153–156; Walter Lippmann, *The Public Philosophy* (Boston: Little, Brown, 1955), pp. 113–140.

35. Robert Bellah, et. al., *The Good Society*, (New York: Knopf, 1991), p. 139.

36. For a complete overview of the place of the First Amendment in contemporary life, see Rodney Smolla, *Free Speech in an Open Society* (New York: Knopf, 1992).

37. We tend to oversimplify with regard to governmental censorship in other countries. Iran, for example, has had a long history of public dissent in its media, as has China on occasion. Even so, media in so-called "command" economies such as China have far less flexibility in opposing "official" governmental perspectives. See, for example, Tsan-Kuo Chang, Jian Wang, and Chih-Hsien Chen, "News as Social Knowledge in China: The Changing Worldview of Chinese National Media," *Journal of Communication*, Summer 1994, pp. 52–69.

38. E. J. Dionne, Jr., *Why Americans Hate Politics* (New York: Simon and Schuster, 1991), p. 10.

39. For analyses of these two presidents' inaugural addresses, see Craig Smith, "President Jimmy Carter's Inaugural Address, 1977," and David Henry, "President Ronald Reagan's First Inaugural Address, 1981," in *The Inaugural Addresses of Twentieth-Century Presidents* ed. Halford Ryan (Westport, CT: Praeger, 1993), pp. 245–270.

40. The Federalist Papers of John Jay, Alexander Hamilton, and James Madison, published in 1987 and 1988, represent the basic discussion of the nature of a federal government as conceived in the Constitution. See Madison, *Federalist Papers*.

41. Seymour Martin Lipset and William Schneider, *The Confidence Gap: Business, Labor, and Government in the Public Mind* (New York: Free Press, 1983), pp. 13–40.

42. Steven Kelman, *Making Public Policy* (New York: Basic Books, 1987), pp. 271–276.

43. Kathleen J. Turner, *Lyndon Johnson's Dual War* (Chicago: University of Chicago Press, 1985), pp. 8–14.

44. John Morton Blum, *The Progressive Presidents* (New York: Norton, 1980), pp. 168–169.

45. Karlyn Kohrs Campbell and Kathleen Hall Jamieson, *Form and Genre: Shaping Rhetorical Action* (Falls Church, VA: SCA, n.d.), pp. 9–32.

46. See, for example, Dan Nimmo and James Combs, *Mediated Political Realities*, 2d ed. (New York: Longman, 1990).

47. Two classic examples of work from this general perspective include Edward Jay Epstein's *News From Nowhere* (New York: Vintage, 1973), and Stephen Hess's *The Government/Press Connection* (Washington, DC: Brookings, 1984).

48. For additional discussion of political communication research, see Dan Nimmo and David L. Swanson, "The Field of Political Communication: Beyond the Voter Persuasion Paradigm," in *New Directions in Political Communication* (Newbury Park, CA: Sage, 1990), pp. 7–47.

1

THE MEDIA, THEIR OWNERS, ADVERTISERS, AND INTERCORPORATE STRUCTURE

> *Concentrated control of the media is not the most urgent danger facing society. . . . But the ability to cope with larger problems is related to the peculiar industries we call the media, to their ownership and the nature of their operation. They create the popular base of information and political values out of which all critical public policy is made. In a world of multiple problems, where diversity of ideas is essential for decent solutions, controlled information inhibited by uniform self-interest is the first and fatal enemy.[1]*

If a foreign visitor to New York City were to ask a tour guide to show her where some of the most influential of all Americans work, they might be surprised at where they would end up. In the political world, power is frequently reflected in public architecture. The great civic monuments of municipal buildings, executive residences, and courtrooms are meant to impress us with the legitimacy and power of those who reside in them. But within the mass media, power is exercised behind almost anonymous facades.

One of the great media giants of North America, for example, sits among a row of bland brick warehouses on the western edge of Manhattan's 57th Street. Among the buildings that occupy the south side of the street just before it gives way to the industrial wharfs of the Hudson River is the CBS Broadcast Center. Its nearly windowless exterior and sparsely decorated lobby gives no clue that this is the heart of one of the great opinion-making machines in the nation.

The inner sanctum of the Broadcast Center is the studio and set for the "CBS Evening News." After careful screening by security guards, a visitor makes the trip to the studio down several long hallways broken only by occasional pictures of the journalist-celebrities—Paula Zahn, Harry Smith, and others—who invest network news with much of its credibility. The studio is entered through a narrow tunnel that suddenly gives way to reveal the large, two-story circular space known as the goldfish bowl. An upper ring of glassed-in offices overlooks the studio floor, with its massive elevated anchor desk in front of a wall of brightly lit maps, multiple color monitors, and a huge "Eye on America" logo. These are the familiar backdrops for anchorman Dan Rather, who spends most of his late afternoons at work behind a curtained office on the second-floor ring. As managing editor, he will have a considerable role in setting the news agenda that will reach the CBS-affiliated stations and about 15 million of their viewers.

Earlier, in another control room upstairs, technicians began gathering location reports to be fed to local affiliates for use in their own newscasts, and also the "Evening News." Pictures of unexpected events often dominate television news. And on this day in February of 1992 the pace of the staff in the satellite-relay room is brisk. A military cargo plane has crashed into a hotel on the outskirts of Evansville, Indiana, killing the crew and scores of bystanders on the ground. A young reporter from CBS's Indianapolis affiliate is at the location, along with a KU-band truck, which is capable of linking the crash scene to West 57th Street via satellite. The reporter draws admiring comments from the technicians for his ability to remain calm under the pressure of covering a fast-breaking national story. Within a few moments he has finished one report to a midwestern station, and is told to stand by to provide a live insert about the crash to CBS's New York affiliate, WCBS, which is in the first half hour of its local newscast. Later, a different three-minute pretaped "package" will be introduced by Rather as the lead story, bumping to second position a five-minute package on the Bush presential campaign's proposal for health-care reform.[2]

From this building once occupied by a milk-processing plant, the American news agenda can be maintained or altered. Our national attention may be focused on a midwestern field where a plane has crashed. It may also concentrate on the White House, the Capitol building, or a briefing room at the Pentagon. All are almost instantly accessible to the network and to the nation. Along with a handful of newspaper and network production offices in New York, Washington, and Atlanta, the unassuming compound of the CBS Broadcast Center represents one of the primary sources of our national conciousness.

If CBS's day-to-day editorial decisions are made at the Broadcast Center, the long-term financial and organizational planning for the network is calculated elsewhere, at both the network's Sixth Avenue headquarters, and 300 miles away at the Pittsburgh offices of its new Westinghouse parent. The reporters and studio staff at West 57th Street know that their fates are closely tied to the decisions of those in these offices. Their sense of vulnerability is legend in the industry, where a long history of tension has given special meaning to the popular nickname for the networks's New York offices, known to all as Black Rock. The clash of cultures representing advertising's Madison Avenue, the investment community on Wall Street, and the idealism of the journalists on 57th Street has been not easily accommodated at CBS, and represents in miniature many of the pressures that indirectly influence the content of the opinion-leading mass media.

In this chapter we consider how the business of the media guides the use of resources—both human and financial—for the presentation of political issues. As we shall see in the next two chapters, the decisions of newsworkers are affected—if sometimes unclearly and indirectly—by commercial pressures and the weight of tradition. We will pay special attention to the ties of media corporations to other key institutions in business and government, and the direct and indirect pressures that audiences, advertisers, and investors can have on the fabric of political and informational discourse.

CORPORATE CONTROL: THE PATTERN TOWARD BIGGER PLAYERS

It is a given in American life that the discussion of virtually every kind of topic and issue can be found in some form of media. But the apparent diversity of outlets is *not* necessarily matched by a comparable diversity of content. As we have noted with regard to cable, part of the reason for the lack of content diversity is that different outlets are doing essentially the same things, a matter we will consider shortly when we look at commercial pressures favoring large audiences who seek "mainstreamed" rather than specialized content. The other cause of this effect is what might be called the "Bagdikian argument," the well-documented assertions of press critic Ben Bagdikian that we are losing a diversity of media owners.

In his influential book *The Media Monopoly*, Bagdikian cites long-term trends of consolidation within the press and entertainment worlds, where a combination of closures and buyouts by large conglomerates is having the effect of reducing the number of independent media voices. Advances in journalism, he argues, have been offset by a dangerous concentration of corporate control in newspapers, magazines, radio, television, books, and movies. "Modern technology and American economics have quietly created a new kind of central authority over information—the national and multi-national corporation." Fewer corporations—perhaps less than twenty-five—now represent the majority of all major American media. These corporations have been "interlocked in common financial interest with other massive industries and with a few dominant international banks."[3]

Bagdikian sees the large media corporation—Westinghouse-CBS, Time Warner, Gannett, and others—as essentially "private ministries of information," where owners are apt to impose their own values and corporate culture on the scores of wholly owned local media outlets that millions of Americans depend on. His concern springs from a long-honored article of faith enshrined in the First Amendment and the idea of democracy itself that a plurality of different voices enriches public discussion and debate. We are a stronger nation for permitting a wide variety of competing and different views to be heard.

Consider several examples. Time Warner is a huge media giant created by the 1989 merger of Time Incorporated and Warner Communications. The decisions taken by the management of this company influence what all of us read, see, and probably think. Imagine a weekend where a significant amount of time is spent with various forms of media content. In the course of forty-eight hours a person may look at issues of *Time* or *People* magazines; watch a program on cable's HBO or CNN; rent one of the popular "Lethal Weapon" films; watch TV situation comedies like "Friends" or "Full House"; listen to Paul Simon's 1986 "Graceland" album; and read a mystery by novelist Ruth Rendell. All of these specific forums and media are owned or distributed by subsidiaries of Time Warner.[4]

The 1995 purchase of Capital Cities–ABC by the Walt Disney Company has created a similar behemoth that includes newspapers (the *Kansas City Star*), cable networks (ESPN, Lifetime, Disney), theme parks (EuroDisney), motion picutres (Touchstone and Hollywood Pictures), TV programming ("Home Improvement"), and, of course, radio and television stations in addition to ABC itself.[5] It will take years to tell if a company that specializes in fantasy and family entertainment will have an interest in presenting the harder realities represented by Capital Cities' news and public affairs divisions.

Concentration of media ownership and control means that more sources of information come from the same corporation. In some regions of the country, for example, an individual traveling through several cities may read a national newspaper such as *USA Today*, a local newspaper, watch television, and listen to the radio without ever leaving media owned by the Gannett Company. The effect of this may be to limit the number and diversity of voices reaching the American population.

The conclusion that our media are falling into fewer and fewer hands is undeniable, and is a cause for concern. What is less certain is whether the continued buyouts and consolidation of media will weaken the ability of

Dominant 25 Media Corporations with U.S. Operations

The following list of media giants indicates the broad reach of a handful of American and international corporations, including the publisher of this book. Each year the list gets shorter. A 1994 draft of this list included Capital Cities—ABC,CBS, and Turner Broadcasting. Since then all are no longer separate entities, having merged with larger corporations.

1. Bertelsmann A.G. (German; books, recordings); sample holdings: RCA Records, Doubleday Books, Bantam Books

2. Cox Enterprises (newspapers, broadcasting); sample holdings: *Atlanta Journal* and seventeen other newspapers, Cox Communications (cable)

3. Dow Jones (newpapers); sample holdings: *Wall Street Journal*, and twenty-two newspapers of the former Ottoway Chain

4. Gannett/Multimedia (newspapers, television production, cable), sample holdings: *USA Today* and eighty-two other newspapers, Multimedia Entertainment (television talk shows)*

5. General Electric Corporation (industrial electronics, broadcasting); sample holdings: NBC Television network, CNBC, WNBC (New York)

6. Harcourt Brace Javanovich (books); sample holdings: Academic Press

7. Hearst Newspapers (newspapers, magazines); sample holdings: *San Francisco Examiner, Good Housekeeping, Cosmopolitan*

8. Ingersoll (newspapers); sample holdings: *New Haven Register* and thirty-six others

9. International Thomson (Canadian; 120 daily newspapers, book publishing)

10. Knight Ridder (newspapers); - sample holdings: *Philadelphia Inquirer, Miami Herald* and twenty-seven others

11. Media News Group (newspapers); sample holding: *Dallas Times Herald*

12. Newhouse (newspapers, books, magazines); sample holdings: *Staten Island Advance*, Random House Publishing

13. News Corporation (Australian; magazines, newspapers, television); sample holdings: 20th Century Fox, Fox Television Network, *TV Guide*

14. New York Times (newspapers, broadcasting); Sample holdings: *New York Times, Boston Globe*, WQXR Radio

15. Readers Digest Association (magazines, books); sample holdings; American and foreign version of *Readers Digest*

16. Seagrams (films, publishing, music); sample holdings: Universal Pictures, MCA Records, G.P Putnams publishers.*

17. Scripps-Howard (newspapers); sample holdings: *Rocky Mountain News* and twenty-two others.

18. Sony Corporation (Japanese; film and television production, records), sample holdings: Columbia Pictures, Tri-Star Pictures, Sony Music (formerly CBS records)

Continued

Continued

19. Tele-Communications Inc (cable systems); sample holdings: Liberty media, America One, Prime network

20. Time-Warner (cable television, magazines, records, books, motion pictures); sample holdings: Warner Brothers Pictures, CNN, Turner Entertainment, *Time* magazine, *Sports Illustrated*, Scott Foresman publishers*

21. Times Mirror (newspapers); sample holdings: *Los Angeles Times* and seven others

22. Tribune Company (newspapers); sample holdings: *Chicago Tribune*

23. Viacom (books, motion pictures); sample holdings: MTV Networks, Blockbuster Video, Simon and Schuster publishers, Allyn and Bacon publishers, Paramount Pictures

24. Walt Disney Company (movies, theme parks, television networks and stations, radio networks and stations, publishing); sample holdings: ABC television, ESPN, Hollywood Pictures*

25. Westinghouse-CBS (electronic equipment, broadcasting); sample holdings: CBS television network, Group W Productions, Family Channel, Genesis Entertainment, television stations*

Sources: Ben Bagdikian, *The Media Monopoly* 4th ed. (Boston: Beacon Press, 1992), pp. 21–24; various company reports; and issues of the *New York Times* and *Broadcasting and Cable.*
*Companies engaged in mergers or buyouts initiated in 1995.

news and information units to freely present vital information to the American public. Bagdikian himself provides better evidence of concentration of ownership than proof of corporate efforts at censorship. Indeed, it is unlikely that editors at Warner Books, for example, would ever be given a management-imposed political agenda forced on them and others who work in other divisions of the far-flung Time Warner empire.

But it would be dangerous to underestimate Bagdikian's concerns, even though the political and social costs of centralized ownership are more subtle and often very difficult to document. One effect may include a corporation-wide emphasis on profits that reduces interest in innovation or risk taking. When the Coca-Cola Company owned Columbia pictures, to cite a vivid instance, it replaced its studio head, David Puttnam, within a year. Puttnam's desire to take greater risks by moving beyond standard formulas for popular commercial films put him at odds with many in Hollywood. Soon the soft-drink maker lost interest in the "high concept" films such as "The Last Emperor" that Puttnam had sought to do.[6]

Another effect may be an organizational emphasis, common to very large corporations, on using professional managers rather than trained-in-the-media specialists to run various divisions. Journalists are especially quick to criticize management shake-ups that place nonjournalists in charge of news-gathering operations. They argue, quite reasonably, that every medium requires special sensitivities that are best acquired through years of work "in the trenches." For example, in its recent history CBS has been managed (and mismanaged) by the former head of the food corporation Pillsbury, and by a stock and investment speculator with very little knowledge of television. Even so, it is a given in American business that management is a profession, and that management skills are often more important than a manager's familiarity with the products or services a company provides.

An additional effect of control by a large corporation is the natural tendency of its leaders to foster a positive image of itself and its various activities. Corporations want to protect and nurture favorable public impressions about their work, a priority that can come at a high cost to the public if it is challenged by journalists on the corporate payroll who value editorial independence. For example, it is not an empty question to inquire into the willingness of reporters and news producers at NBC to challenge interests that its corporate parent—General Electric—might like to protect. One would hope that producers of the "NBC Nightly News" and the popular "Today" show have been free to deal with issues as they see fit. But the network's owners have made huge investments in nuclear power plants, commercial aviation, combat weapons systems, and many other areas that touch on sensitive policy issues. On one occasion the network's former news president recalls having received a phone call from GE Chairman Jack Welch, urging the "NBC Nightly News" to downplay the sudden drop of stock market prices. The problem, according to Lawrence Grossman, was that Welch feared such news "would certainly not help the stock of NBC's new parent company."[7]

Anecdotal evidence of editorial interference from Time Warner is also not encouraging. In 1990, one of its book subsidiaries, Little, Brown, began a final round of prerelease publicity for a new exposé linking some American corporations to organized crime. The manuscript for the book, to be called *Connections: American Business and the Mob*, had already been completed when the publishers took the unusual step of cancelling its publication. A small segment of the exposé linked *Time* to a company allegedly involved in illegal activities. Had the publisher's superiors intervened? The unflattering reference to *Time* seemed to be the probable cause for the book's late rejection, even though executives at Time Warner denied this as their motive.[8]

THE MYTH OF THE MEDIA APART

Arguably one of the greatest contributions that American culture has exported to developing countries is the idea of a genuinely free press. We share the view that newspapers and publishers have the right to function as independent agents free to comment on affairs of government, business, and society. This bold concept of public empowerment originated in the Europe in the 1700s, but received its greatest impetus in the decisions of the American patriots to rebel against British Colonial rule.[9]

This freedom of the American media to offer information, criticism, and interpretation of even the most powerful individuals and groups in society is genuine, and has been the model for nations in Latin America, Africa, and Eastern Europe, as they have established private development of print and some of their broadcast media.

But having a "free press" is not the same thing as having a press that is free from political or economic pressure. The American mass media are remarkably unencumbered with formal governmental controls and restric-

---

Limited Governmental Restrictions on the Press

Mass media law is complex in its application, but simple in its general scope. Four important exceptions exist with regard to the freedom of the American mass media.

First, broadcasting comes under nominal regulation of a government agency, the Federal Communications Commission. The FCC licenses radio and television broadcasters (but not cable programmers) based on the availability of broadcast channels and the financial stability of its applicants. With the exception of a narrow category of "indecent" content, it generally does not regulate programming.

Second, all media are subject to libel laws, which hold operators accountable for the distribution of blatantly false information that defames or harms others. Libel is difficult to prove in court, because the burden rests on those allegedly defamed to prove that the media outlet acted with malice and disregard for the truth. Adding to the difficulty are the courts' frequent reminders to public figures such as politicians that inaccurate and injudicious reporting is the price they must pay for being in the public eye.

Third, all media are subject to local laws on obscenity, which is not considered a protected form of the press. Beyond child pornography, there are vast regional differences in how the states and municipalities define obscene content. And there are relatively few prosecutions in most states, largely because Supreme Court rulings have defined acceptable content broadly.

Fourth, all media must honor general legal guidelines on the use of copyrighted material. Copyrights give authors, publishers, and other media producers rights of ownership over their work. Rebroadcast or duplication of all media forms is restricted to brief "fair use" excerpts. Whole duplication is restricted, especially when the making of additional copies would deprive the copyright holder of additional revenues.

tions. If the ideal of a "free press" means a press without government interference, we have surely achieved the promise of the First Amendment. Yet the media are not free from many complex entanglements that can compromise its independence. In different ways the media are intricately tied to the web of institutions that influence how the nation's resources will be spent, and how the ebb and flow of national affairs will be portrayed.

There are three general kinds of pressure points that are sometimes established between the corporate, governmental, and media "elites" that pose different problems for the free flow of information.

Adversaries and Sweethearts

As the famed political analyst Walter Lippmann noted, "Cronyism is the curse of journalism."[10] The most romantic notions that we have about the free press is that, in their roles as news gatherers, they will function as watchdogs or adversaries. The press serves as our eyes into official Washington and its counterparts in the states, national and state agencies, and the boardrooms of America's richest corporations. The press in its adversarial role provides the vital information that must be present to create an informed and involved citizenry. The oversight it provides works best when there is a robust degree of skepticism regarding the actions and public rhetoric of official Washington and other powerful interests around the country. In this view, the press functions as an agent to its readers and viewers, providing them with impartial intelligence about the larger forces at work in the society.

In the last century the great newspaper tycoon Joesph Pulitzer noted that it was the task of journalism to comfort the afflicted and afflict the comfortable. For many Americans in this century the archetypal example of this adversarial role of the press is perhaps still the Watergate story. The idea that two reporters at the *Washington Post* could be given the freedom to dig into the connections between a burglary at the Democratic Party headquarters and the 1972 campaign of Richard Nixon is a vivid reminder of the impact of an aggressive and impartial press.[11]

The opposite pattern—a sweetheart role—occurs more than we care to admit. In sweetheart relationships, as William Rivers notes, individuals within the media foster positive relationships with the people they are reporting about. The standard journalistic guise of objectivity conceals a desire to "get along with" and even support the person or institution they are writing about.[12] From a personal view, positive cooperation between writers and their subjects is understandable. Media workers, like the rest of us, want the approval and support of those with whom we have a professional relationship. Many also feel that they need to maintain cordial ties with the people they talk about in order to maintain their access.

Consider, for example, the problems facing reporters assigned to cover America's space programs. Space exploration has long been a source of national pride. Reporters who wrote skeptical reports about aspects of the program or NASA (the National Aeronautics and Space Administration) risked appearing unpatriotic, or at least seeming a sour presence in an otherwise noble American adventure. Even CBS's normally skeptical Walter Cronkite made no secret of his support for the ambitious and costly plans of NASA. He and other journalists were assisted in their reporting by a very publicity-conscious space agency. In turn, their generally enthusiastic reports increased pressure on the agency to maintain their ambitious flight plans.

After the riveting adventures of the Apollo lunar program in the late 1960s, the development of the Space Shuttle promised new problems to solve and interesting crews with "the right stuff" to write about. But as William Boot describes it, there was at least one important news story about that program we did *not* see prior to the disastrous crash of the Shuttle *Challenger* on January 28, 1986. Boot wishes that we could have seen a story that might have begun this way:

> *CNN is broadcasting a live progress report from the Cape when the anchorwoman in Atlanta suddenly breaks in. "We have an important announcement about the space shuttle. A panel of engineers from Morton Thiokol, which designed the crafts solid-fuel rocket booster, has unanimously urged NASA to scrub this morning's launch. According to a company memo provided to CNN, the rocket experts are afraid cold weather might cause problem-plagued rocket-booster parts called o-rings to malfunction, allowing hot gases to burn a hole through the booster. This, the experts say, could cause a catastrophic explosion."[13]*

Had it occurred, such a report could have led to a postponement of the flight.

Hindsight criticisms are notoriously easy to make. And yet Boot is correct in noting that the signs of trouble with the booster rocket were present for enterprising reporters who might have been less in awe of NASA's achievements. NASA's desire to keep journalists and the American public involved and optimistic about the shuttle program at least inadvertently deflected attention from its inherent high risks. Too many reporters accepted the agency's assurances about the safety of the shuttle, missing the paper trail of memos from engineers and others about serious problems in various systems, including the booster rockets. As William Broad of the *New York Times* conceded, "If [journalists had] really dug into it they might have been able to save seven lives."[14]

Darts and Laurels to News Organizations from the *Columbia Journalism Review*

The *Columbia Journalism Review* regularly critiques the work of colleagues in the print and broadcast media. Each issue cites examples of journalists who either resisted or succumbed to commercial or ideological pressures in the course of reporting the news. As the two examples below illustrate, the ideal of the adversarial or "watchdog" role of the press is still a vital anchor of journalistic values. The "Dart" identifies a "sweetheart" relationship; the "Laurel" is the Review's recognition of two writers for upholding journalistic standards, acting as agents to their readers rather than the powerful.

DART to the Orange County, California, *Register*, for unholy journalism. Under the byline of one Chris Meyer and accompanied by a photograph credited to one Ron Londen, the *Register* of Monday, November 28 offered in the page-one, above-the-fold spot of its Metro section an inspirational piece on a fund-raising campaign of a local church. What was not revealed is the both Meyer and Londen attend the church and are *Register* editors too.

LAUREL to the Minneapolis *Star Tribune* and reporters Sharon Schmickle and Tom Hamburger, for an exposé of the most honorable kind. In a page-one series "Who Owns the Law?" (March 5–6) Schmickle and Hamburger revealed that over the past twelve years seven Supreme Court Justices, including four (O'Connor, Stevens, Scalia, and Kennedy) still on the bench, as well as a number of federal justices around the country, had enjoyed first-class, all expenses-paid winter trips to luxury resorts in Hawaii, California, Florida, and the Caribbean, where they gathered to select the winner of the $15,000 prize awarded annually to a judge for "Distinguished Service to Justice" by West Publishing. . . . [O]ver those same twelve years, those very same judges heard cases involving the company which were decided invariably in favor of West.

Source: "Darts and Laurels," *Columbia Journalism Review*, May–June 1995, pp. 23–24.

Political and Corporate Coercion

Because both opinion leaders and the American public perceive that the mass media has so much power, individuals and organizations attempt to influence the ways the media portray the actions of leaders, the effects of policies, and the collective opinions of the American public. In most cases, those with views they want to project to the public use the standard public-relations devices described in Chapter 3, and elsewhere in this book. But members of the media are not immune from the "hardball" politics of influence that include coercion and economic retaliation. In "hardball" politics, a view or a position is not simply presented for consideration; it is made clear that the failure to accept it will result in efforts by the persuader to exact personal or professional penalties.[15] When a film reviewer for the daily trade publication *Variety* wrote a strongly negative review of Paramount's 1992 *Patriot Games*, Paramount responded by withdrawing its advertising from the publication.[16] Given *Variety*'s dependence on revenues from a major studio, Paramount's threat was a form of coercion.

Many owners, producers, and editors show remarkable skill at resisting heavy-handed attempts to guide what is written or discussed. At other times, they may be parties to these tactics as well.

The case of the noted author, David Halberstam, provides a useful case study. Halberstam first gained high visibility as one of the *New York Times'* most important reporters in Southeast Asia. At a time in the early 1960s when much of the American public accepted the conventional wisdom that the United States needed to play an active role in civil conflicts in Southeast Asia, including Laos and Vietnam, Halberstam painted vivid pictures of confused American policies, corruption in pro-American governments, and greed among local business and political figures, who benefited from the portrayal of all reformers as "communists." Many of his most troubling conclusions about this region were described with remarkable accuracy in his early book, *The Making of a Quagmire*,[17] which foretold the high price the United States would pay in Vietnam.

For these reasons and more, Halberstam was seen by many leaders on both sides of the Pacific as an obstacle to winning American support. Along with the AP's Malcome Browne and UPI's Neil Sheehan, he was hated at the White House and State Department. A leading Vietnamese figure expressed the view that he "should be barbecued." The publisher of the *Times* received a personal appeal from President John Kennedy urging that Halberstam be replaced.[18] The *Times* declined the request, but a less secure news organization might have found it harder to resist.[19] Indeed, the same paper *had* acceded to Kennedy's wishes in 1962, when the editors agreed to hold up a story that would have given Americans the news that the Soviet Union had operational missile bases in Cuba. Kennedy asked for and got more time to formulate the eventual naval blockade that brought the world to the brink of war.[20]

Years later Halberstam was again the center of efforts to block his reporting. When he began research on the leaders of the most influential national media that eventually appeared in the book *The Powers that Be*, he encountered intense efforts by CBS's William Paley to discredit him.[21] Halberstam had used some of his research in a series of *Atlantic* magazine articles that portrayed Paley as insecure and insensitive. As was his right, Paley hotly contested these views, both to Halberstam and in an article in the *New York Times*. What is more ironic for a media figure who had himself been the subject of political coercion, he took his case directly to Halberstam's editors at Alfred Knopf, unsuccessfully trying to get them to remove passages that he found objectionable.[22]

While some of the most successful coercion has probably gone unreported, it is possible to sketch other attempts by organizations to use coercion to alter the way they are portrayed in the press.

- In 1971, CBS journalist Daniel Schorr discovered that he was the subject of an FBI investigation, ostensibly because he was going to be offered a job in the Nixon Administration. The offer was a highly suspicious cover story, since the Nixon staff considered Schorr one of the most hostile and objectionable of all network reporters.[23]
- At the height of the Vietnam War, President Lyndon Johnson ordered a security check of CBS's Morley Safer, no doubt hoping to find a reason to keep him from doing further reports on the ambiguities of jungle warfare and American military attempts to "pacify" the local population.[24]
- During the Watergate affair that gained visibility in the reporting of the *Washington Post*, the Nixon administration retaliated by ordering the FCC to take an "obstructionist" view toward the renewal of the Post's broadcast station licences.[25]
- Before CBS aired a documentary in 1976 entitled "The Guns of Autumn," the National Rifle Association, fearful that the program would portray their members in a negative light, began a letter-writing campaign against the network. Letters were directed to advertisers who had purchased part of the six commercial minutes available in the program. This campaign was successful in getting all but one of the corporate sponsors to back out of their participation in the show.[26]
- General Foods Vice President Kent Mitchel indicated that in the 1970s his corporation was regularly withdrawing its advertising from roughly 100 television programs a year because the content did not match the views the company held. General Foods is the second-largest purchaser of television advertising in the United States. In one instance the company withdrew their sponsorship of an episode of a TV drama with a plot built around a poorly run nursing home. "It wasn't as balanced as we would have wished," he noted.[27]
- Gloria Steinem, the founding editor of *Ms.* magazine, recalls the painful experience of losing real and potential advertisers because the politics of feminism were thought to be a hostile selling environment. She notes that Philip Morris dropped their ads—$250,000 worth—after complaints from readers about the sales pitch for their Virginia Slims cigarettes ("You've Come a Long Way, Baby"). Clairol similarly pulled most of its ads after the magazine reported studies that suggested some hair colors could leach in to the skin and cause health problems. And

General Mills, Pillsbury, Dole, and other companies were approached to buy ad space, but with no success. The missing ingredient was the lack of food recipes in the magazine, an apparent prerequisite for purchases of space in women's periodicals. Eventually the owners of *Ms.* took the unusual step of publishing without ads, using the magazine's subscription price and funds from a foundation to support its existence.[28]

- Almost two years before his own company was purchased by Time Warner, Ted Turner charged that the media giant was pressuring him to give up plans to purchase NBC. Time Warner then owned just 20 percent of the Turner Broadcasting System, including CNN, TBS, and many other holdings. Turner alleged that Time Warner was interested in establishing or buying its own network, and did not want competition from another source. With two seats on Turner's board of directors, he noted, they had the power to veto any deal he could arrange.[29]

Interorganizational Alliances

A single corporation often seems to be an entity unto itself. We often view media companies and their staffs in this light, assuming that in an industry as competitive as the media, the loyalties of employees to their organizations must run very deep. Yet no organization can be characterized so simply. Alliances are an important part of what makes the organs of mass communication so powerful. They share with other industries a basic need to protect their common interests, especially against governmental regulation and control. The National Association of Broadcasters, for example, is a powerful trade association with generally clear ideas of what is or is not in the industry's interests. In 1992, an official from the NAB complained to a reporter that the costs of lobbying Congress for favorable treatment were "soaking up money faster than I can make it." The NAB spent over one million dollars just lobbying members of the United States Senate on just one bill affecting cable television.[30]

Contacts with leaders in industry are even more common. Many of the members of a specific media corporation's board of directors are apt to sit on the boards of other major industrial corporations. Some of those who have sat on the board of the *New York Times*, for example, have also been on the boards of Merck Pharmaceuticals, Morgan Guaranty Trust, Bristol Myers-Squibb, Johns Manville, American Express, Bethlehem Steel, IBM, Scott Paper, Sun Oil, and First Boston Corporation.[31]

Leaders in politics, media, and business are apt to find themselves at the same White House state dinners, Washington diplomatic receptions, and New York charity benefits. Over the last four decades virtually all of the major network presidents have been on familiar terms with the president and major political party leaders. CBS's founder, William Paley, for example, was a strong supporter of Richard Nixon, contributing $25,000 to his 1960 presidential campaign, and carrying out specific assignments for the president after 1968, even at a time when the Nixon administration waged a not-so-subtle war against the press.[32] NBC's Robert Kintner went even further. Kintner left his post as president of NBC to work in the administration of Lyndon Johnson. It was no secret that Johnson viewed the ex-newsman as a broadcasting insider who could help smooth over the often rocky relationships that existed between members of the press and his administration. Kintner spent much of his time as a special assistant to the president attempting to put the Johnson "spin" on the reporting of his former colleagues.

Similarly, *Newsweek*'s Ben Bradlee, who later moved to the *Washington Post*, was one of several journalists who become a close friend of John F. Kennedy. Bradlee was later lionized as the epitome of the hard-headed editor for whom no story was off limits. He was, after all, the editor who supported the then-risky efforts of Bob Woodward and Carl Bernstein to piece together part of the Watergate puzzle. Was the Kennedy relationship poison for Bradlee's journalistic independence? "I never wrote less than I knew about him," he later observed. "But obviously, the information Kennedy gave me tended to put him and his policies in a favorable light."[33]

Hollywood is also a source of such corporate-political relationships. Many key entertainment executives have used their positions (and sometimes their corporations) to benefit specific political leaders: a fact that is not insignificant given the power of films and television to consider or avoid topics of social and political importance. Louis B. Mayer, who headed Metro-Goldwyn-Mayer in the 1920s, put his studio at the service of Herbert Hoover and others in the Republican Party.[34] Recently published evidence documents his vital role in recruiting a young producer named Irving Thalberg to make bogus newsreels that would contribute to the 1934 defeat of candidate for governor Upton Sinclair. Sinclair proposed reforms that scared the generally conservative moviemakers. Thalberg passed that concern on to voters by staging news interviews with ostensibly homeless and impoverished tramps who mumbled their support for the big changes that Sinclair would impose on the Golden State.[35] In more recent times, the Disney Company's Michael Eisner and Fox's former president Barry Diller have worked on behalf of a wide range of Democratic candidates.[36]

Reporters themselves have entered into relationships that can reduce their independence, or at least raise questions about it. It is not unusual for influential members of the press to be hosted at elaborate fetes sponsored by the political leaders they cover. Among the guests who dined on sturgeon and veal at a 1992 White House state dinner for Russia's Boris Yeltsin were journalists who cover the president, including NBC's Andrea Mitchell, UPI's

Presidents and other high-ranking officials have often hired members of the press and other media leaders to represent their interests. In making such a change, a former member of the media does a 180-degree change, working to represent a political figure or agency to the media.

In the memo below, White House Special Assistant Robert E. Kintner addresses President Lyndon Johnson, indicating that a number of White House staffers have been assigned the task of briefing "backgrounding" a number of important national reporters about one of Johnson's speeches. Kintner resigned as president of NBC prior to joining the Johnson administration. The reporters Kintner targeted for this 1967 version of "spin control" included columnists Roland Evans, Joseph Alsop, William S. White, and Charles Bartlett, and the *New York Times'* Max Frankel and the *Los Angeles Times'* Robert Donovan. Note, also, Kintner's promise to "do some work" with his former colleagues at the three television networks.

MEMORANDUM

THE WHITE HOUSE
WASHINGTON

January 11, 1967
11:05 a.m., Wednesday

CONFIDENTIAL

MR. PRESIDENT:

I had a meeting with Harry McPherson, Doug Cater, Joe Califano and Walt Rostow particularly in relation to the meaning of the Civil Rights portion of your State of the Union address, but also in relation to the principal points of the talk. We divided up various key people in town to background including Wiggins, Evans, Frankel, Chapman, Kilpatrick, Kraft, Wicker, White, Donovan, Grant, Bartlett, Joe Alsop, Stewart Alsop, etc. Harry McPherson is also going to talk with Louis Martin of the DNC.

In addition, I will try to do some work with the news chiefs of ABC, NBC and CBS.

Robert E. Kintner

FIGURE 1-1   A Media Leader Goes to Work for the President

Helen Thomas, and ABC's Kathleen Delaski.[37] A more apparent conflict was evident in 1980 when columnist George Will coached Ronald Reagan as he prepared for his debates with incumbent Jimmy Carter. After one of the debates, Will then went on television as a journalist and commented favorably on Reagan's performance.[38]

More troubling because of its scope is evidence from many sources that present a disturbing pattern of give and take between segments of the media and the Central Intelligence Agency. Such a relationship may have included William Paley; it most certainly involved a significant number of American correspondents covering foreign affairs during the Cold War.[39] Some presumably briefed the CIA on what they had seen or heard at distant outposts, especially in eastern Europe. It is difficult to imagine how reporters could retain their credibility or their independence as observers while providing services to an American agency.

As we have seen, then, media leaders sometimes make friends and professional contacts that conflict with their obligations to be neutral observers.

THREE COMMERCIAL PRESSURE POINTS: AUDIENCES, WALL STREET, AND ADVERTISERS

Thus far we have considered the media in terms of their widespread use by Americans, their increasingly concentrated ownership patterns, and the interorganizational processes that make the them very much *in* rather than *apart from* the rest of American institutional life. It remains to briefly outline some of the commercial pressures that influence part of what Americans see and read.

It is obvious that most of the American media are "commercial." That is, they sell time or space to advertisers, thereby creating a revenue stream that makes other forms of content such as news and entertainment possible. Over-the-air broadcasters by and large have a *single revenue stream* of advertiser support for programming. Magazines, newspapers, and cable television function with *dual revenue streams* made up of both subscription (or point of sale) charges as well as advertising. With some exceptions such as "premium" cable services and the film industry, advertising generates the largest source of revenue for all media.

Consumers tend to view the media as providers of specific forms of content: programs we want to see or items we want to read. But the media themselves, along with those who evaluate them as potential investments and advertisers, generally consider the media as *audience-delivery* systems. With the exceptions of film and recorded music, virtually all media present themselves to potential advertisers on the direct promise that they have the right "environment" for selling products and services to an important segment of the American public. In more prosaic language, a television network executive may describe his or her task as "selling eyeballs."

The great marketing machine of mass-mediated culture is fueled by the right mixture of content, audience, and advertising message. Thus the *New York Times* presents itself as the medium that can deliver high-income, college-educated readers to advertisers who want to promote luxurious services and products. NBC decides to cancel a long-running situation comedy series because it is failing to attract the younger audiences most advertisers want to reach. A radio station favorably positions itself in a given "market" by picking a music format that draws audiences particular advertisers want to reach. "Top 40" is still a reliable net that can be used to capture younger audiences, perfect for companies merchandising fast food, films, concerts, and skin-care products.

But all audiences are not equal. Virtually every specific media outlet has a measurable demographic signature that effects its ability to attract advertisers. Audiences can be surveyed and defined by sex, age, income, race, education, and geographical location. In broadcast television, for example, the most sought-after audience is generally women between the ages of eighteen and forty-nine. Marketing analysts for many kinds of food and household products have determined that these women represent the primary purchasers of goods in the United States. More recently, the Fox network has made it a high profile-strategy to go aggressively after younger viewers.[40]

Even the ostensibly "noncommercial" programs of public television are considered in terms of the potential goodwill that certain audiences may feel toward their increasingly visible underwriters. Thus the Boeing Corporation has funded a PBS program on the president's airplane, Air Force One, a product made by that corporation. And various drug companies have supported shows on health care, but not on more controversial health issues such as insurance cost containment programs or malpractice.[41]

This commercial necessity of selling audiences to advertisers has a number of obvious and important implications that must figure in virtually every assessment of the popular media. Our focus is largely on some of the problems this equation imposes on the breadth and flow of information.

Satisfying Audiences: The Push for Higher Ratings and Larger Circulation

In general the larger the audience for one media outlet the more it can charge for advertising space or time. This basic commercial rule is subject to certain variables. There are instances when smaller audiences are extremely desirable, if they contain high numbers of the kinds of people particular advertisers want to reach. But the correlation between audience size and commercial success is rather rigid in settings where similar media are competing in the same market for the same audiences.

A vivid case in point is seen in behavior of the major broadcast television networks. CBS, NBC, ABC, and Fox all compete for national audiences, as measured by several national ratings services. A *rating* is an estimate of the percent of all television households in the United States tuned to a network program. It is based on systematic surveys of a limited number of more or less randomly selected households. Nationally, one rating point equals 955,000 households. A related audience measurement figure is a *share*, which is an estimate of the percent of all households *using* television that are tuned to a network program. For the week of October 9, 1995, for example, the ratings service of A.C. Nielsen indicated that the NBC drama series "ER" was the most-watched network show. It had a rating of 24.7 and a share of 40, huge numbers by the standards of 1990s. Nielsen's estimate amounted to the conclusion that about 24 million American households watched the program, representing 40 percent of all households using television in that prime-time hour.[42]

The lowest-rated programs in many weeks are programs that deal with public affairs. In 1992, for example, a special half-hour on CBS devoted to summarizing the returns from the "Super Tuesday" presidential primaries in a number of states had a modest rating of 6.0 and a share of 9.[43]

Advertising costs in these two shows, like all of television, increases as ratings increase. The specific prices that networks charge advertisers are subject to variations, but the cost of a single thirty-second commercial in a top-rated network program could range from $300,000 to $350,000. The lower-rated program of election returns would have sold each of its thirty-second segments of commercial time for far less. Because network production and administrative costs are more or less fixed, it is easy to see why programmers want to maximize audience size. Large audiences increase the distance between just breaking even and making extremely large profits. The commercial logic of television is essentially to develop and promote popular programs that can maximize revenues from advertising.

The parallel effect in print has editors scrambling to find editorial content—often "soft news" and features—that will heighten the interests of readers, thereby increasing circulation. Like the television industry, newspapers and magazines provide rate cards to potential advertisers listing their daily circulation figures, along with the attractive demographic features of their readers.

The more arcane details of audience measurement and demographic analysis need not concern us here. Our point is more basic. In most of the "mainstream" commercial media such as network television and large city newspapers, audience size is the primary measure for determining suitable content. Ratings and circulation figures of competitors in a given market take on the status of absolute benchmarks of success or failure. Television networks talk about "winning" specific time periods with higher ratings than their competition. Magazines and newspapers describe their status as "the number one medium for adults with high household incomes."

With regard to television and political discussion, the commercial logic that seeks to maximize audiences tends to evoke two very different kinds of judgments. Defenders of the American system of broadcasting by and large see the industry as democratic. In this view, television is a medium that goes to great lengths to win the approval of large segments of the viewing public. The aggregate of viewer response, as measured by nightly program ratings, makes television truly the people's medium. Viewers "vote" with their channel selectors. If programs cannot find their audience on one of the major broadcast networks, they will be replaced by different programs that will be more acceptable to a larger number of people.

In the 1960s this logic lead to such hit shows as "Green Acres," "Mayberry R.F.D.," and the weekly saga of a transplanted Appalachian family of childlike dimwits, the "Beverly Hillbillies." Of the very popular "Hillbillies," CBS's William Paley noted that it was "well done." A "vast majority of television viewers enjoyed that show," he noted, "which was why it was so successful on television."[44] In the mid-1990s the big audience-pleasers were also light comedies—though with a decidedly less rural feel—including "Roseanne," "Home Improvement," "Seinfeld," and "Grace Under Fire."

Critics have made what are, by now, familiar but important objections to the equation of high ratings with "success." If mass culture is the standard by which the most important television content is measured, they note, and if television sees itself as being primarily in the entertainment business, then the culture has been severely handicapped in its abilities to engage in public discussion.[45]

Two realistic options for maintaining serious public discussion in a mass entertainment medium are possible, if not very satisfactory. Either serious consideration of issues must be minimized in this lucrative milieu, a pattern seen in the dramatic decline in once-common hour-long network documentaries. Or issues-discussion must be "packaged" in the structure and pacing of the entertainment programming that defines the medium.

One of the many "worriers" about the effects of television on the quality of public discourse, Neil Postman, has noted that we have generally followed the second option. In *Amusing Ourselves to Death* he argues that serious (meaning extended, in-depth) discussion has been driven from our attention by news programs that must match the pacing and variety of mass entertainment. He quotes one-time NBC correspondent Robert McNeil, former co-anchor of PBS's "McNeil/Lehrer Newshour," who notes that the pattern in contemporary broadcast journalism is "to keep everything brief, not to strain the attention of anyone but instead to provide constant stimulation through variety, novelty, action, and movement." The nexus of audience and advertiser needs in television imposes stiff financial penalties for the medium that wants to focus sustained attention on a single idea. "You are required," McNeil writes, "to pay attention to no concept, no character, and no problem for more than a few seconds at a time."[46] Postman draws the obvious conclusion:

> *If you were a producer of a television news show for a commercial station, you would not have the option of defying television's requirements. It would be demanded of you that you strive for the largest possible audience, and, as a consequence and in spite of your best intentions, you would arrive at a production very nearly resembling McNeil's description.*[47]

Thus, in the past few years the networks have shown that they are willing to curtail much of their coverage of national political conventions that occur in election years. ABC has had difficulty keeping its "bottom -line"-oriented affiliates interested in carrying future "Nightline" broadcasts.[48] The affiliates have found that they can make more money carrying various forms of late-night entertainment. And the only large newspaper that was designed specifically with younger, television-trained consumers in mind—Gannett's single-paragraph-per-story *USA Today*—is the only major American daily to show significant circulation increases.[49]

Satisfying Wall Street

Most of the large media businesses in the United States are public corporations, which means that they sell shares of the corporation to investors who, in return for providing capital, hope to share in its profits. As opposed to private companies such as the Newhouse Group and Reader's Digest, public corporations carry the burden of making themselves attractive to stock purchasers by increasing profit margins and paying dividends. Members of a corporation's board of directors will often recognize that their first obligation is to those who own its shares.

In terms of serving the stockholders, "prudent management" can mean many things. It may involve starving the company's growth to build profits and pay dividends to investors. It may involve using money on hand to invest in equipment, talent, or new ventures. When an economy is in a recession and the management is not farsighted, the need to please shareholders may come at the expense of the company's or the public's long-term needs.[50] In the mass media such a scenario is not uncommon, and frequently results in the decision by management to cut back on various public service efforts, or on labor-intensive operations such as news.

The recent history of CBS is illustrative. Prior to its sale to Westinghouse Electric in 1995, the quality of CBS's highly regarded public affairs programming—including news—suffered significantly from a series of financial dealings in the 1980s. Trouble for the corporation began in 1984 when a group of political conservatives, including North Carolina senator Jesse Helms, announced their intention to purchase sufficient shares of the company to be able to control what they felt were its left-leaning news staff. It was doubtful they could ever achieve their goal, but the takeover attempt was enough to "put the company into play" as a takeover target. The following year Atlanta media mogul Ted Turner made a more serious attempt to purchase CBS by using a Byzantine arrangement involving the use of so-called junk bonds. He, too, had little chance of success, but the CBS management and board took defensive action by purchasing back much of its stock, cutting staff, and selling profitable operations such as its St Louis affiliate, KMOX- TV.[51]

At the same time, the shrewd chief financier of the Loews Corporation, Larry Tisch, began to buy large blocks of CBS stock, and was soon invited to its board of directors. One reason the invitation was extended was the fear that Tisch, too, was interested in acquiring CBS. After a failed attempt by CBS chief Tom Wyman to convince the board to accept a friendly takeover by the Coca-Cola Company, Wyman was forced to resign, and the Chairman of Loews was asked to take his place.

Tisch was known as a generous benefactor to many New York cultural institutions, but he was notably stingy in his leadership of CBS. In a period of just several years, control of one of the greatest American corporations had gone from William Paley, a man who—even with his limitations—loved broadcasting and respected the company's special obligations to the American public, to a financier who admitted that he knew little about the entertainment business. One of Tisch's first acts was to sell the very profitable CBS Records Division to the Sony Corporation, and to downsize news and entertainment division staffs. He also sold the company's research center in Connecticut, its book publishing operations, and its American and Latin American musical publishing divisions.[52] In Peter Boyer's words, by 1988 CBS was no longer a media giant, "but a relatively small broadcasting company with a lot of cash."[53]

Tisch's reign over CBS generally had the effect of maintaining its short-term attractiveness as an investment, but weakened it as a media corporation with a unique history and identity. The "CBS Evening News" lost its reputation as the "newscast of record" to the more ably managed ABC and to the more cost-efficient CNN.

The fear of gutting a respected media giant in order to keep its attractiveness as an investment is not just the product of the takeover period of the 1980s. It has haunted other news operations, most notably the *Washington*

Post and the *New York Times*. Both are public corporations, but their boards took precautions to provide buffers between investors and the staffs responsible for management and editorial judgments. Issuing stock is a way to finance the purchase of new equipment or upgrade the staff. The trick is to find a way to do it without sacrificing control. The *Times'* solution to this problem was ingenious, and has since been copied by other corporations. In 1968 the company issued a bare 51 percent of voting stock to the Sulzberger and Ochs families, who wanted to continue to run the newspaper with an eye on quality rather than maximizing profits. At the same time they issued nonvoting Class A stock to the general public.[54] Presumably quality is attractive to investors, even if they do not have the right to vote out a paper's management or board of directors.

Satisfying the Formula: Determining Commercial Saliency

There is something ennobling and romantic in the old publisher's admonition to publish now and worry about the consequences later. As Ellis Cose notes, the news business used to be populated by "oddballs and erratic visionaries,"[55] most of whom maintained modest goals for financial success. To be sure, they had their failings, but as a class they were less inclined than their modern counterparts to reference their worth in terms of the commercial saliency of their institutions. With increasingly rare exceptions (found mainly in opinion periodicals like Charles Peter's *Washington Monthly* or television's Ted Turner) media owners and managers see themselves largely in marketing terms, shaping their "products" to fit specific demographic and entertainment objectives.[56]

In many ways the standards of newsgathering have never been higher. Journalists are better trained than they used to be, and newsgathering has emerged as a profession with recognizable values and ethics.[57] And some of those working in the "prestige press" note that they have been relatively free to ignore the business sides of their organizations.[58] But many others must contend with a modern-day complication that was far less apparent in the precorporate age. Those responsible for producing content in all forms of media are now inundated with data about audience and advertiser acceptance of their work. The line that separates the marketing of the media and the production of its content is far less distinct than it once was.

The print media's newest major newspaper, *USA Today*, for example, was constructed and formatted from a marketing point of view. Before its official launch in 1982, prototypes were tested with a wide variety of opinion leaders and potential readers, and content was altered to deal with their objections.[59] The suitability of anchorpersons for national and local television newscasts are judged in part by their Q-ratings, which have nothing to do with their journalistic skills, but are derived from audience surveys of how well they are liked. To the regret of many broadcast journalists, stations often hire consultants called news doctors to tinker with the pacing, story selection, and format of local news "shows." And news directors distribute to their staffs ratings results, which remain the determining variable considered by advertisers in deciding where to place ads.

What all of this indicates is an inexact but clear shift away from the idea of news as *information* to news as a *commodity* designed for the marketplace. Certain news stories dealing with national politics and unexpected events will always remain well; if not even better-covered. But the layers of reporting that have been added to ever-thicker newspapers and extended hours devoted to local news often exploits individuals and events as vehicles for winning the attention of preselected audiences.

One sign of this is the increasing tendency of broadcast stations to insert stories in their late-evening newscasts that build on a plot line developed in a television movie. Teasers for such stories start in the early commercial breaks of the film. And the presence of stories on adoption, teen suicides, incest, and child abuse enjoy a superficial kind of relevance that frequently conceals their real purpose: to hold the viewer a little longer through the evening.

In such an environment it is difficult for anyone to resist a process of automatic self-censorship that calculates the suitability of certain approaches and topics in light of their acceptability to audiences and advertisers. In one sense, this process is healthy. Communicators of all sorts need to consider the effects of their efforts on those to whom they are directed. But self-censorship becomes a problem when it begins to impose unnecessarily restrictive limitations on information.

During the 1991 Persian Gulf War against Iraq, to cite an interesting case, advertisers were reluctant to buy commercial time.[60] War and other national crises are considered inappropriate "environments" for selling products and services on television. "When we use TV," noted an advertising executive recently, "we're not using it to support First Amendment rights or artistic freedoms, we're using it because it's a good business decision for our client, and nobody wants the result of a business decision to be a loss of customers rather than gains."[61] To their credit, the networks sacrificed millions of dollars of revenues to carry extensive reporting. But a similar event in the future may make them more conservative about defining their responsibilities to their viewers.

In candid moments, reporters and assignment editors will sometimes admit dismissing their journalistic judgment in favor of covering a story because of its unattractiveness. Citing two useless stories he covered when working as a street reporter at WCBS in New York (one on a "hippie" commune, another on a suicide), Bob Teague admitted that his sense of journalistic ethics became secondary to his role as a gatherer of superficial if fascinating events.[62] There is, he notes, a constant battle between producers "who think in terms of production values" and reporters who "have to fight like hell to persuade them that a particular story deserves more time." Sadly, self-censorship can quickly become a survival strategy for journalists who "tend to stop battling after losing four or five in row."[63]

CBS's Morley Safer is even grimmer, noting that "reporting as I knew it has all but disappeared." In a 1992 speech to news executives, he argued that even some of the network's news segments are now indistinguishable from those of video tabloids such as a "Current Affair" or "Hard Copy," which now offer stiff competition to more traditional early evening news programs.[64] He and many others in television news wonder how far networks will go in using audience ratings as a basis for determining the content and depth of news.

SUMMARY

In this chapter we have surveyed some of the important attributes and pressures that exist within the mass media industries. Certain fundamental features of these industries must be considered in assessing the processes of newsgathering, political reporting, and—even in the context of entertainment—the discussion of political issues.

The primary characteristic of the media as vital elements in an increasingly competitive corporate climate is their tendency to allow circulation figures and television ratings to define success or failure. One of the ironies of the news business as a corporate activity is that content may be seen as something to be shaped by public opinion rather than to lead it. Such a view squares better with the marketing models used by industries promoting consumer goods than to communicators entrusted with the task of contributing to constructive public discourse.

No industry can afford to be indifferent to its economic health. The protective mechanisms of the information industries are not unlike those employed in other settings. They include the increased concentration of ownership of most of the nation's newspapers, broadcasting stations, and entertainment enterprises. The virtues of concentration sometimes make sense financially; large enterprises usually have the financial resources needed to take risks on the development of new projects. But there are also costs, the most basic of which is the need to avoid criticism of institutions of American life where an industry may have a financial stake. These financial interests may dictate not getting involved in reporting on issues affecting another business owned by the parent company, or avoiding negative comment and reporting on the actions of an important advertiser.

We have also argued against the idea that the mass media exists apart from the pressures and constraints that affect and sometimes govern the behavior of other kinds of industries. Like many other corporations, enterprises in the business of contributing to the public dialogue seek out alliances in business and government that will solidify their financial success. They are the objects of political and economic pressure. And they sometimes engage in lobbying and the development of "sweetheart" relationships with other institutions for whom they are ostensible observers.

The mass media in the United States thus coexists in worlds that sometimes require very different sensibilities. As industries, they must remain profitable and attractive to their consumers. And as agents of social and political interaction, they are irreplaceable as agents for the maintenance of our national life.

NOTES

1. Ben Bagdikian, *The Media Monopoly*, 4th ed. (Boston: Beacon Press, 1992), p. 237.

2. Abstract of the CBS Evening News, February 6, 1992, Vanderbilt News Archives.

3. Bagdikian, *Media Monopoly*, p. xxvii.

4. For a recent look at the Time Warner empire from the perspective of its former head, Steve Ross, see Connie Bruck, *Master of the Game* (New York: Simon and Schuster, 1994).

5. Geraldine Fabrikant, "Walt Disney to Acquire ABC in $19 Billion Deal to Build a Giant for Entertainment," *New York Times*, August 1, 1995, pp. A1, D5.

6. The "resignation" of Puttnam from Columbia is a complex story, told with interesting detail by Andrew Yule in *Fast Fade: David Puttnam, Columbia Pictures, and the Battle for Hollywood* (New York: Delacorte Press, 1989). A further example of Hollywood's desire to avoid risky subjects is seen in the 1992 film "The Player," a sharp satire as seen through the experiences of a major studio head. It is probably not a coincidence that Robert Altman's film was financed by the New Line Cinema Corporation, an independant film company separate from the "big six" Hollywood studios.

7. Lawrence K. Grossman, "Regulate the Medium," *Columbia Journalism Review*, November–December 1991, p. 72.

8. Roger Cohen, "Killed Book is Haunting Time Warner," *New York Times*, April 16, 1990, pp. D1, D8.

9. For a more thorough review of these events see Gary C. Woodward and Robert E. Denton Jr., *Persuasion and Influence in American Life*, 2d ed. (Prospect Heights, IL: Waveland, 1992), pp. 32–39.

10. Quoted in William Rivers, *The Adversaries: Politics and the Press* (Boston: Beacon, 1970), p. 68.

11. This story is told by the journalists Bob Woodward and Carl Bernstein in their book *All the President's Men* (New York: Simon and Shuster, 1974), and raised to the level of an American myth in the 1976 film of the same name.

12. See Rivers, *The Adversaries*, pp. 68–133.

13. William Boot, "NASA and the Spellbound Press," *Columbia Journalism Review* July–August 1986, p. 23.

14. Ibid, p. 24.

15. For an extended discussion of political gamesmanship, see Christopher Mattews, *Hardball* (New York: Summit Books, 1988).

16. Bernard Weinraub, "Paramount Withdraws Its Ads After a Bad Review in Variety," *New York Times*, June 10, 1992, p. C15.

17. David Halberstam, *The Making of a Quagmire* (New York: Random House, 1965).

18. See Gay Talese, *The Kingdom and the Power* (New York: World Publishing, 1969), pp. 443, 466.

19. For many examples of successful political coersion at the local level see Rivers, *The Adversaries*, pp. 91–133.

20. Tom Wicker, *On Press* (New York: Viking, 1978), p. 235.

21. David Halberstam, *The Powers That Be* (New York: Alfred A. Knopf, 1979). The book is also a fascinating examination of how the lives of media leaders are intertwined with the political and corporate world.

22. Sally Bedell Smith, *In All His Glory: The Life of William S. Paley* (New York: Simon and Schuster, 1990), p. 510–511.

23. See Daniel Schorr, *Clearing the Air* (New York: Houghton Mifflin, 1977), pp. 71–74.

24. Peter Stoler, *The War Against the Press* (New York: Dodd and Mead, 1986), p. 66.

25. Michael Parenti, *Inventing Reality: The Politics of the Mass Media* (New York: St. Martin's, 1986), p. 231.

26. Eric Barnouw, *The Sponsor: Notes on a Modern Potentate* (New York: Oxford, 1978), p. 136.

27. Todd Gitlin, *Inside Prime Time* (New York: Pantheon, 1983), pp. 257–258.

28. Gloria Steinem, "Sex, Lies, and Advertising," in *Mass Media 94/95*, ed. Joan Gorham (Guilford, CT: Dushkin, 1994), pp. 62–71.

29. Harry A. Jessell, "Turner Takes a Swing at Time Warner," *Broadcasting and Cable*, October. 3, 1994, p. 17.

30. Don West, "DeSales Street," *Broadcasting*, April 27, 1992, p. 15.

31. Bagdikian, p. 25.

32. Smith, p. 479.

33. Benjamin C. Bradlee, *Conversations with Kennedy* (New York: Pocket Books, 1976), p. 21.

34. See Ronald Brownstein, *The Power and the Glitter: The Hollywood Washington Connection* (New York: Pantheon, 1990), ch. 1.

35. Malcolm Jones, Jr., "Lights, Action, Politicking!" review of Greg Mitchell's *The Campaign of the Century*, in *Newsweek*, June 1, 1992, p. 70.

36. Brownstein, *The Power and the Glitter*, ch. 10.

37. "White House Dinner: The Guest List," *New York Times*, June 17, 1992, p. A12.

38. Jack W. Germond and Jules Witcover, *Whose Broad Stripes and Bright Stars? The Trivial Pursuit of the Presidency, 1988* (New York: Warner, 1989), p. 428.

39. See, for example, Parenti, *Inventing Reality*, pp. 232–233, and Schorr, *Clearing the Air*, pp. 274–280.

40. Bill Carter, "As Cable Makes Inroads, Networks Cast a Wider Net," *New York Times*, March 29, 1993, pp. D1, D8.

41. Pat Aufdeheide, "A Funny Thing Is Happening to TV's Public Forum," *Columbia Journalism Review*, November–December 1991, pp. 60–63.

42. "People's Choice: Ratings According to Nielsen, Oct 9–15," *Broadcasting and Cable*, October 23, 1995, p. 32.

43. "Broadcasting's Ratings Week, March 9–15," Broadcasting, March 23, 1992, p.34.

44. William S. Paley, *As It Happened: A Memoir* (New York: Doubleday, 1979), p. 273.

45. See, for example, Robert M. Entman, *Democracy Without Citizens: Media and the Decay of American Politics* (New York: Oxford, 1989); "Is TV Debasing Politics," *Columbia Journalism Review*, September–October 1973, pp. 41–48.

46. Neil Postman, *Amusing Ourselves to Death* (New York: Penquin, 1986), p. 105.

47. Ibid, p. 106.

48. Bill Carter, "Ted Koppel Says 'Nightline' Is in Jeopardy," *New York Times*, June 4, 1992, p. C20.

49. "ABC FAS-FAX Totals for Top 25 Newspapers," *Editor and Publisher*, May 9, 1992, p. 18.

50. The "takeover madness" that regularly occurred in the 1980s was driven largely by the interests of managers and boards to make huge sums of money for investors, including themselves. For a full account of this greed at the expense of the long-term interests of a corporation, see Bryan Burrough and John Helyar, *Barbarians at the Gate* (New York: Harper and Row, 1990).

51. Peter Boyer, *Who Killed CBS?* (New York: Random House, 1988), pp. 197–199.

52. Ken Auletta, *Three Blind Mice: How the TV Networks Lost Their Way* (New York: Random House, 1991), p. 414.

53. Boyer, *Who Killed CBS?* p. 323.

54. See Ellis Cose, *The Press* (New York: Murrow, 1989), pp. 216–217.

55. Ibid, p. 21.

56. Others who might be on a short list of individuals or groups for whom content is central to their business mission might include—from days past—C. K. McClatchy of the *Sacramento Bee*, Harold Ross and William Shawn of the *New Yorker* and—presently—the managers of C-SPAN, the publishers of the *Christian Science Monitor, Ms., Atlantic Monthly,* and *National Review.*

57. See Stephen Hess's description of reporters in the nation's capital, *The Washington Reporters* (Washington, DC: Brookings, 1981), pp. 82–83.

58. See, for example, David S. Broder, *Behind the Front Page: A Candid Look at How the News Is Made* (New York: Simon and Shuster, 1987), p. 325.

59. Peter Prichard, *The Making of McPaper* (Kansas City: Andrews, McMeel and Parker, 1987), pp. 105–121.

60. Bill Carter, "Few Sponsors for TV War News," *New York Times*, February 7, 1991, pp. D1, D20.

61. Jeff Silverman, "TVs Creators Face a New Caution," *New York Times*, December 8, 1991, Sec. 2, p. 31.

62. Bob Teague, *Live and Off Color: News Biz* (New York: A and W Publishers, 1982), pp. 88–90.

63. Ibid, pp. 99–100.

64. Rich Brown, "CBS's Safer Blasts Network News," *Broadcasting*, February 3, 1992, p. 14.

2

NEWS IN THE TELEVISION AGE: PATTERNS OF ORGANIZATION AND NEWS SELECTION

At its best, journalism is a kind of window on the world, one that offers an inevitably limited but useful view of what is going on. At something less than its best, journalism is a screen on which deceptive images dance—today's seeming truths, tomorrow's undoubted foolishness.[1]

By any measure it was a sad and bizarre event. The story was political, but also something more: in its own way a perfect drama made for television. A public figure—the state treasurer for the Commonwealth of Pennsylvania—would conclude a 1987 news conference near his office in Harrisburg by doing the unthinkable, taking his own life as horrified journalists and aides looked on. "You don't want to take down your equipment yet," R. Budd Dwyer said to the few television camera crews who attended the conference he called to defend himself against charges of official corruption. He then pulled a .357 magnum from a large manila envelope and placed its short barrel in his mouth. In an instant he had pulled the trigger, ending his life.[2]

Had the midmorning news conference taken the expected pattern of a routine meeting between reporters and a leader in state government, it is unlikely that it would have been given time on the state's television stations. Print journalists might have found some value in the statements of a State Treasurer under a cloud of suspicion for the misuse of funds. But television usually requires something more dramatic and vivid. With the bloody footage of this suicide, it had what it needed. Just days before, viewers had seen almost the same scenario on episodes of NBC's popular "L.A. Law" and CBS's "The Equalizer."

The state's most successful station, the ABC affiliate in Philadelphia, ran the footage in its popular noon newscast. Its news director later defended the decision, noting that it was a "difficult decision," but "to properly tell the story, we felt it was appropriate." Even the Harrisburg ABC affiliate, which did not have a noon newscast, decided to break into its regular programming to run the footage, focusing especially on the tragic epilogue to the news conference. An exception was the decision of NBC's Philadelphia affiliate to tell the story rather than show it. News director Randy Covington believed that showing the suicide served no purpose and was "disrespectful of the family of the deceased."

For the networks and CNN it was also a dicey call. Had Dwyer's news conference ended with his reaffirmation of his innocence, it would have remained buried in the back pages of the Pennsylvania's newspapers and ignored by national broadcast journalists. But now newsroom decision makers had to decide if they now had too much of the kind of graphic footage that is usually sought out by producers. In the end, ABC's World News Tonight and CNN opted for stopping the sound and video before the suicide. CBS and NBC had their anchorpersons verbally summarize the story.

By itself this was an exceptional and tragic event. But it illuminates some of the essential features and troubling issues facing the medium that for several decades has reshaped American politics and the way Americans think about their civil (and sometimes not so civil) affairs.

In this chapter we will look at television news in the United States from two perspectives. The first third focuses on the importance of television news in the national consciousness, and how video journalism has evolved at the local and national levels. This perspective suggests that news is a vital national institution with a profitable but unstable corporate base. The remainder of the chapter explores theories and concepts of news selection. Based in the fundamental models of agenda setting and gatekeeping, the chapter documents newsgathering routines, especially the gatekeeping values that govern the selection of materials for local and national versions of news. The chapter concludes with a summary of eight common features of video journalism, which both enhance and limit the possibilities for effective public discussion.

TELEVISION AS POLITICAL THEATER

Television is now the primary narrator of the American experience. Citizens of diverse backgrounds are likely to recall the "defining moments" in our recent political history by reference to the images and events witnessed on the small screen: the charges of Anita Hill against Supreme Court nominee Clarence Thomas, the agonizing congressional debate over the commitment of American ground forces to the 1991 Persian Gulf War, the murder trial of O. J. Simpson, the governor of California trying to account for the explosions of violence and rage in South Central Los Angeles. As we approach the end of the twentieth century, the public dimensions of American culture are best understood in the context of the private traumas, fantasies, and national rituals that appear on the nation's television screens. No medium so clearly ties us together with dramatic visions of victory and defeat, pride and shame, success and failure.

In the print media, politics is often about ideas, unseen actions, arguments, or abstract proposals. But television news owes more to the elements of storytelling than information giving. It uses narration to present us with a vast panorama of players caught up in struggles that end in victimage or vindication, acceptance or rejection, triumph or defeat.[3] Thus, the Dwyer story stood by itself as a public tale about a private horror. On television the political circumstances that led to his decision to stage his own death seemed to matter less than the details of the final moments of his life. In Richard Sennett's useful phrase, television is "compulsively personalistic, always making the private life of the politician the center of interest."[4]

Like the novel or film, television encourages us to view the action seen through the camera viewfinder as representative of larger trends. We view the events recorded in television news as symbols of the collective poverty or wealth of our culture. News functions as a barometer of the nation's morality, issuing cautionary warnings about our successes and failures, and suggesting uncountable similar events that have occurred away from the glare of television coverage.[5]

The Pervasive Nature of Television News

The glow of the television set is almost a constant presence in the American home. A significant part of what viewers consume from America's 2,400 broadcast television stations and 12,000 municipal cable systems includes news and discussion. On any given night as many as one-half of all adult Americans may view one of the newscasts carried by CNN or one of the television networks. Nearly three-quarters now identify themselves as regular news viewers.[6] In 1991, even after several rounds of corporate belt-tightening, CBS, NBC, and ABC spent nearly one billion dollars feeding this enormous appetite for video information.[7] In just one nine-month sample of CBS, analyst Doris Graber and her associates recorded over 4,800 individual stories covering more than 8000 topics. More than two-thirds dealt with political issues.[8]

Americans are not only attracted to television for much of their information about local and national events, but they believe that television versions of events are more accurate than competing accounts offered by radio, magazines, and even newspapers. In recent Roper Polls, a cross section of Americans were asked to choose which medium they would believe "if you got conflicting or different reports of the same story from radio, television, the magazines, and the newspapers." Over half of all respondents (55 percent) said they were "most inclined" to believe television, with newspapers coming in a distant second (21 percent). Radio and magazines were the first choices of less than 8 percent of those responding.[9]

The relative credibility of television news sometimes suffers from setbacks, as when NBC faked a truck explosion for one of its news segments. The segment essentially duplicated a stunt that is common in action/adventure programming, but at a significant cost to the network's prestige. NBC publicly apologized in early 1993 for planting explosives in the truck to "simulate" the alleged dangers of its vulnerable gas tank.[10] There is also no shortage of critics and press-monitoring groups who claim to see a crippling bias (usually liberal or conservative) in the mainstream video media, such as ABC's "Nightline" or the "CBS Evening News."[11] However, as we shall see in the last half of this chapter, the larger bias of television is not in its politics, but in its structure, especially its fascination for interesting stories and pictures.

TELEVISION NEWSGATHERING AT THE LOCAL AND NATIONAL LEVELS

Television news is gathered by three types of organizations. They include local broadcasters operating on one of the channels in a regional market; television networks, who have traditionally set the highest standards for broadcast news; and news services both print and video, which augment the supply of text and pictures available to the first two.

Local Television News

At the local level, commercial television stations—especially the more affluent network affiliates—employ staffs of reporters, writers, camera persons, and managers to produce segments for their news programs. Typically, a station affiliated with a network will generate local inserts blended into the network's morning news shows. It will also produce a noon broadcast and a financially profitable and very competitive local news program before and after the network's prime-time schedule.[12]

On any given day, a station in a middle-sized television market (such as Sacramento-Stockton, Denver, or Pittsburgh) may have four to six video crews available to cover stories. Most crews (cameraperson and perhaps one technician) are assigned a reporter. There can be wide day-to-day variations, but generally each team will contribute material for two or three stories, one of which may be video only (to have a voice-over added by the news anchor in the studio) or an entire package (original video, with narration by the reporter on the scene).

The events crews are chosen by the station's news director or senior producer, based on three criteria: the availability of crews to cover a story, an estimation of what is journalistically defensible, and the judgment of what may hold or attract viewers. Consider, for example, a producer's task in deciding how to deploy three crews on a more or less typical news day. Many groups have faxed press advisories and called the station asking for coverage. Assume each crew (camera person, reporter, and technician) can produce two stories. Where would you assign these crews?

- A press conference by the mayor announcing her intention to run for a second term
- A press conference by a local hospital on a new procedure for treating fire victims
- A press conference by the representatives of a Native American group announcing a lawsuit against the state over river fishing rights
- The demolition of an old five-story factory by a team of explosives experts
- A conference of economists at the convention center conferring on the future of the American banking industry
- The official opening of a "magnet school" catering to gifted science students
- A strike of teachers in a suburban school district
- A press conference by a federal prosecutor on the effects of drug raids on local drug users
- The offer of one of the state's senators—running for reelection—to hook up by satellite from Washington for an interview with one of the news anchors
- The opening of the city's annual flower show at its convention center
- Hearings by a members of the State Assembly on auto insurance rates
- Planned eviction of several poor families that had illegally taken over apartments in city-subsidized housing
- City council debate on the placement of a trash collection center in a middle-class neighborhood.

Note that most of these events are not stories to be "discovered," but events planned by others who may benefit from television exposure. News is "manufactured" as much as it is "covered."[13] Note, too, that even this very limited list represents twice the number of stories three crews could cover. Moreover, assignments to any of these stories will be contingent on whatever spot news items (accidents, fires, and other unexpected but "urgent" stories) develop over the period.

In addition to local occurrences, the station also has a choice of relaying thousands of stories supplied to it by its wire services, typically Reuters, United Press International, and the Associated Press. It may also use a number of video packages devoted to national and international events that are fed to it throughout on an almost continuous basis from a network and other video news services. For example, NBC's service to its over 200 affiliates is called NBC News Channel, which the network started in 1991. The range of stories offered to a station may include business news, foreign war coverage, election results from other nations, obituaries of leaders or celebrities, reports from international trade meetings, and trend stories describing important political or social changes in another country. In actual fact, however, local stations exclude most national and international news unless they deal with natural or manmade catastrophes.[14]

There are many choices that must be made in a short period of time. To focus for a moment on only the station's important half-hour newscast at the end of the evening prime-time schedule, it becomes apparent that the limits imposed by both time and the desire for high ratings will dramatically narrow down what finally gets on the air. A half-hour newscast actually has about twenty minutes for various segments, after commercial breaks are figured in. In addition, stations have determined that significant percentages of the newscast will go to non-news elements. In middle-sized markets, according to Stephen Hess, sports news represents 17.2 percent of the newscast, with weather close behind at 14.2 percent.[15] There are also transitional "billboards" about what is coming up next, along with soft news items such as film reviews and "back of the book" human (or animal) interest stories. The actual time for "news" may be as little as eleven minutes, which usually translates into about twelve items with an average length of only fifty seconds.[16]

In such a small space what kinds of stories merit coverage? Several values can be said to dominate local television reports. First and most basic, events become "news" when they symbolize important conflicts or issues within the community. The mayor's announcement to run for a second term is likely to be covered because much of any city's future is perceived to ride on the fortunes of its top elected officials. A second value places emphasis on stories with interesting pictures. As we shall see when we focus on the traits of network news, with few exceptions producers have little use for stories—even important ones—for which they do not have interesting pictures. This visual bias of television is so pronounced that the odds would favor providing time for footage of the warehouse demolition, even if that segment has virtually no long-term importance. These basic values are elaborated more fully in the section on gatekeeping later in this chapter.

Network Television News

The networks began their news departments when radio was the dominant home entertainment medium and television was still under development. In the mid-1930s expanded news services were put together by David Sarnoff at NBC and William Paley at CBS for both altruistic and practical reasons. The original goal was to provide Americans with up-to-date information on World War II. Especially at CBS, the tradition of hiring first-rate reporters and giving them wide latitude was established when William Paley choose Edward R. Murrow as the cornerstone of an independent news organization within the network.[17] Murrow was a legend in his own right, first for his insightful radio reporting in the hot spots of Britain and Europe during World War II, and later for his courageous television documentaries that could be highly critical of popular American institutions.[18] Murrow was one of a handful of industry pioneers that helped television broadcasters live up to their federal license obligations to serve the "public interest, convenience, and necessity." As the networks matured through the 1950s and 1960s, it was understood that news had a public-service function and would be financed by the revenues generated from lucrative entertainment programs.[19]

By the 1990s, however, news divisions no longer functioned as quasi-independent units within the networks. Not only had the federal government generally given up its interest in holding broadcasters to the original "public interest" standard—encouraged by a wave of deregulation that reached its height under President Ronald Reagan—but networks increasingly looked for profits rather than prestige in informational programing.

Eric Sevareid, who held the important position of providing commentaries on the "CBS Evening News," claims that this shift started with the success of CBS's "60 Minutes." Once this program gained huge ratings, programmers set their sights on news as a profit center tied to ratings rather than a semi-autonomous unit removed from the intense commercial pressures of the industry.[20]

However different they are today from their earlier network roots, the news divisions of the networks—along with Cable News Network—represent key forces in the informational life of Americans. Because they have created a vital common link of information and experience, the networks have provided much of the "glue" that binds together the diverse strands of American culture. What we claim to know about events and individuals in much of the world is largely "mediated" through the lens of these organizations. Critic Michael Arlen's description of the Vietnam conflict as "The

Living Room War"[21] could be applied to an endless string of conflicts and events Americans have "witnessed." The networks still represent a vital pool of common experience about events beyond our immediate lives.

Story selection is one of the most discussed dimensions of network news. In his seminal book, *Deciding What's News*, Herbert Gans described the kinds of activities the networks typically portrayed in their newscasts over a two-month period. The top five were crime scandals and investigations (28 percent), government conflict and disagreements (17 percent), disasters, actual or averted (14 percent), government decisions, proposals, and ceremonies (12 percent), and protests, violent and nonviolent (10 percent).[22] Gans generally confirmed what others have similarly documented over the years. In addition to a steady flow of stories on human accidents, wars, and natural disasters, the networks generally focus on the actions of official Washington. Presidential problems or initiatives, governmental debates and hearings, and tensions between power blocks (unions, industries, agencies, and states) form a sturdy core of typical stories. Gans found that over 70 percent of all figures portrayed in news stories were "knowns," that is, political or professional leaders in official positions, including the president, members of the House and Senate, federal officials, state and local officials, and business leaders.[23]

A political scientist who is highly critical of mainstream news, Lance Bennett, goes even further. He claims that the networks engage in a process he describes as "normalization," which involves giving "official" "mainstream" sources in American life the right to comment on a wide range of events or ostensibly deviant behavior.[24] In the context of congressional coverage, for example, a report on welfare reform may include comments from House or Senate leaders on the politics of the legislation (for example, "According to the Speaker, the president will have a hard time getting what he wants)" and comments from professional analysts, such as academics serving in one of dozens of Washington "think tanks" (for instance, "A scholar at the American Enterprise Institute sees major flaws in the legislation.") Typically excluded in this process of normalization are comments outside these narrow sources, perhaps including potential beneficiaries of the legislation, such as social workers or recipients of existing services.

Taking a somewhat different view, Michael J. Robinson has described the major themes behind television news as often adversarial and antagonistic toward government. Not only must video journalism find stories that are simple and interesting, he argues, but they also profit by a selection process that emphasizes "venality, social discord, bureaucratic bungling, and, especially, the good old days." Robinson continues:

> *Senators fighting with businessmen, bureaucrats, each other, is a popular theme; so are governmental unresponsiveness and governmental laxity.*

David Brinkley, Hughes Rudd, and Charles Kuralt have virtually built their television careers on the theme that our government functions badly and that it used to work far better than it does now.[25]

Robinson's analysis came at the end of the Watergate affair, which had plunged America's faith in the political process to an all-time low. Even so, these major themes persist. Government remains at the center of the network's versions of national news, and probably contributes to the increasingly ambivalent attitudes citizens hold toward those who are responsible for the nation's civil affairs.[26]

Recent Upheavals in Network News

The news divisions of CBS, NBC, and ABC were once the crown jewels of the their parent companies. But it would be difficult to identify another part of the broadcast industry that has faced such rapid and chaotic restructuring. Increased competition from other forms of mass media has led many networks to downsize their reporting staffs and "soften" the reporting they now offer the to public.

A number of factors account for the shock waves that have gone through this industry. Fifteen years ago the three major networks had nine out of ten viewers nightly. But that is now down by a third, due in part to the fact that cable has increased viewing options in the typical American home to four times what it once was.[27] Profits that once were the envy of the corporate world have shrunk. In 1984, for example, the networks together made over $800 million. In 1991, industry analysts projected an astounding $400 million loss by CBS alone, due in part to the high prices it paid to purchase the rights to sports events such as major league baseball and the Winter Olympics.

Since 1992 revenues at the networks have stabilized, but news divisions have not regained their former "protected" status. By 1988 NBC had cut over a quarter of its employees from news.[28] Similarly, a year earlier CBS had sold off its very profitable record division and began a massive downsizing of its news staff. The news budget was cut by $33 million, the staff lost 215 people, and a number of news bureaus were reduced or eliminated. In Germany, for example, CBS removed all of its correspondents and producers, leaving it with little option but to use standard video footage and reports from other news services.[29] Dan Rather became so upset by the changes that he cowrote a *New York Times* op-ed article with Richard Cohen decrying the dismemberment of the division. Entitled "From Murrow to Mediocrity," the piece accused the network of abandoning its mission in favor of putting more money in the stockholder's pockets.[30]

Nowhere were these cutbacks felt more dramatically than in the Washington operations of the networks. Since 1993, there have been sub-

Network newscasts work in a confined framework. As this Vanderbilt News Archive summary of a 1995 program from ABC indicates, the time to develop stories is at a premium. The total program length is just over 28 minutes, with 7 minutes for commercials, and slightly more than 1 minute promoting upcoming items (called "billboards" or "bumpers" in the industry.) The "news hole" that is left is about 20 minutes long and, on this night, includes 9 stories.

In the last few years networks have generally decreased their foreign coverage and included segments exploring a domestic issue. In this installment of the ABC Evening News the longest item is the last, a mini-documentary on the teaching of a classic American novel that is not politically correct. The second longest item opens the newscast: the announcement of the proposed purchase of CBS by Westinghouse. Other stories remain close to the mainstream news agenda, including a report on civil war in the former Yugoslavia, and the highly publicized murder trial of sports celebrity O. J. Simpson.

```
ABC evening news

1995.08.01      PREVIEW/INTRODUCTION    FORREST SAWYER (New York)
5:30:00-5:30:40                 Tuesday             ABC

1995.08.01      BUSINESS: CBS—WESTINGHOUSE MERGER
5:30:40-5:34:30                 Tuesday             ABC
    (Studio: Forrest Sawyer)  Report introduced.

    (New York: John Martin)  The transformation of the media world with
the announcement that Westinghouse Electric Corp. proposes to take
over CBS featured.  [Westinghouse chairman & CEO Michael JORDAN, CBS
chairman & CEO Laurence TISCH — talk about the deal.]  The recent
problems at CBS television reviewed.  [Media analyst Chris DIXON —
comments.]  The scope of the combined power of CBS & Westinghouse in
network—owned TV & radio stations explained; map shown.  Concern that
a bidding war may come about outlined.  [Media analyst Tom WOLZIEN —
says Ted Turner & others might look for a network outlet.]

    (Studio: Forrest Sawyer)  Announcement from the four major networks
of funding for a system to let viewers block out programs noted.

1995.08.01      STOCK MARKET REPORT (Studio: Forrest Sawyer)
5:34:30-5:34:40                 Tuesday             ABC

1995.08.01      UPCOMING ITEMS (Studio: Forrest Sawyer)
5:34:40-5:35:00                 Tuesday             ABC

1995.08.01      (COMMERCIAL: Buick Park Avenue; Mylanta; Tylenol.)
5:35:00-5:36:10                 Tuesday             ABC

1995.08.01      WACO, TX / CONGRESSIONAL HEARINGS / RENO
5:36:10-5:38:40                 Tuesday             ABC

    (Studio: Forrest Sawyer)  Report introduced.
```

Continued

FIGURE 2-1. A "typical" network newscast: ABC Evening News, August 1, 1995

ABC evening news

(Capitol: Tim O'Brien) Testimony by Attorney General Janet Reno at the Congressional hearings into the government's handling of the siege of the Branch Davidian cult compound in Waco, TX, featured. [In response to questions from Representative John Mica, RENO — talks about the children & tear gas; reiterates that David Koresh broke promises; defends going in & President Clinton's actions.]

1995.08.01   FLORIDA / HURRICANE ERIN
5:38:40-5:40:40   Tuesday   ABC

(Studio: Forrest Sawyer) The course off Florida of Hurricane Erin updated.

(Palm Beach County: Linda Pattillo) Preparations in eastern Florida for Erin featured; scenes shown of people evacuating areas of Miami & other cities. [RESIDENT — comments.]

1995.08.01   MANTLE HEALTH
5:40:40-5:41:20   Tuesday   ABC

(Studio: Forrest Sawyer) News from former baseball great Mickey Mantle, who recently had a liver transplant, that his cancer has spread reported. [MANTLE — says he has lung cancer.]

1995.08.01   (COMMERCIAL: Aleve; Channel 2 News; Transitions Lenses; Phazyme; "Nightline".)
5:41:20-5:43:40   Tuesday   ABC

1995.08.01   POLITICS & ENVIRONMENT / EPA RULES
5:43:40-5:45:50   Tuesday   ABC

(Studio: Forrest Sawyer) Report introduced.

(White House: Brit Hume) Reaction of President Clinton to the House moves to curtail the EPA's powers featured; details given of the vote to cut its budget. [CLINTON — criticizes this stealth attack on the environment; promises to veto this "polluters' protection act."] [Senator Tom DASCHLE — responds.] The President's threat to also veto the telecommunications bill noted.

1995.08.01   BOSNIA / CIVIL WAR / ARMS EMBARGO
5:45:50-5:48:20   Tuesday   ABC

(Studio: Forrest Sawyer) Report introduced.

(Capitol Hill: John Cochran) House vote to lift the embargo against the Bosnian government examined. [On the House floor, Representatives Ike SKELTON, Larry COMBEST, Richard GEPHARDT, Gerald SOLOMON — debate the implications of lifting the embargo.] The question raised as to whether or not the move will matter in the war in Bosnia.

(Studio: Forrest Sawyer) New & broader threat from the NATO allies of air strikes against the Bosnian Serbs noted.

FIGURE 2-1. *Continued*

```
ABC evening news

1995.08.01      UPCOMING ITEMS (Studio: Forrest Sawyer)
5:48:20-5:48:20              Tuesday                ABC

1995.08.01      (COMMERCIAL: Ensure; Advil; Ragu; Thompson's Water
Seal; Dentu-Creme.)
5:48:20-5:50:20              Tuesday                ABC

1995.08.01      LOS ANGELES, CA / SIMPSON MURDER CASE / THE TRIAL
5:50:20-5:51:50              Tuesday                ABC

   (Studio: Forrest Sawyer)  Report introduced.

   (Los Angeles: Aaron Brown)  Package of photos & videotapes relevant
to the O.J. Simpson murder trial that was sent by the FBI to Judge
Lance Ito featured; photos shown of O.J.'s gloves. [Defense Co-
counsel Johnnie COCHRAN — addresses Ito about the photos.] [UCLA law
school professor Peter ARENELLA — analyzes whether the photos can be
introduced.]

1995.08.01      AIR TRAFFIC CONTROL / COMPUTERS
5:51:50-5:52:10              Tuesday                ABC

   (Studio: Forrest Sawyer)  FAA plan to put new air traffic control
computers in five major airports reported; map shown.

1995.08.01      UPCOMING ITEMS (Studio: Forrest Sawyer)
5:52:10-5:52:20              Tuesday                ABC

1995.08.01      (COMMERCIAL: The Olive Garden Restaurant; Bengay;
Imodium A-D.)
5:52:20-5:53:50              Tuesday                ABC

1995.08.01      AMERICAN AGENDA (EDUCATION: TEACHING "HUCKLEBERRY
FINN")
5:53:50-5:58:10              Tuesday                ABC

   (Studio: Forrest Sawyer)  Report introduced.

   (No location given: Catherine Crier)  The controversy over teaching
racially sensitive literature like "Huckleberry Finn" in the classroom
examined; scenes shown from a converence to teach English instructors
how to teach Mark Twain's novel. [University of East Texas professor
Jocelyn CHADWICK-JOSHUA — teaches about the novel.]  Parents in New
Haven, CT, said getting the novel removed from the junior high school
reading list. [Parents Robin BARNES, Marcella FLAKE, student Doron
FLAKE — oppose the language & tone of the book.]  Exchanges in the
play between Huck & slave Jim shown to illustrate the aims of the book
shown. [CHADWICK-JOSHUA — calls it a psychological journey of
discovery.]

1995.08.01      GOOD NIGHT
5:59:10                     Tuesday                ABC
```

Source: Vanderbilt News Archive. Used by permission.

FIGURE 2-1. *Continued*

stantial cuts in the number of reporters and producers covering the State Department, the Supreme Court, and agencies such as the Environmental Protection Agency. CBS and NBC traditionally had about thirty correspondents based in Washington. In 1994 they were down to about thirteen each, with CBS going even further by restricting its ability to do live production from the nation's capital.[31]

Part of what motivated managers to cut their news operations was the unexpected success of Ted Turner's Cable News Network (CNN). Turner started the Atlanta-based video news service as an adjunct to his other cable offerings. Broadcasters at first admired his effort, but they hardly took the twenty-four-hour service very seriously. That has now changed, a fact dramatically illustrated by the 1995 decision of the media giant Time Warner to buy the entire operation. While its viewership at any one time usually remains smaller than the network's scheduled newscasts, it has arguably provided more coverage in more places with less money. CBS's Larry Tisch was known to admire the economic efficiency of CNN, which in 1986 had less than half of his own network's news budget ($300 million) and yet still produced a profit.[32]

CNN's legitimacy as a fourth significant news service was cemented in early 1991 during the Persian Gulf War. The decision of the networks to pull most of their reporting staffs out of the Middle East in efforts to save money was painfully evident during the war. Some local network affiliates declined to clear their own network's news segments in favor of reports from CNN. At one point in the conflict NBC was reduced to having its anchor, Tom Brokaw, interview CNN's Bernard Shaw in Baghdad.[33]

This changed organizational climate for gathering video news has resulted in reporting patterns that in some ways resemble the print media's much older Associated Press. Like most American newspapers, the networks are increasingly dependant on their affiliates for gathering and reporting stories. A local print reporter called on to cover a disaster in his or her region may have the story picked up by the AP and distributed nationally to other papers. The pattern is now similar for networks, who are using the services of local reporters employed by one of their affiliates to augment the work of their own staffs.

The dependence on local affiliates, however, comes at a stiff price. The quality of reporting at some stations leaves a lot to be desired, largely because regional stations often hire reporters for their on-camera appearance rather than their journalism skills. Research of issues and investigative reporting is not rewarded at most stations. In addition, there is sometimes no substitute for maintaining a news bureau, as NBC discovered after the 1989 San Francisco earthquake. It had just closed its news bureau there. With its affiliate knocked off the air, the network virtually ceded coverage to ABC, which was in the midst of covering the World Series at Candlestick Park at the time of the earthquake.[34]

The networks are also making more extensive use of video news services that distribute pictures for events far removed from the normal "beats" of the increasingly limited number of network reporters. The largest is Reuters (formerly Visnews), which began in 1957 as a cooperative effort run by the BBC and other British Commonwealth broadcasters. NBC, Fox, and scores of other broadcasters around the world use its feeds from the thirty-five bureaus it operates.[35] The second largest, WTN, is owned by ABC, Britain's ITN, and Channel Nine Australia. In 1994 both CBS and the BBC signed deals with WTN.[36] The effect of these services is to present viewers with an armchair seat to far flung events, such as the attempted takeover of the Soviet Union by the military in August 1991.

But network dependance on external news services also has a journalistic cost. Unlike print reports that carry the originating wire service's name in subscribing newspapers, most of this footage runs as if it originated with the newsgathering staff of the networks. What viewers rarely know is that the networks have closed most of their own bureaus (CBS, for example, now has less than ten) and are now frequently providing little more than studio-based narration to video footage supplied by free-lance crews working for these news agencies or reporters employed by their affiliates.

The Networks in Cyberspace

There is no shortage of speculation about how traditional media like television will be affected by the rapid but chaotic growth of computer-accessible data, video, and voice. It has been apparent for some time that information databases and networks provide many tantalizing opportunities for reporters to extend their reach. A journalist in Alaska preparing an environmental story, for example, can easily locate past news releases and statements by the president or members of Congress via internet sites.[37] But the effect these sources will have on the news business and the general public is less clear.

As we enter the last half of the 1990s, however, several trends have begun to emerge. In late 1995 optimistic estimates placed the use of on-line communication networks in the United States and Canada at over 20 million households. Casual users seeking current news and information are increasingly served by news summaries offered by Reuters, CNN, America Online, and others. And one study commissioned by a computer network provider indicates that users are watching somewhat less television.[38] Many news viewers have also begun to find that stories covered by the television networks are developed in multimedia packages through various media "homepages." At this writing, CNN has perhaps made the most extensive use of on-line follow-up to stories, with an extensive on-line service known as CNN Interactive. Users are given a menu of categories (U.S. News,

Politics, International News, Sports, and so on), and invited to view headlines or longer summaries. Other networks have more limited on-line data, sometimes amounting to little more than their news schedule and promotional ads resembling press kits.

It is too early to know if on-line services will become a profitable second tier of service for news providers. But many in television see on-line data as a natural form of content to package for computer networks. The difficulty that exists presently is that media groups are not sure how their on-line services can be sold to advertisers or consumers. Advertisers are skeptical of the still limited numbers who can access such services.[39] And there is considerable consumer resistance to user fees for what is still relatively skimpy information available on most World Wide Web sites supported by news gatherers.[40] To the extent these conditions remain, growth of the internet into a true medium of political information for the general public is probably some time away, at least until phone or cable systems are ready to provide inexpensive and nearly universal access to on-line users. ATT has already made such an arrangement with CNN Interactive. The phone giant will offer CNN's financial and business news to subscribers.[41] But upgrades to most individual homes through cable and phone access are still in the future.

NEWS SELECTION AND CLASSIFICATION THEORIES

Thus far we have looked at television news by reviewing its importance to most Americans, some elements of its history, and how it operates in its corporate environment. In short, we have seen what it is from a structural standpoint. What remains is to account for what it does, specifically in terms of its content. News content is notoriously difficult to study, but we are aided with research and analysis centered on several important concepts of news-selection including agenda setting, gatekeeping, and "need to know" versus "want to know" journalism. After reviewing these concepts, we will explore gatekeeping theory by looking at eight values that govern story selection.

Agenda Setting

The idea that the press in the United States generally guides us to certain issues and away from others is the core idea of agenda-setting theory, which accounts for the diffusion of political information throughout society. In the words of one of its early researchers, agenda setting "captures the idea so long cherished by social scientists that the mass media have a significant impact on our focus of attention and what we think about."[42] In one of the earlier studies of agenda setting, for instance, Maxwell McCombs and D. L. Shaw found that newspapers in North Carolina were "the prime movers" in defining the issues voters would focus on in the 1972 presidential campaign. "Issues emphasized by the newspaper in the late spring and early summer exerted a major influence on what voters regarded as the major issues during the fall campaign."[43] Television, they found, played a similar role in highlighting other issues as election day approached.

Consider the process of agenda setting on the single issue of abused children. As Barbara Nelson notes, the problem of battered children has been known and discussed by a wide range of social welfare groups over the last hundred years. But public awareness of the problem surfaced only after specialists writing for professional journals were able to comment on the problem in general interest media, such as *Newsweek* and *Life* magazine. She notes that these accounts (starting, largely, in the 1960s) then triggered more news reports of the crime of child abuse, creating an upward curve of public awareness. "Once child abuse was rediscovered as a social problem, newspapers began to cover cases more frequently and intensively."[44] Such coverage then provided a level of public awareness that would enhance the likelihood of future reporting on the issue.

One specific case of child abuse indicates how potent the agenda-setting function can be. The decision of several television stations to carry live televised coverage of the 1988 trial of Joel Steinberg, a Manhattan attorney charged with the beating death of his six-year old daughter, triggered intense public interest. New York City's CBS affiliate alone devoted more than eighteen hours to court testimony over just six days, contributing to coverage of the trial in other city and national media over the same period.[45]

Recent research tends to confirm the power of media agenda setting. Heavy consumption of newspaper or television content on certain dominant issues tends to correlate with broad public perceptions of the relative importance of those issues. Individuals tend to refer to events that have been featured prominently in recent news coverage.[46] Even so, there are no guarantees that readers or viewers will rank stories exactly in the same way as the media they observe. As Doris Graber has noted, audiences will sometimes seek out sensationalistic news stories, even when they are relegated to the end of a newscast.[47]

If television has the power to increase dramatically the awareness of certain types of crimes, the "elite" print media retains an important role in setting the political news agenda. Print sources such as the *New York Times*, *Washington Post*, the AP *Budget*, (a list of top stories of the day) and the *Los Angeles Times* have enormous clout, shaping coverage of major television news outlets. The aggressive reporting of the *Washington Post* following the 1972 burglary of the Democratic Party National Headquarters is perhaps the textbook model of one source setting the agenda for others. The story of Watergate and the fall of the Nixon administration initially rested on the enterprise reporting of the *Post*, and on the chaining out of their reports to other media across the country.[48]

In political campaigns the essential features of agenda setting seem especially dramatic. The importance that the American public attaches to certain issues or individuals is largely a function of news coverage. In political campaigns, as Roger Simon has observed, candidates no longer "count the house" to estimate their prospects on election day. "Today, they count the cameras."[49] In the early stages of presidential campaigns, for example, the success of candidates is likely to be tied to the decisions of the local and national media to feature or ignore them. Media writer Tom Rosenstiel has called this the "invisible primary." Reflecting a widely held view among reporters and candidates, he notes that the first presidential primary is preeceded by an invisible one "conducted by a closed circle of journalists and Washington insiders that decides which candidates could raise money, build an organization, and win party support."[50]

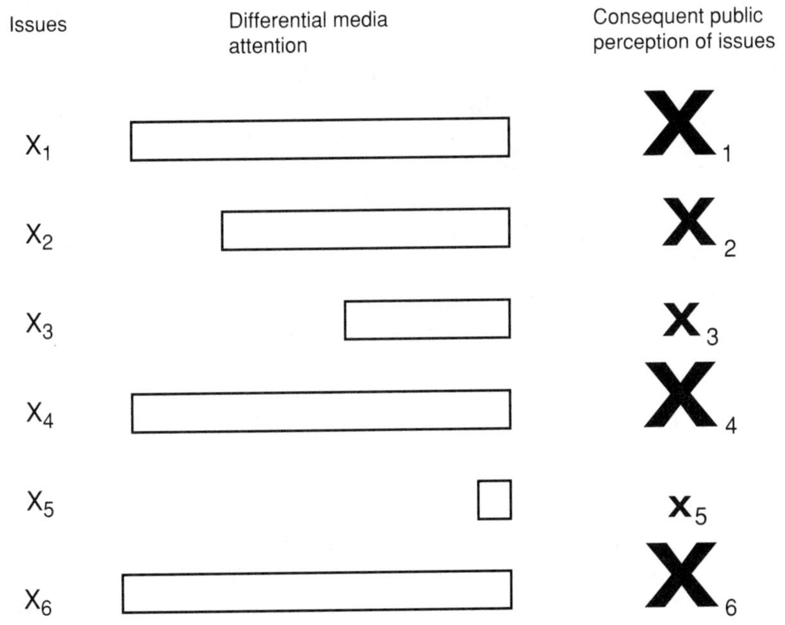

Source: Dennis McQuail and Sven Windahl, *Communication Models*, 2nd ed. (New York: Longman, 1993), p. 105.

FIGURE 2-2. The agenda-setting model: matters given most attention in the media will be perceived as the most important.

"News Priming" as Agenda Setting

Agenda-setting theory has been elaborated in recent years by researchers Shanto Iyengar and Donald Kinder, who have noted that television not only shapes our awareness of events, it also shapes the very standards by which we come to judge the performance of specific public figures, such as the president. Through what Iyengar and Kinder call the "priming effect" of television, they note that we are inclined to judge the agents that appear in stories based on the context the story places them in. For example:

> *When primed by television news stories that focus on national defense, people judge the president largely by how well he has provided, as they see it, for the nation's defense; when primed by stories about inflation, people evaluate the president by how he has managed, in their view, to keep prices down.*[51]

By experimentally altering different video news segments in which the president and others were viewed, Iyengar and Kinder were able to assess how individuals altered their judgments. "By calling attention to some matters while ignoring others," they note, "television news influences the standards by which governments, presidents, policies, and candidates for public office are judged."[52]

Thus if a newscast does a package of stories covering, say, a visit of the president to Japan, priming theory would lead us to believe that how that visit is framed will effect our attitudes toward the president and Japan. Is the story introduced with a reminder that the Japanese government is indebted to the present administration for helping to stabilize its own economy? Or is this package introduced with references to the president's last visit, which was marred by a major diplomatic failure? Priming theory would lead us to assume that the president would fare better in the first cast than the second. In other words, "the more prominent an issue is in the national information stream, the greater . . . the weight accorded it in making political judgments."[53]

Gatekeeping

A related but more complex counterpart to agenda setting is in gatekeeping theory. The word itself is a useful metaphor that describes the editing process "by which billions of messages that are available in the world get cut down and transformed into the hundreds of messages that reach a given person on a given day."[54] The enormous surplus of information provided by wire services, specialized news services, and other sources requires gatekeeping, a process the venerable Walter Chronkite described as the equivalant of stuffing a hundred pounds of news into a one-pound bag.[55] The use-to-reject ratio in journalism of all forms can easily be as high as 1 to 50, meaning news content rejected on any given day is much larger than that which is used.

Gatekeeping takes several identifiable forms. *Ideological gatekeeping* occurs when a media owner or operator consciously imposes a political agenda on the newsgathering process. In this pattern, a story is covered with an eye on communicating a point of view or attitude to the public. Journalism becomes a vehicle for furthering a certain political agenda.

Many Americans are quick to assign the labels "conservative" or "liberal" to various news outlets, believing that media bias is quite recognizable.[56] But studies in this area are notoriously unreliable, and often not confirmed by the work of more neutral academic researchers. One effective search for bias was conducted by Michael Robinson and Margaret Sheehan, who exhaustively surveyed the output of CBS and UPI in the 1980 presidential campaign. CBS has often been cited by observers for its ostensible left-wing orientation, but Robinson and Sheehan found little to support such a view. As they observed, "There are serious deficiencies in political reporting at the national level, but overt subjectivity about issues or about candidates is not high on the list."[57] Even so, as the previous chapter indicates, it would be a mistake to miss the strong possiblity that various economic and political pressures can shape media content. Gatekeepers are in organizations that have stockholders and advertisers to please, investments to protect, and audiences to be won over.

Structural gatekeeping is news selection on the basis of what best fits into the type of media involved, given the organizational and financial constraints that govern it.

Time and space, for example, are significant structural limitations for all media. Available information on any given day always exceeds the size of the existing "news hole." The twenty-four-hour news cycle of the daily press always produces a surplus of potentially valuable or interesting news. The "news hole" of a mid-sized American paper may add up to the equivalant of six or eight pages. Display advertising, classifieds, magazine-type features, sports, and similar items always take up most of the available space. The standard half-hour evening newscast (local or national), after commercials, has space for usually less than twelve stories, most of which will run less than a minute. The text of all these stories would not even begin to fill the first page of a broadsheet (large-format) newspaper.

Many of the eight features of gatekeeping cited later in this chapter illustrate structural gatekeeping. They describe the close connection between the comfortable routines of newsgathering in television and preferences for certain types or approaches to stories.

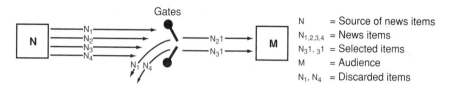

Source: Denis McQuail and Sven Windahl, *Communication Models* 2nd ed. (New York: Longman, 1993), p. 166.

FIGURE 2-3.   A simple gatekeeping model based on the work of D. M. White. The essential feature of gatekeeping is selectivity. Not all items available to newsgatherers are used by them.

Gatekeeping and the Definition of News: "Need to Know" vs. "Want to Know" News

There is a long tradition of journalism as the guardian of a nation's civil culture. The defining feature of this tradition is that news should function to improve the understanding of citizens as responsible participants in a common culture.[58] It values more than a passing familiarity with public issues and ongoing policy debates. What we "need to know" to be active participants may include an acquaintance with the pros and cons of significant issues as revealed in presidential speeches, legislative debates, descriptions of emerging trends, and a sense of why individuals, institutions, or corporations fail. This educative ideal for the press remains largely intact in newspapers such as the *New York Times* and the *Christian Science Monitor*, or television's "Newshour with Jim Lehrer" and "Meet the Press." But these last two examples of television shows noticeably lack what television ostensibly does best, shunning fast-paced movement in favor of static shots of people talking about ideas. (PBS's "Newshour" has been dubbed "the best radio program on television" by broadcast insiders who understand its limited appeal to viewers raised on the frenetic pace of commercial television.)

To many in the extremely competitive news business a restrictive description of news as what viewers *need to know* seems both elitist and a violation of the populist impulse of television to maximize ratings by giving audiences what they *want to know*. This latter category recognizes that news is something less than entertainment but something more than pure information. In the jargon of the social sciences, news is but one category of media content that is selected and consumed because it fulfills an interest or need; it has "uses and gratifications."[59] What we want to see is shaped by a host of factors that may or may not center on our sense of participation in a larger community. In uses and gratifications theory, our interests may be altogether more personal, motivated at times out of needs for diversion, amusement, entertainment, and so on.

In some ways the tension between these two definitions is not new. As early as the 1890s Joseph Pulitzer and William Randolph Hearst discovered that sensationalized and melodramatic coverage of human interest stories could produce impressive gains in circulation for their competing newspapers, the *New York World* and the *New York Journal*.[60] Arguably, we do not need to know about the heroic attempts of a firefighter to save a victim from a burning building. That knowledge will not help news consumers live more productive lives, or produce a better-informed citizens. But unquestionably we want to know.

Consider, for example, Edward R. Murrow's 1960 landmark documentary on the poverty of America's farm workers. In "Harvest of Shame" he documented the exploitation of cheap farm labor, using interviews with destitute workers and a conscience-provoking narration. The impact of the program was heightened by the decision to air the program one day after Americans had feasted on their own Thanksgiving dinners.[61] It was a story the nation needed to be told, carrying out the valuable social function of shining a light into one of the darker corners of American life. It and other documentaries at the time served as a vindication of a medium of which Murrow himself was sometimes ashamed.

Under close scrutiny "want to know" news often seems to represent the darker corners of journalism: mindless sensationalism, voyeurism, gossip masquerading as information. The news segment that allows its viewers to peer into the lives of prostitutes, for example, sells information as a source of gratification. A cover of respectability may be maintained by a script that reassures viewers that the segment is treating an important public health issue. Few viewers or journalists may truely accept that justification, knowing that news gatekeepers are not naive about what draws audiences to their broadcasts.

CONSTITUENTS OF
GATEKEEPING FOR TELEVISION

The remainder of this chapter explores various elements of gatekeeping in television journalism. Because the medium has so little time to cover so much, the formulas and patterns of this influential medium are worth considering in some detail. As will become apparent, the biases that exist in news coverage—especially in television journalism—are generally not ideological but structural. The nature of television as an entertainment medium largely defines what it can and cannot do in its routines.

The Prophetic Murrow

In 1958 Edward R. Murrow addressed a group of broadcast news executives, issuing a warning that still seems relevant in the 1990s. He feared that the values of an entertainment-oriented medium would adversely effect journalistic decisions.

One of the basic troubles with radio and television news is that both instruments have grown up as an incompatible combination of show business, advertising, and news. Each of the three is a rather bizarre and demanding profession. And when you get all three under one roof, the dust never settles. The top management of the networks, with a few notable exceptions, has been trained in advertising, research, sales or show business. But by the nature of the corporate structure,

they also make the final and crucial decisions having to do with news and public affairs. Frequently they have neither the time nor the competence to do this. It is not easy for the same small group of men to decide whether to buy a new station for millions of dollars, build a new building . . . decide what defensive line to take in connection with the latest Congressional inquiry, how much money to spend on promoting a new program, what additions or deletions should be made in the existing covey or clutch of vice presidents, and at the same time . . . to give mature, thoughtful consideration to the manifold problems that confront those who are charged with the responsibility for news and public affairs.

Sources: Edward R. Murrow, Speech to the Radio and Television News Directors, *The Reporter*, November 13, 1958.

The Primacy of the Story Format

The word *story* is such a basic descriptor of a news event that we tend to forget that it defines a unique way for organizing ideas. Storytelling involves the organization of facts and human motives in a definite sequence of stages. To tell a story is to set up a general structure for organizing a set of actors and events in ways that meet certain prior expectations. The story format defines actors moving through a sequence of events filled (usually) with victims, villains, and heroes. Conflict generates our interest, and sets up the search for a final or at least temporary resolution. The story format exists in most general news reporting because it is an efficient structure for reducing complexity to a minimum, and for collapsing a long time frame into a short and interesting summary. Reuven Frank, the former executive producer of the "NBC Evening News," once defined the format for his employees in a memo:

> *Every news story should, without any sacrifice of probity or responsibility, display the attributes of fiction, of drama. It should have structure and conflict, problem and denouement, rising action and falling action, a beginning, a middle, and an end. These are not only the essentials of drama; they are the essentials of narrative.[62]*

Storytelling is not the only way to organize events for presentation to the public. Real-time coverage occurs from time to time in venues like cable's C-SPAN and CNN's long-form coverage of important Congressional hearings or court trials. We leave the framework of narration when we witness events without the benefit of a narrator, and without the compression of time, or when we have unedited access to a source of information (a speech, press conference, or debate).

But the basic impulse to find meaning for an event in the narration of an observer is potent. Even most sports enthusiasts prefer television coverage of games with the dramatizing narration of play by play and "color" commentators. An NBC decision in the early 1980s to present an NFL football game without play by play—only the sound of the crowd in the stadium—was considered a resounding failure.

There are enormous consequences in the use of the story format as the primary way to organize news. The most significant effect is the tendency to look to the action of particular actors as central to the causes of conflict and to its eventual resolution. Storytelling is a dramatic form that typically places responsibility for an individual's condition squarely on the human participants involved. To a large extent, therefore, stories tend to underestimate the hard-to-dramatize structural causes of human actions in favor of the drama of individual combat.

In coverage of political campaigns this pattern plays out in stories that present the candidates as competitors actively engaged in defeating each other. We are much less interested in their explanations of social conditions as the products of large institutional changes than we are in seeing candidates assign individuals or groups with specific blame. For example, the problem of high unemployment in the manufacturing sector is often understood by professional economists as a function of changing markets and the globalization of trade. From their view the issue is less in finding fault than identifying long-term trends beyond the control of any single political figure. But the expression of this view is inherently less newsworthy than a political leader's attack on the "failures" of a president to deal with job losses, or the alleged crafty manipulations of foreign companies guilty of "stealing" the jobs of American workers. Storytelling needs real or potential villains, so that political campaigns and public discussion is framed, in Paul Weaver's phrase, as a contest "of figures deeply and totally embroiled in an all-out struggle."[63]

Even television coverage of a natural disaster like a hurricane may ultimately be reframed in terms of the unnatural failure of specific groups to perform as expected (such as the National Weather Service, or zoning boards that approved buildings in certain vulnerable areas). In the framework of storytelling, events do not simply occur, to be observed on their own terms. Events are the result of specific human agents with honorable or dishonorable motives.

The Search for Expressive "Moments"

Where journalists such as Ed Murrow and Walter Lippman talked about the press as conduit to citizens about great public issues, news producers today think more in terms of private traumas and social victims. One former CBS news chief, for example, concluded that the best events for news are those that have "moments" of high emotional intensity. Vivid images of people experiencing the anguish of their lives generally fit in well with television's commercial imperative to capture large audiences for its advertisers. "What the moments doctrine amounted to," notes Peter J. Boyer, "was a deftly designed cover for the infiltration of entertainment values into the news":

> It completely changed the way CBS reported the day's news because it completely changed what news was. There were no moments to be found in a minute-fifteen report on unemployment told by a CBS News correspondent standing outside the Department of Labor in Washington, D.C. There was, however, a moment of the highest sort if the CBS News camera studied the strained and expectant face of a young Pittsburgh mother as she stood (babe in arms) beside an employment line as her husband asked for a job.[64]

In a basic sense the "information" communicated in the face of an impoverished mother is less about government employment programs than it is the universal experience of sharing another person's misery.

Television, as Joshua Meyrowitz has reminded us, is full of expressive content. It saturates us with opportunities to witness other people's feelings and attitudes. Seeing people react to the events around them is one of the primary pleasures of watching television. As Meyrowitz notes, the archetypical television game show technically contains "information." But the questions and answers of these programs is often secondary to the experience of watching how other people cope with the pressures and opportunities of winning and losing.[65] In a very basic sense television content saturates us with people engaged in the process of communicating feelings of elation, grief, anger, and reassurance.

Such programs as "Oprah" or "Donahue" that deal with rape, bizarre criminal behavior, and "hot button" social controversies such as sexual harassment cannot be dismissed as irrelevant to the public discussion of vital issues. Some offer touching first-person observations of individuals dealing with the effects of important social problems, including sexual abuse, stresses on the contemporary family, and various forms of abnormal and pathological behavior. Others have drifted into a chaotic world of confrontation and emotional exploitation, merging issues with entertainment, debate with drama, fact with fiction, and a genuine urge to be informed with an irrepressible desire to peer into the abyss of other people's lives.[66]

Synoptic and Decontextualized Coverage

Television thrives on a rapid diversity of content, ranging from the number of individual shots a TV commercial director may use in one thirty-second ad (thirty to forty is not unusual) to the decision of a news producer to cover a variety of topics and stories in a short period of time. By nearly any measure commercial television alters its content at a frenetic pace. Continuous and rapid change of content is a response to the need to interrupt programs for commercials, and a recognition of the fact that rapid-fire pacing is needed to maintain the limited interests and attention spans of television viewers.

A "48 Hours" broadcast on CBS, for example, deals with one subject for one hour, but in six carefully divided segments that may hold the interests of younger viewers unwilling to commit their attention to a more traditionally formatted one-hour documentary.[67] In the space of a few minutes, a network newscast takes us from a Toyota commercial to the description of a new strain of AIDs virus, from the assassination of the Israeli Prime Minister to a pitch for Fancy Feast cat food, and from the Bosnian civil war to an advertiser's plea to wear more cotton.[68]

Few analysts of the mass media have missed the opportunity to point out the incomplete "headline service" provided by television journalism. Even the venerable Walter Cronkite, who anchored the CBS Evening News for many years, readily conceded that he could do little more than introduce the basic elements of a significant story.[69]

One of the effects of a daily television news agenda that is extremely broad but very thin could be called the decontextualization of events. Television news moves us from place to place, event to event, at a speed that leaves us with little time or opportunity to grasp the significance of what we are seeing. As David Webster has noted, the "discontinuity inherent in the process initiated by Samuel Morse and the electric telegraph reached its maturity in the television age."[70]

Cronkite termed this vexing problem "distortion through overcompression."[71] In a typical newscast, the story a viewer sees about Ethiopian famine must coexist in the same short time frame with a commercial for a luxury car and a report on the latest round of a PGA golf tournament. With rare exceptions, such as the 1995 bombing of the federal building in Oklahoma City, a single story of major importance is never allowed to saturate our attention. Not enough relevant details are allowed to burn into an individual's consciousness to make it possible for him or her to have much more than a passing familiarity with the most superficial symbolic (and synecdochic) representations of the problem.

It would be unfair to lay the blame for this superficiality only on television. The rising tide of information that we face has outstripped our abilities to add additional free hours to consume it. But our tendency to consume a high diet of synoptic news has no doubt contributed to a national pattern of indifference and confusion, created by a vague recognition of many topics, but without much understanding of any particular one.[72]

The Primacy of the Narrator

The traditional format for an electronic news story has the effect of putting the actual reporter in the middle of events, both narrating and interpreting what is being seen. Where print journalists remain unseen and largely unknown, their video counterparts take on a strong presence in a story. Print emphasizes attention on the events that are being written about; we are only vaguely aware of the writer's persona as he or she recounts a particular event. But video naturally draws our attention to the narrator as well as the story. Broadcast journalists leave a major imprint on the events they describe, sometimes providing the only sense of continuity and reassurance in an otherwise confusing and turbulent period.

Gaye Tuchman has analyzed the formulas for such stories at length, and offers this typical sequence for a story that features film or video shot on location with a reporter:

> *Reporter in studio: "City Hall buzzed today with talk of a possible solution to the fiscal crisis, as Tom Evans reports."*
>
> *Tom Evans (on film from steps of the City Hall) describes City Council proposal for five seconds.*
>
> *Evans' voice continues giving information about City Council's discussion. Silent film shows Council meeting.*

> *Evans' voice introduces chat with key Council member as silent film continues.*
>
> *Sound film shows Council member talking about the new proposal, including views of its opponents.*
>
> *Evans' voice, explaining depth of opponents' anger, accompanies silent film of demonstration against the proposal outside the City Hall.*
>
> *Evans interviews a demonstrator on sound film.*
>
> *Evans, on steps of the City Hall, sums up the story.*[73]

A striking feature of this very common formula for location reporting is that the reporter is the only continuous presence in the report. Comments from the actual participants occupy less time than the running narrative of the journalist. The story gains meaning only through the frame of reference established by the reporter.

The reasons for the primacy of the narrator are both obvious and subtle. It is clear, for example, that a long meeting of a deliberative body such as a city council cannot be easily presented in its "raw" form. The reporter's most basic job is to tell news consumers what happened, and to achieve this objective quickly and fairly. But a more subtle motivation is also at work. Television journalists live or die by how much "air time" they are able to get. It is an old complaint in broadcasting that electronic journalists covet their time before the camera as a professional necessity. This imperative increases the likelihood that stories will feature a "stand upper" that gives reporters the opportunity to demonstrate their competence and understanding. In actual fact it also means that viewers are left with the irony of watching reporters in the foreground of a camera shot paraphrasing the words of the newsmakers seen in the background.

A Preference for Stories with Dramatic Pictures

To assert that television news needs interesting pictures is to state the obvious. As we noted earlier, television news has a natural visual bias. Reporters can do more than talk about an event; they can often show parts of it, or show others reacting to it. Television news grew out of the riveting photojournalism that for decades captivated readers of *Life* magazine and film audiences watching the weekly newsreels produced by 20th Century Fox and others. "In television," notes ABC News anchor Peter Jennings, "to a very large extent you're obligated to write to the pictures."[74]

Consider the widely studied and largely successful efforts of the White House staff to "sell" the leadership of Ronald Reagan to the American public. Virtually every leader since Franklin Roosevelt has used some of the same devices to influence photojournalistic coverage. One of the primary starting points for the Reagan staff was the knowledge that most Americans get their information from television news. Television cannot resist covering a "photo-op," a peculiar Washington invention that places a public figure in a setting that produces interesting and impressive pictures, enhancing the figure's prestige. News producers know that they are being "used" in these events, but their addiction to interesting visuals is nearly complete.

White House public relations expert Michael Deaver helped execute a string of presidential visits in the president's first term centered on interesting pictures rather than substantive discussion or press questioning. Carefully planned visits to the demilitarized zone between North and South Korea, to an Irish pub (to demonstrate Reagan's solidarity with working men and women), and to a defense plant building the B-1 bomber were among the scores of appearances that helped orchestrate favorable public opinion. ABC's Sam Donaldson noted that Deaver understood "a simple truism about television: the eye always predominates over the ear."[75]

The effects of this visual bias on political content lead us to our next point: a structural emphasis on actions over ideas.

A Preference for Actions to See over Ideas to Discuss

One consequence of the primacy of pictures in shaping the content of television news is that our attention is drawn to the observation of emotions and behaviors as the substance of newsworthy events. Television's tendency in this direction is substantial but not total. Ideas do matter in news content. Policy proposals that can be discussed but not shown represent a presence in all forms of news. But to the extent politics is about ideas and proposals, television frequently cuts against the grain of public discussion by looking for visual forms that can stand in as symbols or representations of key ideas.

A news producer who decides to devote significant amounts of air time to stories on tax reform, the validity of college entrance exams, ethics codes for public officials, or standards for assessing the mental health of defendants in trials faces some difficult choices. These are all significant topics, but they are not easy to portray without resorting to "talking heads." These questions involve abstract concepts such as justice, fairness, intelligence, and compassion. Discussion is their proper forum. But concern for lost viewers will often force the producer to choose a very short segment of discussion, or a pattern of narration over video, in which video approximations are found (video footage of people completing tax forms, elderly patients receiving medical treatment, students in a classroom, or the like) to give the unengaged viewer something to watch.

Arguably, the price we have paid in our recent history for news driven by events rather than ideas is quite high. Of recent major scandals in American life—the Savings and Loan crisis, financial mismanagement in the Department of Housing and Urban Development, and the misuse of federal funds by many universities, to cite just three—none were first uncovered by network television news. These and many other major stories effecting the United State's financial health were brought to the attention of the American public by government investigators or members of the print media.[76]

The Savings and Loan crisis continues to require enormous federal outlays taken from American taxpayers. But as Ellen Hume has noted, its development in the 1980s was rarely reflected in the network's news agendas:

> *It was a numbers story, not a "people" story. . . . Financial stories are particularly hard for television. A reporter or candidate competing to create the most memorable sound bite wasn't about to get one with the thrift question. When asked why TV hadn't covered the crisis much even after it made headlines in 1988, the President of NBC News, Michael Gartner, observed that the story didn't lend itself to images, and without images, "television just can't do facts."*[77]

To the extent that Gartner is right, public discussion via traditional video newsgathering is likely to remain as a rather impoverished form of discourse. There is a difference in focusing on what someone thinks as opposed to what they actually do. A medium that gives preference to movement (events, activities) over thought would seem to leave the polis without an understanding of the intellectual superstructure of their culture. A child's understanding of the American Revolution, for example, may be largely in terms of its events, such as the Boston Tea Party or the meetings of the First Continental Congress. A more mature understanding of the Revolution obviously takes a broader look at the history of ideas that shaped the period, and the generative power of these ideas (particularly from English thinkers) in shaping the attitudes of Jefferson, Madison, and others.[78]

A heavy dependence on visual media would seem to produce a similar childlike incapacity to grasp the vital foundations of political action. Of course television does not prevent the expression of these thoughts. But to the extent they remain unseen, they are at a disadvantage in a medium structured to entertain the eye.

Globalism, but from an American Point of View

One of the evident strengths of television news is its ability to ignore political boundaries to report on significant events in foreign countries. The mastery of geosyncronous satellite technology in the 1970s has made it possible to have dependable broadcast platforms hovering 22,000 miles above one portion of the earth, relaying broadcast signals between continents. Intelsat, a consortium of 122 nations that jointly sponsors satellite ventures, pays for many of these van-sized space relays, which cost about $150 million apiece. Individual companies then lease channels called transponders, which can handle about 120,000 television and telephone signals at one time.

Among the prime users of leased transponders on these four-and-a-half-ton "birds" are television news services. If the result is not fully the "global village" that media theorist Marshall McLuhan predicted nearly four decades ago, citizens of much of the world are still within easy reach of vivid reportage from many of the world's "hot spots" and political capitals. On an average news day in May 1992, for example, the author sat in his living room watching Russian television's evening news show "News 1" (carried in the United States on C-SPAN I). This Moscow-based service included footage of a Los Angeles district attorney announcing the prosecution of policemen in the aftermath of riots brought on by the highly publicized beating of a black suspect. A half-hour later, Public Television's own "Newshour" was running tape of a Tashkint meeting of leaders from various Commonwealth of Independent States nations—including Russia—who were attempting to prevent additional fragmentation in what was the former Soviet Union. On the same day other services carried, among other items, scenes of bloodshed from the Bosnian civil war, and segments of an address to members of Congress by former Soviet leader Mikhail Gorbachev.

Much more than the average American daily newspaper,[79] television attempts to give its viewers a small sample of events from other world locations. Over the recent past most of the coverage has originated from Europe, with Latin America, Africa, and the Middle East (except Israel) falling far behind.[80]

The best way to characterize this pattern is perhaps with the phrase *ethnocentric globalism*. We see ourselves as very much a part of the world, but we also want to be removed from it, and to judge the behavior of other nations in terms of our own national values. With some notable exceptions, foreign news usually has a local or American angle. ABC's Av Westin acknowledges this limited internationalism in our domestic news coverage:

> *There is a crude joke: A producer has to decide whether to order a satellite feed for overseas news. If the story deals with dozens of dead in a South American bus crash, he will pass the story over; if it deals with hundreds killed in a Bangladesh cyclone, he will order the story to be covered and shipped by plane; if the story involves two American hitchhikers who died in a mountain-climbing expedition in Nepal, the producer will shout, "Order the bird!"*

The joke exaggerates the situation some. We are an insular nation, and television news coverage does little to break that insulation down.[81]

In the decade ahead, changes in the fortunes of news organizations may effect some of this ethnocentrism. Ed Turner, Executive Vice President of CNN, notes that perhaps three or four companies will compete in the future for most global news coverage.[82] Among them CNN, the News Corporation's Sky TV, Reuters, and the British Broadcasting Corporation will probably remain dominant, retaining a distinctly Western—but less of an American—orientation.

A Preference for Official Voices

In their analysis of television coverage of the near meltdown of the nuclear reactor at Three Mile Island, Dan Nimmo and James Combs were surprised to discover that a story with implications of regulatory and corporate failure was largely told from the point of view of officials from those two groups. "For CBS," they noted, "TMI was primarily a Washington story, not a localized one."[83]

The agenda-setting and gatekeeping functions of the electronic media favor those in power more than those affected by power. Senate hearings on a controversial proposal, a presidential speech to members of a powerful lobby, the release of official government figures on changes in the economy, and the carefully staged meetings of powerful organizations all influence the daily news agenda. These kinds of events are the easiest and sometimes cheapest to cover. The individuals in these groups are knowledgeable, saavy to the ways of the media, and easy to locate for comments or reactions. But they also contribute to what the *Chicago Tribune*'s Clarence Page calls the "Rolodex Syndrome," meaning a dependence on familiar names and faces as the pressure to finish a story presses in.[84] Part of Page's point is that it is easier to interview a White House official for a two-minute piece on the causes of urban unemployment than a group of individuals waiting for interviews at a state unemployment office. The latter group is less likely to give usable soundbites than the official, who has the rhetorical fluency and interest in summarizing the scope of the problem.

Consider an analysis of ABC's "Nightline" conducted by Fairness and Accuracy in Reporting, a liberal media watchdog group. They tabulated 865 programs featuring 2,498 guests. "With respect to foreign policy," they concluded, "the 'solutions' [anchor Ted] Koppel seeks are essentially outcomes that the U.S. government finds desirable." Eighty percent of all American guests were professionals in government or business. A much smaller 5 percent were from what FAIR described as "public interest constituencies" such as peace or environmental groups. And less than 2 percent were leaders of ethnic or racial groups, or labor unions. "Working, middle class, and poor people and their representatives are provided virtually no opportunity to speak out," they concluded. "Nightline thereby reinforces the notion that non-elites must play by the rules set by the upper classes which have the power to define reality for society as a whole."[85]

There is some room to quarrel with FAIR's political activism and their classifications. But the gist of their argument has found support in the monitoring of many other media observers.[86] It is a paradox of American journalism that, while many reporters privately express their suspicions of official sources and high-level corporate leaders, their broadcast accounts frequently support the interests of those leaders. Because they can initiate news coverage, they help create interest and support for the institutional views they represent. As Lance Bennett has observed, these initiatives are easily recognized in well-established story formulas. For example:

> *President _____ met at the White House today with President _____ of _____ to discuss mutual concerns about _____. Both leaders called the talks productive and said that important matters were resolved.*[87]

News is thus a product of the bureaucracies and individuals that are ostensibly the objects of neutral and unbiased reporting. Access to the media to influence public opinion is, at best, uneven. In many cases the power to define and characterize a news event is shared with the public figures who have the most to lose or gain.

SUMMARY

No medium of human communication has ever equaled the immediacy and drama of television journalism. Communication satellites, compact equipment, and the growth of local and cable newsgathering organizations have all contributed to the popularity of television news. To a large extent, we now define our culture and our place within it in terms of the passing parade of events offered in television news. These endlessly recurring vignettes act as a barometer of our national soul. We accept their images as vital representations of who we are or what we have become, at various times leaving us threatened or reassured about the social and political forces acting on the nation.

The enormous advantage television has over any other medium used for public discussion lies in the nearly universal access Americans have to it. This permeability of television news through the culture implies certain social functions, including agenda setting and gatekeeping. The agenda-setting function lies in the power of the largest and most pervasive news organizations to determine the stories the rest of us will consider. Gatekeeping refers to the allied notion that control over content resides with those who narrate and edit the news.

Both functions are obvious in their basic forms, but subtle in their details. In this chapter we have looked at how television journalism routinely performs the agenda-setting and gatekeeping functions, at both the local and national network levels. We considered a number of common patterns:

- The effect of media "priming," which occurs when the context of a story defines how we will judge those figures, such as presidents, who appear within it
- A general emphasis on "want to know" versus "need to know" stories, particularly in local news
- The tendency of television journalism to exploit the theatrical and narrative aspects of an event, sometimes at the expense of ideas
- The visual bias of television journalism, where stories are constructed around available footage
- The emphasis on synoptic (or summarizing) coverage rather than more detailed "long-form" coverage
- Approaches to international affairs that emphasize a national "angle," and "official" (i.e. governmental) responses

As a general environment for political discourse, then, television is something of a mixed blessing. The economics of the industry have merged the once easy-to-separate categories of "information" and "entertainment" into single forms of content. Broadcast news must now survive in a medium dominated by audience expectations centered on popular amusement. The hybrids of news and entertainment that exist in talk shows, "reality-based" programming such as CBS's "48 Hours," and the networks' newscasts owe less to the idea of information as a resource for successful citizenship, and more to a view of information as a commodity that gratifies and amuses.

NOTES

1. Paul H. Weaver, "Captives of Melodrama," *New York Times Magazine*, August 29, 1976, p. 57.

2. This account is based on a report by David Bianculli and Gail Shister, "How TV covered the Dwyer Suicide," *The Philadelphia Inquirer*, January 23, 1987, pp. D1, D8.

3. The application of the formulas of narration to television have been explored by a number of writers. For a general overview of narrative theory across all media, see Walter R. Fisher, *Human Communication as Narration* (Columbia: University of South Carolina, 1987). More specific applications are made in Sharon Lynn Sperry, "Television News as Narrative," in *Understanding Television: Essays on*

Television as a Cultural Force, ed. Richard P. Adler (New York: Praeger, 1981), pp. 295–312; Edward Epstein, *News From Nowhere* (New York: Vintage, 1974), p. 241; and Fred Graham, *Happy Talk: Confessions of a TV Newsman* (New York: W. W. Norton, 1990), p. 215.

4. Richard Sennett, *The Fall of Public Man*, (New York: Vintage, 1978), p. 284.

5. Literary critics call this pattern of using one event or individual stand for a whole class of individuals *synecdoche*. But its use as a common rhetorical device is equally evident in the ordinary content of television. See Kenneth Burke, *A Grammar of Motives* (New York: Prentice, Hall, 1954), p. 503.

6. Alex S. Jones, "Study Finds Americans Want News but Aren't Well Informed," *New York Times*, July 15, 1990, p. 13.

7. Ken Auletta, *Three Blind Mice: How the TV Networks Lost Their Way*, (New York: Random House, 1991), p. 569.

8. Doris Graber, *Processing the News: How People Tame the Information Tide*, (New York: Longman, 1984), p. 60.

9. Roper Organization/Television Information Office, *America's Watching: Public Attitudes Toward Television* (New York: Television Information Office, 1987), p. 18.

10. Geoffrey Foisie and Sharon Moshavi, "NBC Story Goes Up in Flames," *Broadcasting and Cable*, February 15, 1993, pp. 3, 8.

11. See, for example, L. Brent Bozell and Brent H. Baker, *And That's the Way It Isn't* (Alexandria, VA: Media Research Center, 1990), and Martin A. Lee and Norman Solomon, *Unreliable Sources: A Guide to Detecting Bias in News Media* (New York: Lyle Stuart, 1990).

12. Early evening and late evening newscasts (i.e., 6:00 and 11:00 P.M. EST) are highly valued by stations as carriers of station prestige and sources of enormous revenue.

13. For discussions of this view, see David Altheide, *Creating Reality: How TV News Distorts Events* (Beverly Hills, CA: Sage, 1976), and Mark Fishman, *Manufacturing the News* (Austin: University of Texas, 1980).

14. Stephen Hess, *Live from Capitol Hill!* (Washington, DC: Brookings, 1991), p. 50.

15. Ibid, p. 49.

16. These numbers reflect a general pattern monitored in the 11:00 P.M. newscasts for KYW-TV and WCAU-TV, in Philadelphia, 1989.

17. For an interesting account of this period, see A. M. Sperber, *Murrow: His Life and Times* (New York: Freundlich, 1986), pp. 32–100.

18. See, for example, Sperber, *Murrow*.

19. For a description of network news as a struggle between the public interest and network profits see Fred Friendly, *Due to Circumstances Beyond Our Control* (New York: Vintage, 1968), pp. 212–300.

20. Graham, pp. 206–208.

21. Michael J. Arlen, *Living Room War* (New York: Viking, 1969), pp. 6–9.

22. Herbert J. Gans, *Deciding What's News* (New York: Vintage, 1980), p. 16.

23. Ibid, pp. 9–10.

24. W. Lance Bennett, *News: The Politics of Illusion*. 2d ed. (New York: Longman, 1988), pp. 51–56.

25. Michael J. Robinson, "American Political Legitimacy in an Era of Electronic Journalism: Reflections on the Evening News," in Douglass Cater and Richard Adler

(ed), *Television as a Social Force: New Approaches to TV Criticism* (New York: Praeger, 1975), p. 113.

26. The depth of the American ambivalence toward politics is outlined in E. J. Dionne, Jr.'s, *Why Americans Hate Politics* (New York: Simon and Schuster, 1991).

27. Auletta, *Three Blind Mice*, p. 3.

28. Ibid, p. 484.

29. Peter J. Boyer, *Who Killed CBS?* (New York: Random House, 1988), p. 326.

30. Ibid, pp. 330–331.

31. Penn Kimball, *Downsizing the News: Network Cutbacks in the Nation's Capital* (Baltimore: Johns Hopkins/Woodrow Wilson Center, 1994), pp. 23–33.

32. Auletta, Three Blind Mice, p. 275.

33. Barbie Zelizer, "CNN, the Gulf War, and Journalistic Practice," *Journal of Communication*, Winter, 1992, pp. 71–72.

34. Kimball, *Downsizing the News*, pp. 62–63.

35. Teresa L. Waite, "As Networks Stay Home, Two Agencies Roam the World," *New York Times*, March 8, 1992, p. F5.

36. "WTN Signs $10 million Deal with CBS," *Broadcasting and Cable*, September 19, 1994, p. 42.

37. See, for example, Randy Reddick and Elliot King, *The Online Journalist* (Fort Worth, TX: Harcourt Brace, 1995).

38. Mark Berniker, "Internet Begins to Cut into TV Viewing," *Broadcasting and Cable*, November 6, 1995, p. 113.

39. John Markoff, "If Medium Is the Message, the Message Is the Web," *New York Times*, November 20, 1995, pp. A1, D5. See also Denise Caruso, "Digital Commerce," *New York Times*, November 20, 1995, p. D6.

40. Berniker, "Internet."

41. Mark Berniker, "CNN Interactive Signs AT&T's Online Network," *Broadcasting and Cable*, October 23, 1995, p. 75.

42. Maxwell E. McCombs, "The Agenda Setting Approach," in the *Handbook of Political Communication*, ed. Dan Nimmo and Keith Sanders (Beverly Hills, CA: Sage, 1981), p. 121.

43. Ibid., p. 127.

44. Barbara Nelson, "Making an Issue of Child Abuse," in *Agenda Setting: Readings on Media, Public Opinion, and Policy Making*, ed. David L. Protess and Maxwell McCombs (Hillside, NJ: Lawrence Erlbaum, 1991), p. 168.

45. Paul Thaler, *The Watchful Eye: American Justice in the Age of the Television Trial* (New York: Praeger, 1994), pp. 149, 198.

46. See Everett Rogers and James Dearing, "Agenda Setting Research: Where Has It Been and Where Is It Going?" in *Communication Yearbook, Vol 11* (Beverly Hills, CA: Sage, 1988), pp. 555–594.

47. Doris Graber, *Mass Media and American Politics*, 4th ed. (Washington, Congressional Quarterly Press, 1993), p. 217.

48. The story of Watergate reporting is now a journalistic legend, and is recounted well by the reporters responsible for it. See Bob Woodward and Carl Bernstein, *All the President's Men* (New York: Simon and Schuster, 1974).

49. Roger Simon, *Road Show* (New York: Farrar, Straus and Giroux, 1990), p. 153.

50. Tom Rosenstiel, *Strange Bedfellows* (New York: Hyperion, 1993) p. 47.

51. Shanto Iyengar and Donald R. Kinder, *News That Matters: Television and American Opinion* (Chicago: University of Chicago, 1987), pp. 114–115.

52. Ibid, p. 63.

53. Shanto Iyengar, *Is Anyone Responsible?* (Chicago: University of Chicago, 1991), p. 133.

54. Pamela J. Shoemaker, *Gatekeeping* (Newbury Park, CA.: Sage, 1991), p. 1.

55. Walter Chronkite, Speech to the Radio and Television News Directors, December 13, 1976, in *Rich News, Poor News*, ed. Marvin Barrett (New York: Crowell, 1978), p. 195. A number of classic studies detail the values and norms of journalistic gatekeeping. See, for example, Herbert J. Gans, *Deciding What's News* (New York: Vintage, 1980), pp. 78–115, 146–181, and Epstein, *News From Nowhere*.

56. For a conservative view of media bias see, for example, Bozell and Baker, *and That's the Way It Isn't*.

57. Michael J. Robinson and Margaret A. Sheehan, *Over the Wire and on TV: CBS and UPI in Campaign '80* (New York: Russell Sage, 1983), p. 65

58. For a discussion of some of the features of membership in a common culture, see Robert Bellah et al., *The Good Society* (New York: Knopf, 1991), pp. 138–149.

59. Melvin L. DeFluer and Everette E. Dennis, *Understanding Mass Communication*, 5th ed. (Boston: Houghton Mifflin, 1994), pp. 558–559.

60. Ibid., pp. 88–89.

61. Friendly, *Due to Circumstances*, pp. 120–122.

62. Epstein, *News from Nowhere*, pp. 4–5.

63. Weaver, "Captives," p. 6.

64. Boyer, p. 139.

65. Joshua Meyrowitz, *No Sense of Place* (New York: Oxford, 1985), pp. 97–104.

66. See, for example, Bill Carter, "Killing Poses Hard Questions about Talk TV," *New York Times*, March 14, 1995, pp. A1, A10.

67. Interview with CBS producers, February 6, 1992.

68. ABC Evening News, November 10, 1995.

69. Cronkite, in *Rich News*, pp. 191–198.

70. David Webster, "New Communications Technology and the International Political Process," in *The Media and Foreign Policy*, ed. Simon Serfaty (London, Macmillan, 1990), p. 222.

71. Cronkite, in *Rich News*, p. 197.

72. See, for example, Jones, "Study Finds," p. 13.

73. Gaye Tuchman, *Making News: A Study in the Construction of Reality* (New York: Free Press, 1978), p. 128.

74. Martin Schram, *The Great American Video Game* (New York: Murrow, 1987), p. 58.

75. Mark Hertsgaard, *On Bended Knee: The Press and the Reagan Presidency* (New York: Schocken, 1989), p. 25.

76. Christopher George, "Confessions of an Investigative Reporter," *Washington Monthly*, March, 1992, pp. 36–37.

77. Ellen Hume, "Why the Press Blew the S & L Scandal," *New York Times*, May 24, 1990, p. A25.

78. For a survey of the sources of the American Revolution, see Louis M. Hacker, *The Shaping of the American Revolution* (New York: Columbia University, 1947), Parts I–III.

79. Monitoring of the *New York Daily News* by the author in 1992 indicates an average of slightly less than four article-length international news stories in its daily editions.

80. See, for example, James F. Larson, "International Affairs Coverage on US Evening Network News," in *Television Coverage of International Affairs*, ed. William C. Adams (Norwood, NJ: Ablex, 1982), pp. 15–41.

81. Av Westin, *News Watch: How TV Decides the News* (New York: Simon and Shuster, 1982), p. 67.

82. Ed Turner, presentation to the International Radio and Television Society, Faculty/Industry Seminar, New York City, February 6, 1992.

83. Dan Nimmo and and James Combs, *Nightly Horrors: Crisis Coverage in Television Network News* (Knoxville: University of Tennessee, 1985), p. 80.

84. Lee and Solomon, *Unreliable Sources*, p. 30.

85. Ibid, p. 27.

86. See, for example, Gans, *Deciding What's News*, pp. 116–145; Bennett, *News*, pp. 69–100, and David L. Paletz and Robert M. Entman, *Media Power Politics* (New York: Free Press, 1981), pp. 20–21.

87. Bennett, *News*, p. 107.

3

THE PUBLICITY FUNCTIONS
OF CONGRESS

Lovers of sausages and the law should never watch either of them being made.[1]

Making news . . . has become a crucial component of making laws.[2]

In his masterful study of Washington politics, *The Power Game*, Hedrick Smith recalls a moment from 1986 that epitomizes how the venerable institution of the Congress has changed in the media age. Smith, then a reporter for the *New York Times*, had just witnessed President Reagan's State of the Union address from the press gallery in the Capitol building's house chamber. The State of the Union is always an important national event, one of the few times the president directly addresses the Congress and the nation on the goals and intentions of his administration in the coming year. Some time after the speech, Smith began to thread his way through the labyrinth of hallways in the increasingly deserted Capitol. He recalls his surprise in discovering a gathering of Democratic representatives and senators standing single file outside a second-floor room "like college graduates lined up to receive diplomas." Perhaps forty legislators were patiently standing in a line. The hushed chamber they waited to enter contained lights, a camera, and a well-dressed interviewer. While other Capitol Hill employees quickly dispersed into the chilly February night, "these Democrats were still at work. Some combed their hair and straightened their ties. Most were quietly rehearsing little set pieces like students before an exam." With calm efficiency with they went about their business of relaying via satellite their quick reactions to the president's speech. Their observations would serve as a reminder to their constituents back home that they were more than a passive audience to the president's remarks.

> *Each had forty-five seconds to a minute—no time for fluffs or retakes. The entire operation had to be completed within ninety minutes, if they were going to hit the eleven o'clock local news in New Haven, Cleveland, or San Francisco. The Easterners had to make a feed to Spacenet 1 and the Westerners to Westar 4, two satellites each rented for half an hour for nine hundred dollars by the Democratic Congressional Campaign Committee.*

In turn, every member moved to a spot marked on the blue-carpeted floor, flanked by bookcases and a flag, to record their reaction to the same question: "Congressman, your reaction?"[3]

As minor as this scene is, it serves as a good representation of how the "new" Congress has evolved from the old, and a reminder of the importance of the legislature as a source of *reactions* as well as *laws*. The Congress not only passes federal codes and statutes, but also serves as a forum for debating national priorities and issues.

In this chapter we examine Congress as a setting for communication and lawmaking. Along the way, we will review the traditional functions of Congress, and how some of these functions have recently evolved. We will also look at the publicity personnel and machinery that contribute to the national visibility of Congress, including congressional television and the various forms of the news media that cover Capitol Hill. And our specific focus will be on how Congress has adapted to the age of television.

THE PERMANENT AND CHANGED CONGRESS

A visitor to Capitol Hill is perhaps most impressed with the old symbols of the national legislature and the continuity of its rituals. The interior of the Capitol dome with its impressive interior frieze depicting the nation's early history suggests a timelessness to the institution. The rules of the Congress seem equally old-fashioned, not unlike the Victorian wallpaper that covers the walls of the House of Representatives. Comments about the rhetoric of other members of the House or Senate are still worded in gentle euphemisms, such as "the honorable member from Kentucky," or "the senior senator from Nebraska." And senators continue many of the old customs, such as carving their names into the drawers of their desks, next to earlier occupants such as Daniel Webster and Henry Cabot Lodge. Sessions in both the House and Senate always begin with a prayer for divine help in sorting out the normally messy business of legislating. And most of the formal parliamentary rules for debate have changed little in the 194 years since the government moved from Philadelphia to Washington.

Durable Powers

The general patterns of lawmaking and oversight set forth in the Constitution remain much as they have always been. With regard to oversight, Congress and its committees regularly exercise the right to use hearings to gather information from virtually any corner of American life, ranging from federal agencies and how they do their work, to private individuals whose work may impact on laws pending or approved. In recent years, for example, many members of Congress have taken a well-publicized interest in the ownership and programming of the mass media, as well as efforts by the Federal Communications Commission to regulate broadcasting. In 1988, for example, executives from Time Incorporated and Warner Communications appeared before members of Congress to allay concerns that a merger of the two giants was not another corporate buyout designed simply to make a few stockholders and managers very rich. The new Time Warner, they argued, would be an American-owned entertainment giant capable of competing with the largest foreign media conglomerates.[4]

Congress—notably the Senate—also carries the power of approval and removal for many top federal officials. Impeachment proceedings are rare, involving only a handful of cases against federal judges and—as almost occurred in 1973—a sitting president. But hearings on nominees to high federal office are common, with sometimes one or two per year evolving into a national political drama. The stormy Senate Judiciary Committee hearings of Supreme Court nominees Robert Bork in 1987 and Clarence Thomas in 1991 are two notable examples. Bork was not confirmed; Thomas was, but only after a battle over charges of sexual harassment that left deep wounds on the Senate and those who testified.

The primary task of the Congress is obviously lawmaking. Thousands of legislative proposals or bills are introduced in the Senate or the House in the course of several years. After they are assigned to committees, most are killed, lacking favor with the powerful chairs and leaders chosen from the majority party. Those bills with a good deal of support are frequently the basis of hearings by the relevant committees. We will have more to say later about the importance of hearings in our "mediated" understanding of the legislative process. When a bill is "marked up" or changed, it may be voted out of committee and eventually considered by the entire body in a floor vote. Votes for legislation typically occur several times, starting with procedural votes that measure a bill's support. A later final vote is taken, after a series of amendments have been offered (and usually rejected), and after supporters and opponents have debated the legislation and organized their forces. Favorable action by a majority of the 100 members of the Senate and 435 members of the House usually results in slightly different forms of the legislation, which must be reconciled in a conference that involves representatives from both Houses. Once the final conference report is written, it is voted on again in both houses and forwarded to the president for final approval. A president who supports the legislation will sign it, often with great fanfare. Those who choose to exercise the veto will often state their objections in a veto message. Vetos usually "kill" a bill, but they can be overridden with a two-thirds majority in each house.

As an illustration of some of these processes, consider the fate of several bills introduced in the House and Senate to settle the long baseball strike that abruptly ended the 1994 season and theatened the one planned for the following year.[5] The sport, supporters of the legislation argued, had a special place in American life, a fact suggested by the extensive television news coverage of the standoff between team owners and players.

The major bill (S-376 and HR-870, known as the Baseball Strike Settlement Act) followed on the heals of a well-publicized but failed effort by the president to negotiate a compromise over the issue of salary caps for players. But this proposed legislation, like most bills, immediately ran into trouble. Both the Speaker of the House and the Majority Leader in the Senate indicated a reluctance to get involved in the dispute. Even so, the Senate Judiciary's Subcommittee on Antitrust, Business Rights and Competition held hearings in which owners, labor experts, and the players all testified. In the meantime, new bills were introduced to partly lift special government protections guaranteed to the team owners. But even with hearings and widespread anger over the inability of the players and owners to get together, members of both Houses were too divided for the leadership to risk bringing any proposed legislation to a vote. The Republican leadership declined to schedule time for full House and Senate consideration of any of the bills, and all died a quiet (but typical) death in the spring of 1995, a few weeks before both sides finally agreed to a belated start of the new season without a contract. Like most bills in Congress, the baseball legislation died without a full vote in either house. But also like many pieces of legislation, the bills served as vehicles for Congressional discussion of an issue, in this case one with widespread public interest and significant financial stakes for the businesses involved.

All of these processes—approving high-ranking federal appointees, conducting hearings, and legislating—are largely unchanged functions. And they are preeminently activities of *communication* and *consensus building*. "Legislating" is a collective term for a wide range of essentially rhetorical processes that include motivating like-minded activists outside of Washington, providing information and arguments to the media, defending views that have come under attack, holding together coalitions of supporters in the Congress, and maintaining positive relationships with opponents who may be allies in future battles. Bargaining, posturing, explaining, and persuading are the fundamental tools of legislating.

The widespread public perception that Congress is too often in deadlock

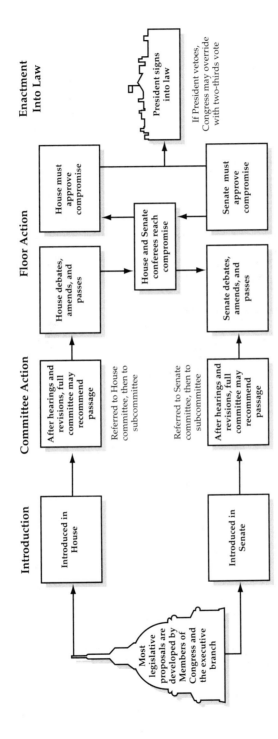

Source: The Benton Foundation

FIGURE 3-1. How a Bill Becomes Law

Here's a typical—but greatly simplified—"legislative road map" showing how bills are enacted into law. Most proposals, however, never make it through this legislative labyrinth. In the 98th Congress, for example, of the 9,769 public bills and joint resolutions introduced in both Houses, only 623 (6.4 percent) were enacted into law.

and overdue for streamlining sometimes misses the essential truth that legislatures are as much about process as product. Indeed, the process of legislating dominates our perceptions of the institution. Less than 8 percent of all bills introduced in the Congress ever attain the status of law. The task of negotiating the interests of 250 million citizens spread over much of a continent rarely occurs with speed or efficiency.[6] Arguably, the framers of the constitution had at least a form of built-in gridlock in mind. For one of its master engineers, James Madison, the Senate was intended to be a foil to quick action, an "additional impediment" against the "intemperate" resolutions of the populist House.[7]

The "Old" and "New" Congress

If the fundamental processes of Congress are largely unchanged, there have been significant transformations in the ways its members communicate influence and power. The Congress our grandparents understood from news reports and the frequent speech making of its members was a very hierarchical institution. With notable exceptions, members knew their place, and more readily accepted party and presidential loyalty as fundamental values. The political professionals around them—the long-serving party leaders in both chambers, and the Speaker of the House—were given powers that were nearly absolute. Many of them now seem larger than life. The role call of the famous senators that John F. Kennedy wrote about in *Profiles in Courage*—John Quincy Adams, Daniel Webster, Robert Taft, and others—suggests a continuity of unquestioned moral authority that is difficult to match in the modern Senate.[8]

Several decades ago, if a freshman Democrat serving his first term in the House ignored the wishes of Speaker Sam Rayburn he or she would have risked more of his or her political future than does a modern counterpart who rebels against the wishes of contemporary legislative leaders. In the old Congress members lived in fear of the power that their leaders could employ to help or hurt them. Christopher Matthews, who served as an aide to former House Speaker "Tip" O'Neil, recalls that Rayburn had a "quiet capacity to deal with congressman after congressman, again and again," turning "the mob scene of the House floor into a disciplined army carrying laws and policies that had seemed unachievable."[9]

Congressional leaders today are probably no less capable than those whose names now adorn the office buildings of Capitol Hill. What has changed are the rules of the political game. Most notably, the parties in Congress have lost some of their clout. The general fragmentation that has occurred in much of American life relating to ethnic, gender, and social issues—issues that create much of the passion in modern politics—has created alliances and commitments that supersede party identification. Newer members are reluctant to serve a long apprenticeship behind senior members. Patience is no longer considered a virtue for those driven into the fast track of national politics. Moreover, as a nation we are no longer so admiring of the power politics that gave legislative leaders disciplinary control over members. Sam Rayburn could activate the Internal Revenue Service and the Army Corps of Engineers for or against a House colleague in the same afternoon. A similar move by the current Speaker today would be subject to public and editorial rebukes for using such political "hardball" against a colleague.

The largest change, however, is that political power is projected differently in Congress than has been the case in its long history. Political leaders and key committee chairpersons still carry enormous weight. But they are no longer the sole forces directing the pace and action of Congress. Competing with formally designated leaders are a larger number of autonomous members with their own agendas and constituencies. It is now possible to survive in legislative life as an independent agent, using a wide collection of public relations skills to offset the now-diminished dangers of rebelling against the president or congressional leaders. A separate base of power can be maintained by relying on the mass media and their audiences. Now it is possible for members to sustain successful political careers even when they are seriously at odds with leaders in their own party.

Reaching Constituents and Building a Political Base in the New Congress

In the "new" congress members increasingly look beyond the institution for support they can establish with external audiences, including members of the press and constitutents in their own districts. Frequent appearances in the district, along with press releases and direct mail "reports" to constitutents, have long served this purpose. They have also been augmented in recent years by the establishment of e-mail addresses and Web sites for individual members. But television has predictably had the greatest effect in making members more independent of the old internal hierarchies. Members have the ability to use Capitol Hill television studios to talk with the anchors of local television news programs, a tool that increases their visibility at home and lessens the rewards of becoming organizational "insiders." They are also aided by the fact that many radio and television stations—especially in middle-sized and smaller cities—are happy to pick up a free satellite "report" or video news release supplied by a member. So common are these member-produced video feeds that many stations around the country have dropped their contracts with Washington-based news services in favor of free material produced by congressional publicity machines.[10] As Christopher Matthews has noted:

The new-breed guys were born in the TV studio, and the old breed were born in the political clubhouse. . . . The old guys worked their way up through the chairs, as [former House Speaker] Tip [O'Neill] puts it. They're very hierarchical. They keep their friendships. They keep their alliances. They dance with the girl they came with. They stick together. The new-breed guys play one-night stands. They're always forming new coalitions. They're always worrying about their image and how to position themselves. They decide what image they want to project, and they position themselves to project that image.[11]

The extent to which nonteam players can now upset the traditional hierarchies of Congress was dramatically seen in 1989, when House Speaker Jim Wright was forced to give up his office because of a highly orchestrated campaign over his acceptance of gifts and external sources of income. The single most potent force toppling the Speaker was the energetic and zealous Newt Gingrich, then an insurgent conservative Republican with little patience for the genteel rituals of Congress. Gingrich went on to assume the Speaker's post in 1995, and fashioned a legislative agenda in the first few months of his first term that momentarily rekindled the image of a majority party unified behind a single leader. But his rise to power—somewhat similar to the rise of Texas senator Phil Gramm in the Senate—had won him few friends in the ranks of the GOP's upper tiers. Numerous Republican legislators privately decried their style of using television interviews to pursue enemies and circumvent leaders in their party. And many also feared the independant power base that Gingrich had established years earlier in the form of a well-funded political action group known as GOPAC. Using his rhetorical skill and GOPAC, Gingrich created as much power for himself than he ever attained as Republican House whip.[12]

Gingrich and Gramm easily fit the mold of the "new" legislator decried by older members who wished to return to the hierarcies and more genteel civility of the historical Congress. Detractors of these newer media-centered leaders talk about "showhorses" rather than "workhorses." As Majority Leader Robert Dole noted about Gramm, "Everybody sees the most dangerous place in the Capitol is between Phil and a TV camera."[13] But there is no doubt that these men fit the rougher and more partisan political envirnoment of the 1990s. Both have understood that the essence of modern legislative leadership includes an eye for publicity and sharply focused attacks on political opponents.

In sum, the "new" congress shares with the old a focus on the processes of negotiation and orchestration of support. But members in the new Congress—if they are to have influence beyond their single votes—have turned outward, using their own considerable publicity-making resources to influence the news media. If the measure of success in the old Congress was

Among the many party-affiliated organizations that have coached incumbents and candidates seeking political office is GOPAC, a republican group organized by Representative Newt Gingrich and others to challenge the Democrat-controlled Congress. In 1990 the group became the subject of news reports and criticism over a mailing it distributed to members suggesting specific words to use against Democrats "in writing literature and mailings, in preparing speeches, and in producing electronic media." As the mailing noted, members had expressed the wish that they "could speak like Newt." Among the "contrasting words" they suggested for members to "define opponents" included the following:

Decay	Traitors	Hypocracy	Radical
Failure	Sick	Pathetic	Unionized
Corruption	Destructive	Self-serving	Intolerant
Welfare	Corrupt	Taxes	Spend
Shame	Disgrace	Cheat	Steal
Machine	Antifamily	Lie	Liberal

Terms proposed as "Optimistic Positive Governing Words" for members to use to characterize their own actions were:

Share	Opportunity	Legacy	Truth
Moral	Courage	Reform	Family
Humane	Liberty	Duty	Citizen
Dream	Freedom	Rights	Workfare
Protect	Pro-flag	Crusade	Hard work
Caring	Principle	Preserve	Prosperity

FIGURE 3-2.   GOPAC

influence and power within its walls, success in the new Congress is often judged by how well a legislator develops or uses public opinion at the local and national level.

COVERING CONGRESS: C-SPAN, THE MAINSTREAM MEDIA, AND THE TRADE PRESS

"The Best Beat in Washington"

For a reporter, Congress is a goldmine of topics and quotes. In any two-year period there is virtually no significant aspect of American life that will escape the scrutiny of hearings and proposed legislation, ranging from the allegedly antisocial lyrics of heavy-metal bands to the clandestine operations of the Central Intelligence Agency. Given enough time, reporters learn how to draw on the expertise and information of the Senate and many members of the lower House. All legislators serve on several committees, and many have gained prominence as experts or savvy observers of the political and economic forces acting on the passing parade of presidential initiatives, outbreaks of crime, foreign events, and difficult social problems.

From the perspective of a reporter working against a short deadline, the Senate is especially a rich resource for thoughtful commentary on major issues of the day, a kind of national speaker's bureau of generally articulate advocates. For example, the observations of New York's Daniel Patrick Moynihan on the causes of urban poverty, or Indiana's Richard Lugar on the politics of Eastern Europe often carry great weight in the public discussion of these issues. Senators are provided with information by a staff of over 7000, (12,000 in the House.)[14] Given this support, Congress unquestionably represents the best single venue for information and expertise on the state of the nation and potential solutions to its problems.

This is not to suggest that the national legislature is the most extensively covered political institution in the United States. Far from it. Studies of Vanderbilt University's Television News Archives show a steady decline in the amount and tone of television reporting from Congress between 1971 and 1993. Between 1972 and 1978, for example, ABC, CBS, and NBC carried an estimated 124 stories a month in their nightly newscasts. By 1992 that number had dropped to only 42 stories a month for all of the networks, with an increasing interest in nonpolicy coverage such as scandals.[15]

The presidency commands much greater attention from the national and local media, and not surprisingly—given the variety of viewpoints that can emerge from 535 members—a greater sense of continuity in terms of viewpoint. The president is easier to write about, photograph, and explain in a compact story. That the president has an enormous advantage in the media—especially the highly compressed reports of the television networks—is virtually never in dispute, though the growth of households capable of receiving C-SPAN has had the effect of increasing at least the potential for public access to congressional work.[16]

C-SPAN: Long-Form Coverage of Congress

After considerable debate about the effects of full-time television coverage of Congress, cameras became a permanent fixture in the House of Representatives at the end of the 1970s. With one important exception, the initial plan for televised coverage still remains as it was first intended. News organizations are free to pick up any portion of the full-time coverage for use in their reporting. And congressional offices are wired to receive coverage of the House floor. The rules of coverage give control of the cameras to a staff under the control of the Speaker. It is also understood that the electronically controlled cameras will stay focused on the "well" of the House, recording the comments of various speakers, but not the presence or absence of members.

The important exception is that few early advocates of House television fully anticipated the rapid growth and widespread acceptance of C-SPAN by the cable television industry. C-SPAN serves as a nonprofit channel devoted to relaying the proceedings of the House, as well as political campaign appearances and seminars on public policy questions. Initially funded in 1979, the Cable Satellite Public Affairs Network is now available to 55 million households.[17] In 1986 it was augmented by C-SPAN II, with a parallel mission to carry coverage of the newly wired Senate.

The networks have held to their original mission of providing gavel-to-gavel coverage of the House and Senate. Their long-form format makes the viewer a witness to congressional action without the benefits and liabilities of editing or accompanying narration. They make what is arguably an even richer contribution to public information, however, when they fill out their twenty-four-hour schedules with additional programming during congressional recesses. C-SPAN I typically offers taped coverage of congressional hearings, public policy forums, addresses at the National Press Club and elsewhere, and extended coverage of political campaign events.

Hearings especially offer viewers a sense of the texture of congressional give-and-take. Hearings involving opponents and proponents of proposed legislation (or oversight of a presidential decision) represent the best chance to hear true debates. Questions from committee members to other members, or to spokespersons who are invited to testify, are as close as we get to true public deliberations. In one such revealing moment, for example, C-SPAN offered full coverage of testimony by the administrator of the Envirnomental Protection Agency before the House Subcommittee on Energy and Commerce. The hearing, like many, was a case study of congressional *realpolitik*. William Reilly faced a panel generally hostile to proposed amendments to the Clean Water Act, serving as a lightning rod for many of the political crosscurrents that faced Congress and the Bush administration at the time.[18] On this particular day the issues involved fuel standards for auto makers, and demonstrated several features of congressional discourse not often seen in more typical news reports: that members thrive within their own areas of policy expertise; that legislation involves many-sided issues, some of which are more political than substantive; and that legislating is partly guided by legislators who have essentially become agents of particular industries. Reilly was especially grilled by the chair, Henry Waxman, who viewed changes in amendments as evidence of weakening resolve on pollution standards.

Although by the usual television standards its audiences are always small, C-SPAN has made members more conscious of their ability to win supporters through their appearances on the House and Senate floors. Access to even relatively small television audiences is an attractive prospect for members who want to increase their visibility or argue the merits and deficiencies of legislation. In his rise to the Speakership, for example, Newt Gingrich often used the Special Orders segment of the legislative day to speak to home viewers. During Special Orders any member can give a short speech *du jour* on any topic. And he estimated that about 200,000 viewers were tuned into C-SPAN at any one time, noting, "that's not a bad crowd."[19]

Some observers point out that the endless floor debates that dominate C-SPAN coverage are not really debates, and not really where decisions are made. Most speeches in the chambers of the House and Senate are undoubtedly given to members who have already made up their minds, and thus may seem to represent little more than empty rituals of posturing.[20] Even so, floor speeches serve the important purpose of publicizing ideas and forcing opinion leaders to deal with the priorities implicit in all legislation. C-SPAN provides a refreshing glimpse at the public reasons that legislators endorse as justifications for their actions; it provides a full and unnarrated video record of the political process and the public rhetoric that goes with it. Viewers see the institution at least partly as its participants see it. As one observer of the network observed, "Everything on C-SPAN goes on for too long, and that's just the point."[21]

The Mainstream Media

The press galleries of the House and Senate are a maze of old offices, closets, and warrens haphazardly tucked away in the Capitol building. Many are on the third floor of the building, a far cry from the formal dignity of the rooms just off the main floors of the chambers. The facilities for Senate print correspondents occupy several cramped rooms packed with the untidy clutter of overstuffed chairs, scraps of paper, old newspapers, press releases, and journalists in various states of concentration or ease, depending on whether or not they are writing against a looming deadline.

The noise and general confusion of the press gallery is a stark contrast to the individual hushed office-closets of the broadcasting gallery, whose members are far better dressed, and often hunched over tiny desks tucked under a few shelves holding congressional reference books and several television monitors. Some of the compact monitors relay pictures of their network; others carry a live video feed from the nearby Senate floor. When they are not scouting the halls and offices for information, they are sometimes in a neighboring studio recording the reactions of members seated in front of a mock-up of a Senate office. And on the days when their network news producers grant approval, they may make a predictable afternoon trek to one of the predetermined locations in the grassy "swamp" on the east side of the Capitol for a "stand upper" that will close what is usually a brief congressional story.

The Standing Committee of Correspondents lists nearly 4000 reporters and support staff accredited to cover the House and Senate. But the number of reporters at work on any given day is far less, usually no more than several hundred.[22] Among the most important are the limited number of reporters committed to Congress as a full-time beat. These include usually two reporters from the major network television and radio news programs, several dozen wire service reporters, and writers for major daily newspapers and national newsmagazines. Some, like former *New York Times* reporter Steven Roberts, the *Washington Post's* Helen Dewar, and ABC's Cokie Roberts have won high praise for explaining the complex personalities and politics of the Senate, and for applying a historical perspective to events that can have a very short shelf life. Others—especially those covering Congress for the networks—note that their stories are often a "hard sell" to their New York producers, who often see the national legislature as a fragmented body of largely anonymous figures.[23] Editors and producers often see news from the national legislature as information that has more appeal to political "insiders" than to the more apathetic American public.[24]

Beyond this limited but important group of national reporters, those who may show up for a committee hearing or a floor debate may represent smaller news services or a chain of regional newspapers. Reporters in this category often have a variety of floating responsibilities, looking for a Washington angle to events as they unfold on Capitol Hill, the Pentagon, and sometimes the underreported activities of agencies like the Department of Energy or Health and Human Services. Their stories will typically cover Congress with an eye on how its actions may effect readers in the towns of the papers that they represent. For instance, reporter Virginia Robicheaux has made a career of writing for publications in the West, reporting to the readers of smaller papers in Idaho, Nevada, and Utah on the activities of their local members.[25] Larger newspapers and chains of modest size will often have at least a small Washington bureau with several staffers who work on stories about Congress and other institutions inside the beltway.

The watershed elections of 1994 gave the reigns of power in Congress to a vocal conservative majority, and partly revitalized press interest in the body. Many reporters longing for more time or space to describe the emerging battles between the vocal Speaker of the House and President Clinton successfully argued that the election was a historic moment. For months after those elections, journalists on Capitol Hill found that they were newly reinfranchised. And they often covered the House as a more powerful institution that had partly taken over the national political agenda from the president.

The Trade Press

One area of press coverage that has been largely ignored by congressional observers and most Americans is the vast array of specialized trade publications that regularly report to their readers about legislative activity.

Nearly every profession in the United States is represented in Washington by professional lobbyists. They serve organized business and public interest groups who have strong financial or ideological incentives to protect their members. Among the most powerful are broadcasters, home builders, realtors, mortgage and investment bankers, auto makers, gun owners, unions, drug manufacturers, and scores of others. Even a small change in the federal tax codes, for example, may be seen as producing unwanted effects for individuals in the home-building, advertising, and mortgage businesses. Proposed alterations in Medicare—a perennial issue because of its enormous costs—similarly send up the antennas of those in the health-care and senior citizen lobbies.

All such groups are assisted in their tracking of Congress by the wealth of information that the institution makes available in the *Congressional Record*, from staffers and committees, on C-SPAN, and daily summaries available on the internet. In addition, there are privately published newsletters from long-time congress-watchers, and the extensive weekly updates and electronic data banks of the *Congressional Quarterly*, a virtual Talmud of authoritative assessments about the politics and details of pending legislative action.

The informational counterpart to the lobbying arms of these industries are the hundreds of trade journals that keep specialized constituencies informed of changes in their industries or areas of interest. These publications are often an important part of the machinery that drives the lobbying efforts of organized groups. Some are sponsored by a formal group, such as the American Legion, American Association of Retired Persons, or the American Medical Association. Others are independently financed, such as *Advertising Age, Broadcasting, Modern Machine Shop, Electronic Business, Chronicle of Higher Education*, and *Publisher's Weekly*. But they all share an interest in reporting Washington news with an eye on those points where the political process intersects with their own professional welfare.

What these often glossy publications lack in high circulation numbers they make up in targeting readers who are strongly motivated to press their views on lawmakers. Many have at least one staff member assigned to the political beat, with editors who often link legislative stories with calls for action to forestall changes that would adversely effect their group. While it would be an overstatement to conclude that members of Congress are al-

FIGURE 3-3. Congressional Quarterly advertisement

ways impressed by the orchestrated campaigns these publications sometimes promote, there is no question they are useful to the specialized communities who seek to influence legislation. In many cases these professionals and activists are more apt than the general population to give money to political candidates, engage in letter-writing campaigns, and deploy skilled lawyers and lobbyists on Capitol Hill.

LEVELS OF COVERAGE

The press covers Congress on three different levels. Individuals may be the primary focus of stories, especially when a few members or leaders are presented as strong advocates of or adversaries to legislation. Coverage may also focus on the collective actions or work of committees or special interest caucuses (such as the Congressional Black Caucus). And some reporting—especially in television reports and the weekly newsmagazines—focuses on features of the whole body or its two parts. While much of the reporting of Congress is a blend of these different areas, they are useful to explore separately.

Publicity and the Coverage of Individual Members

Overall, the coverage that the print media gives to individuals is usually less than it gives to the institutional actions of the House and Senate. According to their comprehensive study of newspaper reporting, for example, Charles Tidmarch and John Pitney, Jr., found that the *Chicago Sun Times* followed a pattern similar to other papers by devoting roughly 37 percent of its stories from Capitol Hill to collective actions, with only 27 percent to individuals. The remainder of their coverage linked the actions of one House to its opposite, to the president, or to the federal bureaucracy.[26]

The goal of securing favorable press coverage for each member is evident in the fact that nearly all members of the House and Senate have press secretaries who oversee the care and feeding of the media. They routinely field phone questions from reporters working on stories. They know many of the news producers at the television stations within their districts. They usually take care of arranging satellite interviews or videotapings in one of the Capitol Hill studios, such as the House studio located in an unused subway tunnel under the Capitol. And they help schedule appearances in Washington and in the frequent weekend trips that members take back to their states and districts. Many are also former journalists, using their knowledge of the news business to plan future appearances and to instruct their bosses on ways to deal with the press.

Several systems are used to reach the press. The newest involve video satellite links (frequently paid for by the parties) to local television stations, where reporters interview the member. On the radio side, a common approach is to put a message of the day on a phone system, so that stations can call in and tape a short response to a particular issue. The sound bites typically feature the member's reaction to presidential or congressional actions.

Even in the age of electronic communication, the primary vehicle used by members to communicate with the press remains the ordinary press release. Because political reporting within most districts is more complete in the national and local print media, their basic targets are almost always daily and weekly newspapers within the members home district or state. The so-called permanent campaign that keeps members in good standing between elections involves a steady stream of publicity about their effectiveness and work in Washington. Even the several hundred members who maintain relatively low profiles—rarely seeking out or appearing in the national news media—are careful to feed a constant supply of stories to local outlets.

Distributed handouts typically serve a number of purposes. As a source of good news, they give credit to the member for providing government support for a district ("More federal money is heading for Lorain County, Congressman Don J. Pease [D-13 Ohio] announced today"), describe his or her view on legislation that is moving through Congress ("Danforth Seeks to Expand Telecom Exports: Would Use AT&T as Negotiating Lever"), or announce an appointment or honor of local interest ("Aspin Welcomes Helwig as Janesville Office Intern").[27] Senators generally put out more releases than their counterparts in the House, with key figures such as Senate Majority leader Bob Dole producing nearly three hundred a year.[28]

Because print releases and their electronic counterparts mimic the general conventions of journalism, they are sometimes run in local media as is.[29] At larger outlets with more resources and a stronger sense of journalistic rigor, they often serve as advisories to editors about members or events they may want to cover. In every case, however, they encourage a member-centered approach to an issue. The slanted viewpoint of the publicity always makes the member an agent for positive reform. He or she is presented as someone who has convictions, is an advocate for an important agenda, and is a defender of the needs of the community in Washington's halls of power.

The success of this press agentry is difficult to measure.[30] Many journalists reject releases as useless and self-serving. But their continual presence on the desks of local editors and reporters undoubtedly helps frame issues to the advantage of incumbents. One indirect sign of their influence is the paradox of public opinion that has surrounded general American attitudes toward Congress for years. As an institution Congress gets low marks from the public. And yet when individual citizens are asked to comment on the quality of their members, they are much more positive.[31] Members portrayed as individuals generally escape the dulling effects of an essentially anonymous body. Their publicized work makes them more human, something that is harder to attribute to an institution built on the premise of competing factions. We associate them with their families, or with sets of personal traits. We recall news accounts about their work on behalf of individuals, industries, and groups in "our" region. And we are forgiving of their limitations, knowing that they cannot easily impose their will in a place where they represent only one of many decision makers.

The release below from the House Judiciary Committee prominently features the actions of its chair to the press and public. The chairs of major committees have enormous powers in shaping or delaying legislation, and in promoting issues they have an interest in. This press release was accessed via the Committee's World Wide Web site.

104_011

April 6, 1995

CONTACT: Sam Stratman

OFFICE: (202) 225-4561

For IMMEDIATE Release

Chairman Hyde Announces Oversight Hearings on Terrorism; Testimony Begins Thursday

(WASHINGTON) - Responding to recent terrorist incidents here and abroad, Congress must now act to safeguard American citizens, U.S. Rep. Henry J. Hyde (R-IL) suggested today.

Hyde, Chairman of the House Judiciary Committee, said domestic law enforcement agencies need additional recources to better coordinate anti-terrorism efforts, and he announced that the Committee will begin extensive hearings on the issue Thursday.

"In this post-cold war world the threat of terrorism, and our response to it, ranks as one of our greatest national security priorities and challenges," Hyde said.

"We need to strengthen the ability of U.S. law enforcement agencies to uncover and root out potential terrorist campaigns which target our citizens," he added.

Hyde warned of mounting evidence of clandestine groups in the United States that are actively raising funds to support international terrorist activities - a development he called "alarming." He also voiced concern about the growing worldwide trade in enriched uranium smuggled out of the Ukraine and Russia, and the potential of terrorist states to acquire weapons of mass destruction.

"We have learned much from the World Trade Center bombing - most importantly the weaknesses in our law enforcement efforts in fighting the terrorist threats," Hyde said.

Last month, the Clinton Administration sent to Congress a legislative proposal intended to curb illegal money laundering schemes in the U.S.; establish procedures to freeze assets of groups or individuals in the U.S. found to be violating fund raising prohibitions; and establish new courts to hear deportation cases brought against persons accused of illegal fund raising activities.

FIGURE 3-4.   A Sample Press Release

One of Congress's most effective advocates was Les Aspin, who gained a reputation as a first-rate specialist in foreign policy and military issues. Aspin died in 1995, after leaving the House of Representatives to serve as the Clinton administration's first Secretary of Defense and, later, as a defense advisor. While still in the House, he described general guidelines he followed in gaining press access: a "users guide" to gaining legislative power by influencing the national news media.

1. Go after coverage in the most influential media: the wire services such as the Associated Press and major agenda-setting papers like the *Washington Post* and the *New York Times.*
2. Anticipate where a story is going. Be days ahead of it so that your information or quotes actually further the reporting.
3. Pick a slow news day—usually Monday—to release new or useful information. Your story is more apt to get favorable coverage. Press releases should be prepared on Thursday and held or embargoed for Monday release.
4. Know the respected journalists in a given specialty, and give them useful information. In defense reporting, for example, there are a relatively small number of reporters who can give a story special legitimacy and importance.
5. Television coverage is hard to obtain. It is often triggered by important stories in the agenda-setting print media. But television is usually not very interested in policy discussion. For TV, "if it moves, it's news, and if it doesn't move, doesn't wiggle, there's nothing to see."
6. Sometimes the trivial and unusual pieces of information will give a member visibility. The information may come from staff research or information given to a committee of which you are a member. For example, a brief item about Army tests of poison gas on beagle puppies produced large amounts of coverage and mail.

Source: Katherine Winton Evans, "The News Maker: A Capitol Hill Pro Reveals His Secrets," *Washington Journalism Review*, June 1981, pp. 28–29, 32–33.

FIGURE 3-5.   Coverage of Les Aspin's "Advice for Managing Congressional News"

Covering the Committees

Hearings involving the committees of Congress are one of the fixed reference points of the nation's political journalism. Among other uses, hearings serve the function of allowing members and other interested observers to weigh in on the merits and weaknesses of proposed legislation. Hearings are such a common event "on the Hill" that their occurrence is sometimes taken for granted. But they can have unexpected effects, as members discovered in 1987 when the president of the former Soviet Union began to respond to comments made before the Joint Economic Committee. Apparently the testimony of Reagan administration officials before the committee estimating Mikhail Gorbachev's chances of pulling off planned economic reforms had caught the Soviet leader's attention. To the surprise of committee members, references to the generally pessimistic assessments of the administration suddenly started showing up in Gorbachev's speeches in Moscow.[32] Somehow the leader of what was still the Soviet Union had decided that these hearings deserved serious counterarguments that would affirm his domestic reforms and peaceful intentions. It would not be the first time that others attached more importance to this routine congressional process than did some of the members of the committees.

In their most important work, the committees of Congress engage in policy-making rather policy-enacting activities. The nominal function of most committees is to consider the testimony of experts and outsiders on national or regional problems that are likely targets for legislative action. Members may study proposed legislation or hold hearings in advance of concrete proposals. Committees may also investigate the work of federal agencies, and several—such as the powerful Senate Judiciary Committee—make recommendations on high-level federal appointees. In their various forms, they represent the most obscure and, occasionally, the most gladiatorial arenas to be found in American politics. The panels of knowledgeable testifiers slated to appear in one of the many rooms on Capitol Hill are sometimes only the minor players in what can become a debate waged in front of the cameras by members who have very different views about the merits of a bill or a federal appointee. In the spring 1995, for example, the Clinton Administration's nomination of Dr. Henry Foster to the position of Surgeon General began an intense struggle for public opinion waged between the White House and key Republican leaders, who opposed the nomination because Foster had performed some abortions in his duties as a gynecologyst. Confirmation hearings for Foster became the center of the ongoing battle in the United States over the legitimacy of existing protections for women seeking abortions.

No subject is too large or small, too specialized or too general, to be the subject of an inquiry. On one spring day in 1988, for example, the Joint Economic Committee's Subcommittee on Education and Health met in a more or less typical four-hour session. Congressman James Scheuer led the hearing, ostensibly to listen to the views of experts on how to streamline the United States' patchwork system of health-care services. He heard first from former Secretary of Health and Human Services Joesph Califano, and then from two panels of specialists from the Reagan administration and several universities. About eighty-five people came to at least part of the session, including several reporters, a number of lobbyists representing pensions and medical insurance programs, and a handful of student interns.[33] By all accounts the meeting was typical, a small moment in a long history of public discussion over a problem with no simple national consensus on a solution.

Most hearings such as Scheuer's go unreported in the mainstream press. But trade journals are careful to cover them if anything is proposed that could effect the interests of the industries they represent. Readers of the trade publication *Broadcasting*, for example, regularly see summaries of the views of members serving on the Senate Commerce Committee, the House Energy and Commerce Committee, and its Subcommittee on Telecommunications.

Republicans have booked some of the nation's top communications chief executives for their March 8 "megaconference" on telecommunications. Among the CEOs who have accepted invitations are BellSouth's John Clendenin, Pacific Telesis' Philip Quigley, Time Warner's Gerald Levin, NBC's Bob Wright, Comcast's Brian Roberts and Tribune's James Dowdle. The conference is sponsored by the National Policy Forum, a policy group supported by the Republican Party. Also expected are Senate Republicans Bob Dole (Kan.), the majority leader; Commerce Committee Chairman Larry Pressler (S.D.); Finance Committee Chairman Bob Packwood (Ore.); and House Telecommunications Subcommittee Chairman Jack Fields (Tex.). The conference comes just two months after Democrats held a post-election telecommunications summit with state and local regulatory officials.

Fin-syn is coming back for what could be its last act on the Washington policy-making stage. In April, the FCC is expected to begin a proceeding to determine whether what's left of the financial interest and syndication

rules—a prohibition against the Big Three broadcast networks entering the domestic syndication business—should be allowed to lapse into regulatory history this November. After a long and bitter fight between Hollywood and the networks, the FCC two years ago gutted the fin-syn rules, which blocked the networks from virtually any role in producing or syndicating programs on their own prime time schedules. It set the syndication prohibition to expire this November, but said it would give Hollywood one last chance to make a case for its preservation. That chance comes in the April proceeding.

The coalition of big studios, independent producers and TV stations that wants to keep programing restraints on the networks already is gearing up for the proceeding. "Our position is the same as it has been," says Warner Bors,' Barbara Brogliatti, a spokeswoman for the pro-finsyn forces. "Without rules, the networks are apt to abuse the power they derive from the control of prime time network TV." Hollywood will have an uphill fight: James Quello and Andrew Barrett, two of the commissioners who voted for the sunset in 1993,

Continued

FIGURE 3-6. *Washington Watch,* **broadcasting's weekly report to readers.**

are still around. And FCC Chairman Reed Hundt has indicated that the burden of proof on those advocating an extension of the rule will be a heavy one.

Local broadcasters will be in town this week for the National Association of Broadcasters annual state leadership conference. Key Capitol Hill policy-makers, including Senate Communications Subcommittee Chairman Bob Packwood (R-Ore.) and House Telecommunications Subcommittee Chairman Jack Fields (R-Tex.), will speak to the broadcasters, most of whom represent state broadcasting associations. FCC Commissioner Susan Ness also will address the group. And FCC officials will provide an overview of commission activity during a panel discussion that will feature Mass Media Bureau chief Roy Stewart, Audio Services Division chief Larry Eads, Enforcement Division chief Chuck Kelley, Video Services Division chief Barbara Kreisman, Policy and Rules Division chief Douglas Webbink, and Compliance and Information Bureau chief Beverly Baker.

FCC Inspector General Walker Feaster is one of several federal inspector generals who have been summoned to Capitol Hill this week to testify about their agencies' budgets. A sub-committee of the House Appropriations Committee is looking for places to cut the federal budget. Subcommittee members also may want to hear Feaster's opinion on the

quality of the FCC's bookkeeping. Feaster's predecessor, James Warwick (now retired), last year reported that the FCC's books were such a mess that they were "unauditable." At the time, the commission blamed its bookkeeping problems on another federal agency that handled its accounts. The FCC since has switched federal accountants. FCC Chairman Reed Hundt is expected to make his way to the Hill on March 21 to testify before the subcommittee that oversees the commission's budget.

C-SPAN marked President's Day last Monday by airing an interview with President Clinton. C-SPAN Chairman Brian Lamb asked the President what he thought was the best method by which to get his message across to the public. Clinton said it is his annual State of the Union address, but he also enjoys "town hall meetings." "I love the town hall meetings, and they're the best forum because there you have an honest dialogue with people," Clinton said. However, there can be difficulties with that format: "If there are 40 questions and 38 are positive and two are negative, and you're slightly off, the real hazard…is that one then becomes an evening news story, and 100 million people hear one thing and then maybe 1 million people hear the town hall meeting." Clinton received a statue of Abraham Lincoln and Stephen Douglas from C-SPAN as a commemoration of C-SPAN's coverage of the re-enactment of the 1858 Lincoln-Douglas debate.

Source: *Broadcasting and Cable,* February 27, 1995.

FIGURE 3-6. *Continued*

All of these legislative groups have the power to propose or question the regulations governing the ownership of stations and programming.

But if the average hearing goes unnoticed by most Americans, the exceptions still represent a large component of national news coverage. Hearings frequently represent the largest kind of congressional action covered by television news.[34] The reason goes to the heart of Congress's most potent informal power. If the manifest function of the legislature is to pass laws, its nearly equal latent function in the age of the mass media is to use committee hearings to publicize the concerns of its most powerful members. Current rules continue to give chairs wide latitude in deciding when to organize informational hearings and investigations. The results have sometimes served neither truth nor the rights of participants, as in the landmark Army-McCarthy hearings in 1954. That widely covered witch-hunt for phantom communists in government and the military turned a senator's name into a noun of reprobation.[35] "McCarthyism" remains a label for the special kind of demagoguery that weds the worst impulses of political life with the most irrational fears of the public. But useful public discussion has been served in scores of hearings over the long history of the modern Congress, notably in the Senate's inquiry into Vietnam policy in 1966,[36] the landmark Watergate inquiry of 1973, and the Iran-Contra investigations of 1987.[37]

On countless other occasions hearings have served as forums for the debate of social issues, such as the memorable meeting of the Senate Commerce Committee to hear witnesses for and against a proposal to print parental advisories on record albums with "offensive" music lyrics. The testifiers ranged from a member of the group Twisted Sister, who opened his defense against the action with the observation that he wasn't sure whether it was morning or afternoon, to the wife of then-senator Al Gore.[38] In addition to full coverage on C-SPAN, that session made its way onto two network television news shows and countless newspapers. If such meetings are unlikely to result in legislative action, they serve to air opposing views on subjects of broad concern. On this day the alleged effects of popular culture on America's youth surfaced as a national issue.

Covering the Institution

Content studies differ, but two general patterns stand out as prominent features of reporting about the institution of Congress. First, in the print media most of the reporting that originates on Capitol Hill focuses on the actions of the body rather than specific individuals.[39] Second, much of the coverage presented in all media is tinged with negativity. The first is self-evident. The formal actions taken by Congress, along with the institution's strengths and weaknesses, are represented as news about the group as a whole. Final votes on legislation, attempts to override presidential vetoes, and the more or less fixed laundry list of institutional problems—ranging from its 1992 banking and post office scandals to deeper issues such as the building of huge campaign "war chests"—are usually represented as features of the whole institution. In their study of ten major newspapers, Charles Tidmarch and John Pitney found that roughly two to three times as many stories are devoted to institutional processes as compared to individual statements or actions.[40]

The second feature represents a continuous cloud that hangs over the legislative branch. No public attitude better symbolizes the crisis in confidence about American political institutions than reporting characterizing the Congress as a body. Humorist P. J. O'Rourke surely captured prevailing American attitudes when he titled his scathing satire of Washington politics *Parliament of Whores*.[41] His best-selling broadside reflects the views of virtually every modern President since the end of Lyndon Johnson's term in 1968 who has railed against the Congress as a body of provincial individuals, far more concerned about protecting their own interests than considering the broader "public interest."[42] It also is indicative of the general tone of much national reporting. As Representative David Obey has observed, national reporting has "a smirking way of covering this institution . . . just one more raindrop eating away at the rock of a very complicated institution."[43]

There can be little doubt that Congress is an easy target. Nothing so clearly symbolizes the alleged failings of "divided government" than a system that permits the election of a president from one party and majorities in the House and Senate to come from the other party. Further, with members of the House never far from a campaign for reelection, and with a purposively regionalized Senate that gives tiny Rhode Island the same number of senators as California, the Constitution has virtually guaranteed that the national legislature will be fractured and pluralistic. No group charged with truly representing so diverse a country as the United States could be otherwise. Given human nature, and the diverse political and cultural geography of the United States, Congress is unlikely to act as a single disciplined unit.

Reporting from Congress is thus dominated by the continuing dilemma of accounting for a single unit made up of 535 individuals. Its members rarely share the same priorities, motives, and legislative goals. Commenting on them as if they were a coherent unit requires a certain degree of semantic fudging in the use of collective pronouns and verbs. In real terms, "they" or "them" rarely fits all of its members.

Since nearly all of the popular media need clarity and simplicity, reporting on Congress rarely leaves its dignity in tact. Reporters love the diversity of sources and subjects built in to the Congress, but editors and television producers generally reflect their audiences' impatience with subjects that will not yield to simple summaries and characterizations.

SUMMARY

On its own terms, Congress is clearly an impressive governmental institution. It serves as a national forum for most of the issues that concern most Americans. It has taken advantage of new communications technologies to bring the views of its members and those who lobby it to the news pages and television screens of any Americans who are interested. And it attracts bright and frequently articulate people, not only many of those who are elected to serve from every region of the nation, but hundreds of staffers who support its operations as information gatherers, policy specialists, and troubleshooters for constituents. Moreover, Congress has proven itself to be one of the more durable political institutions yet devised for the purpose of legislating. Since 1789 it has kept intact a structure of formal and informal procedures that makes it easy to talk about legislation, but appropriately difficult to implement it. The committee system, the growth of personal staffs, and power sharing with the president and the courts emphasizes extensive private and public discussion in advance of legislative action.

Even given its strengths, this chapter has described a body that is now alien to many Americans. The inefficiencies that have always been built into the legislative process now seem magnified by the very communications innovations that have made the body so accessible to most Americans. These newer communications methods—modern press relations, satellite links to home television stations, extensive coverage on C-SPAN and other media—have helped Americans see what it has always been. Congress now prominently displays many features of its eighteenth-century origins that many Americans no longer admire. In our era we tend to honor institutions with clearer lines of authority and faster-paced methods of achieving change. With sometimes embarrassing clarity Congress displays the fractures and fragmentation of American life that generations raised on the fantasies and simplicities of television would sooner forget. It reminds us that we are a nation of competing interests, not the single community that presidents rhapsodize about in their more inclusive rhetoric.

NOTES

1. Peter Theroux, *Sandstorms: Days and Nights in Arabia* (New York: Norton, 1990), p. 24.

2. Timothy E. Cook, *Making Laws and Making News* (Washington: Brookings, 1989), p. 168.

3. Hedrick Smith, *The Power Game: How Washington Works* (New York: Random House, 1988), pp. 128–129.

4. Connie Bruck, *Master of the Game* (New York: Simon and Schuster, 1994), pp. 271–272.

5. This sequence is reconstructed from David Hosansky, "President Swings and Misses at Baseball Strike," *Congressional Quarterly Weekly Report*, February 11, 1995, pp. 447–449.

6. See, for example, George E. Reedy, *The U.S. Senate* (New York: Mentor, 1986), pp. 30–46.

7. Alexander Hamilton, James Madison, and John Hay, *The Federalist Papers* (New York: New American Library, 1961), pp. 378–379.

8. John F. Kennedy, *Profiles in Courage*, memorial ed. (New York: Perennial Library, 1964).

9. Christopher Matthews, *Hardball: How Politics is Played—Told by One Who Knows the Game* (New York: Summit, 1988), p. 50.

10. See Mary Collins, "News of the Congress and by the Congress," *Washington Journalism Review*, June, 1990, pp. 30–34.

11. Quoted in Smith, *The Power Game*, p. 135.

12. Adam Clymer, "House Revolutionary," *New York Times Magazine*, August 23, 1992, pp. 41, 47–48.

13. Ruth Shalit, "Bob Dole's Vision Thing," *New York Times Magazine*, March 5, 1995, p. 58.

14. Martin Tolchin, "Congress's Influential Aides Discover Power But Little Glory on Capitol Hill," *New York Times*, November 12, 1991, p. A22.

15. S. Robert Lichter and Daniel R. Amundson, "Less News is Worse News: Television News Coverage of Congress, 1972–92," in *Congress, The Press and the Public* ed. Thomas E,. Mann and Norman J. Ornstein (Washington: Brookings, 1994), pp. 134–136.

16. There is no clear consensus on how underrepresented Congress is. Arguably, there was intense coverage of the GOP's 1995 "Contract with America," which consumed the first several months of work in the Congress in its first 1995 session. That was partly due to the ability of Speaker Gingrich to use speeches and press conferences to generate interest. It was also due to the 1994 elections, which pitted GOP majorities in both houses of Congress against a Democratic president. For additional different perspectives see Greg Schneiders, "The 90-Second Handicap: Why TV Coverage of Legislation Falls Short," *Washington Journalism Review*, June, 1985, pp. 44–46, and Stephen Hess, *Live from Capitol Hill* (Washington: Brookings, 1991), pp. 33–61.

17. Thomas J. Meyer, "No Sound Bites Here," *New York Times Magazine*, March 15, 1992, p. 46.

18. C-Span, broadcast of proceedings of the Health and Environment Subcommittee to the Energy and Commerce Committee, July 24, 1989.

19. Cook, *Making Laws*, pp. 99–100.

20. Paul E. Corcoran, *Political Language and Rhetoric* (Austin: University of Texas, 1979), pp. xi–xvii.

21. Meyer, "No Sound Bites Here," p. 57.

22. Cook, *Making Laws*, p. 36.

23. Schneiders, "The 90-Second Handicap," p. 45.

24. Stephen Hess, *The Utlimate Insiders: U.S. Senators in the National Media* (Washington: Brookings, 1986), 89–91.

25. Cook, *Making Laws*, p. 37.

26. See Charles M. Tidmarch and John J. Pitney, Jr., "Covering Congress," *Polity*, Spring 1985, p. 473.

27. These examples are from Hess, *Live from Capitol Hill*, pp. 9, 82, 89.

28. Ibid., p. 151.

29. Collins, "News of the Congress," pp. 30–32.

30. Tidmarch and Pitney, "Covering Congress," pp. 473–474. In their 1985 study of congressional coverage in ten large newspapers the authors found that at least one, the *Philadelphia Inquirer*, completely ignored all members in their circulation area for an entire month.

31. Richard Fenno, *Home Style*, (Boston: Little Brown, 1978), ch. 5.

32. Clyde H. Farnsworth, "Gorbachev Lends an Ear to Proxmire's Hearings," *New York Times*, November 9, 1987, p. B8.

33. Robert D. Hershey Jr., "Hearings on Capitol Hill and Who They Attract," *New York Times*, May 6, 1988, p. A22.

34. Michael J. Robinson and Keven Appel, "Network News Coverage of Congress," *Political Science Quarterly*, Fall 1979, pp. 414–415.

35. For a concise summary of this period, see Robert J. Donovan and Ray Scherer, *Unsilent Revolution: Television News and American Life* (New York: Cambridge University Press, 1992), pp. 23–34.

36. See Fred Friendly, *Due to Circumstances Beyond our Control* (New York: Vintage, 1968), pp. 212–265.

37. Smith, *The Power Game*, pp. 616–637.

38. For an account of this hearing see ibid., pp. 119–122.

39. Tidmarch and Pitney, "Covering Congress," p. 473.

40. Ibid.

41. P. J. O'Rourke, *Parliament of Whores* (New York: Atlantic Monthly Press, 1991).

42. It is important to note that widespread criticism of Congress is not new. It has been more or less a fixed feature of American life. Consider the start of an article written in the last century by Mark Twain, who covered Congress as a journalist: "Dear Reader: Suppose that you were a Congressman. And suppose that you were a thief. But I repeat myself." Quoted in Michael Green, "Nobody Covers the House," in *Congress and the News Media* ed. by Robert O. Blanchard (New York: Hastings House, 1974), p. 329.

43. Schneiders, "The 90-Second Handicap," p. 45.

4

WINNING AND HOLDING THE PRESIDENCY: A CAMPAIGNS PERSPECTIVE

The president is a ubiquitous electronic presence, always on the go and on the tube, in some vivid new tableau that is a masterwork of the campaigner's art.[1]

Campaigning is the ugly price they pay for the opportunity to practice statecraft.[2]

This chapter examines both a *process* and a *subject*. The process is the political campaign, the subject is the presidency, and our goal here is to explore the enormous common region where they intersect. Newly elected presidents used to leave their campaigns behind, glad finally to be rid of the need to feed the daily journalism and publicity machine that generated votes. But no more. Executives must now function in continual media-based campaigns. The communication of power and the orchestration of public opinion in the modern presidency owes a great deal to the introduction of campaign methods to the governing process.

Campaigns occur in many phases of American life. We are a nation constantly "on the make" in business, religion, social action, and politics. The messages of campaigns are as close as our mailbox and as pervasive as television newscasts. They may be undertaken by the United Way, McDonalds, the American Association of Retired Persons, or the Republican Party. Institutions now routinely organize their calendars by determining outcomes and goals they seek from the press or public—as votes, purchase decisions, or attitudes—and then strategizing to achieve them.

After a brief overview of the weakened state of the presidency in the 1990s, this chapter discusses the concept of the campaign as a permanent fixture of presidential politics, and summarizes the historical shifts that have encouraged this development. We will then explore the features of modern political campaigns, especially media-based strategies for waging them, as well as the dominant "process" orientation used by the news media to cover them. The chapter closes with a look at two models that describe contrasting impressions of relations between the president and the press.

THE CAMPAIGN IMPERATIVE: DEALING WITH A TROUBLED PRESIDENCY

There have been many changes in the nature of the institutionalized presidency that have oriented the office to a more permanent campaign mode. Most obviously, it is a more public office than it used to be. Presidents are expected to be heard from on a regular basis, and they have willingly obliged.[3] Two less noted changes in the character of presidential politics have also encouraged presidents and their advisers to think in terms of campaigns approach to their ongoing work. And both point to developments that now seem to diminish rather than enhance the office.

One of the two has to do what recent presidents and legislative leaders have called "gridlock." In its common usage, the term refers to the tendency of the executive and legislative branches of government to neutralize each other's power, making effective governance difficult. Gridlock forces presidents to think in term of massive campaign efforts to achieve modest short-term goals.

The makers of the Constitution foresaw and even welcomed divided government. But they probably did not intend a system where, in their words, "factions" would fracture and sometimes paralyze the legislative process. There have been exceptions. The most famous, perhaps, was the New Deal. With the help of a supportive Congress, President Franklin Roosevelt set out a legendary set of economic and employment programs in 1933. In the first one hundred days of that administration Roosevelt was momentarily able to enact a vast web of initiatives defining a new level of governmental activism in creating jobs and federal activism in spuring a weak economy.

But today Congress is stunningly independent, with members more likely to seek their own routes to election that partly bypass the old party channels. Magnifying this trend, members feel equally empowered to define a role that permits dissent from a president in their own party. Party discipline is, at best, a sometime thing. Gridlock has made the president legislatively more impotent,[4] and more dependent on massive public-relations exercises to sway a suspicious public and a reluctant Congress. In Hillary Rodham Clinton's words, it is now necessary "to run a campaign for policy just like you do for elections."[5]

A second contributing cause for engaging in full-fledged persuasive assaults to win the hearts and minds of Americans has to do with the increasingly shrinking distance between constituents and office-holders. The presidency has lost much of its mystique and, with it, the aura of authority that made it relatively easy to gain public deference to presidential decisions.

On one hand the presidency still confers enormous prestige and legitimacy on its occupants and their actions. It gives holders of the office the chance to dress their intentions in the rhetoric of moral leadership, a rhetoric that can be followed up with awesome military and political power. "Are you better off today than you were four years ago?" candidate Ronald Reagan asked Americans about the chief executive he sought to unseat. That many Americans apparently took the question seriously as a measure of the effectiveness of President Jimmy Carter is evidence of the power we continue to assign to the presidency. The question assumes that he or she can be the agent responsible for the economic success or well-being of ordinary citizens. Figures including George Washington, FDR, Dwight Eisenhower, and John Kennedy were heroes in their time partly because we identified the success of the nation—and sometimes ourselves—in their achievements. But that leap of faith about the legitimacy of their leadership was possible, in part, because we did not know them in the same ways as we know their modern counterparts.

Just when the majesty and mystery of the office began to disappear is difficult to determine. Certainly the widespread disaffection with the Johnson and Nixon administrations in the late '60s and early '70s contributed to the loss of distance and respect. Johnson's relentless pursuit of a disastrous Vietnam policy and Nixon's involvement in Watergate soured public regard for the presidency. These events also unfolded at a time when the news media's intensified public interest in the private lives of national figures was gaining momentum. Biographies of FDR, Kennedy, and Eisenhower in this period, for example, revealed that all three had engaged in affairs that had strained their marriages. These factors and others combined to undermine whatever "mythic" roles we had assigned to earlier leaders.[6]

Presidents have thus been demythified. Under the intense daily exposure of the press, and in a coarsened and somewhat poisoned climate of public discourse,[7] chief executives have been partly recontextualized in personal rather than political terms. We recognize their specialness, but we want to see their ordinariness as well: individuals with dysfunctional family members, rocky marriages, and familiar medical problems. At times, presidents are agents in this trend, seeking ways to display their own hu-

A President Works Through an Image Problem

On Memorial Day 1993, Bill Clinton made an appearance and brief speech at the Vietnam Veterans' Memorial. The black granite wall carries the names of 58,000 dead soldiers who died in a war that fragmented and polarized the nation.

To these veterans the President's appearance at the memorial was bound to be provocative. In the 1992 campaign Clinton represented himself as "the man from Hope," the son of a backward part of the country, and the product of hard work rather than privilege. But the campaign waged against Clinton communicated a different story of a young man who used his glibness and guile to avoid the war. The image of a draft evader and war protester partly stuck, creating a long-term problem with the military and its traditional supporters. In the few minutes that it took on the warm May day to deliver his comments the president drew scattered applause, especially when he promised to release additional information on missing MIAs and POWs. But he was heckled mercilessly by a sizable minority of Vietnam vets during the first half of the eight-minute speech. Even a carefully inclusive introduction of the president by Joint Chiefs of Staff Chairman Colin Powell could not curb the hostility. Front-page stories in the nation's newspapers described the "angry taunts"[1] and "raucous . . . reception"[2] the president received. All three of the major network's nightly newscasts lead with the story, some showing placards bearing words like "hypocrite," "for shame," or "Never trust a draft dodger."[3] Clinton's dilemma was perhaps reflected most completely in the placard carried by an eight-year veteran, who seemed at once to capture the lost hope of many veterans and the epidemic of national cynicism that now surfaces in our national discourse. It read: "Dodge the Draft, Smoke Dope, Cheat on Your Wife, Become President—The American Dream."[4]

We are not used to seeing a president heckled and booed. Presidents do not often have to say, as Clinton did a few minutes into his speech, "To all of you who are shouting, I have heard you. I ask you now to hear me."[5] "Let us continue to disagree, if we must, about the war," he noted, "but let us not let it divide us as a people any longer."

Many volumes have been written about this war and those complicated times, but the message of this memorial is quite simple. These men and women fought for freedom, brought honor to their communities, loved their country, and died for it. They were known to all of us. There's not a person in this crowd today who did not know someone on this wall. Four of my high school classmates are there, four who shared with me the joy and trials of childhood and did not live to see the three score and ten years the scripture says we are entitled to.

Continued

Continued

No single speech or press event can transform a president's image. But by the end of his remarks, Clinton had clearly won the admiration of some of those present.[6]

[1]Paul Richter and Howard Libit, "Against the Wall: Clinton Heckled, Hailed at Vietnam Memorial," *Trenton Times*, June 1, 1993, pp. A1–A7.
[2]Thomas Friedman, "Clinton, Saluting Vietnam Dead, Finds Old Wound Is Slow to Heal," *New York Times*, June 1, 1993, p. A1.
[3]Vanderbilt New Archives, Abstracts for May 31, 1993.
[4]Richter and Libit, "Against the Wall," p. A7.
[5]Transcript of Clinton Speech at Vietnam War Memorial, *New York Times*, May 31, 1993, p. A14.
[6]Friedman, "Clinton," p. A14.

manity.[8] But in such a climate of personalized coverage, they must use the public relations apparatus of the White House to refocus attention on their political objectives.

THE CONCEPT OF THE PERMANENT CAMPAIGN: FROM EPISODIC TO CAMPAIGN POLITICS

Sidney Blumenthal is the author of the important notion that the ownership of politics has shifted partly from leaders and policy makers to public relations professionals who are now central to the process of governing, as well as getting elected. Blumenthal argues that politics is increasingly dominated by the need to engineer and maintain consent.

> *The permanent campaign is the political ideology of our age. It combines image-making with strategic calculation. Under the permanent campaign governing is turned into a perpetual campaign. Moreover, it remakes government into an instrument designed to sustain an elected official's public popularity. It is the engineering of consent with a vengeance . . . truly a program of statecraft.[9]*

A concern for public opinion remains the central focus of any campaign. While we may sometimes romanticize defiance of popular approval as an act of political courage (as admirers of Harry Truman like to quote his aphorism "If you can't stand the heat, get out of the kitchen"), the links between political success and public acceptance are real, if extremely complex.

Presidential power is especially easy to equate with presidential approval ratings, however imperfectly they are measured. It is an iron law of the presidency that high public support lessens political and rhetorical opposition. In his first term, for example, Ronald Reagan was able partly to silence a hostile press and Congress and win a number of legislative victories because of generally strong approval ratings. Many members of the press and congressional opponents seemed unwilling to take him on.[10] In political terms, favorable public opinion is an enabling power; low acceptance is enormously crippling.[11] As Emmet John Hughes has written, "historians of the Presidency concur that the loss of the people's trust is the one mortal disaster from which there can be no real recovery."[12]

It is helpful to trace the origins of the permanent campaign in a historical oversimplification. Politics in American life has changed in part because it has moved from being a relatively closed and episodic activity to a much more public activity tied to the daily news cycle. This conclusion misses some important exceptions, but it catches the essence of an important historic shift. Presidents and other national leaders prior to the early 1900s expected that they could do most of the public's business in private, and at their own pace. But many events began to change this way of functioning. One of the most dramatic was the decision of Franklin Roosevelt in 1933 to establish a White House Press Office. A place for the press near the president had the effect of giving the Roosevelt the power to comment on the daily news agenda. As the object of daily press attention, and as a leader who gained energy from the

---

What Is a Campaign?

According to William Safire, the word campaign is derived from a French term referring to the open countryside. It soon became associated with military operations, referring to the length of time troops were in the field. The American usage in the eighteenth century was adapted from this combat context, referring to "the business of getting elected to office."[1] In the twentieth century it was expanded to the vocabularies of advertising and public relations, whose strategies and skills are employed in politics as well as industry.

Some of the essential features of the campaign include:

- The development of consistent messages, repeated for maximum positive effect on public opinion
- The identification of target audiences to maximize the effects of messages
- The use of market or audience research to improve message effectiveness
- The development of a well-defined end goal (i.e., legislative approval of a presidential initiative)
- When necessary, the inclusion of messages calculated to minimize success of the opposition while maximizing your own

[1]William Safire, *Safire's Political Dictionary* (New York: Ballantine, 1978), p. 92.

audience's rapt attention to his words, Roosevelt became a prime public interpreter of the American scene. Along with Eleanor, who wrote a popular newspaper column called "My Day," FDR became a commentator to the nation. The routinized task of gathering and reporting presidential news gave the president clout and provided a way to prepare public opinion for the programmatic experimentation that was central to the New Deal. For their part, reporters repaid this sudden and extensive access with a fondness and protectiveness that would seem unimaginable in the modern White House.[13]

The historic presidency prior to Roosevelt was often far different. The actions of earlier leaders were generally more leisurely, and less the center of national attention. Statecraft in the old office was centered on the interpersonal cooperation or struggles of major political leaders at the White House and the Congress. Presidents were largely oriented to the internal power structure within a relatively limited number of major institutions, what would be called today an "inside game" involving powerful senators, a handful of influential editors, and vocal reformers. Speeches were given far less often, reflecting a political culture less dependent on orchestrating and developing public opinion. Lincoln, for example, gave an average of only sixteen significant speeches a year.[14] By the second McKinley administration in 1900 the average was up to sixty-five and climbing. With the loquacious Theodore Roosevelt a few years later came the recognition that the presidency could indeed be a "bully pulpit" for arguing how people should live as well as what policies they should accept.[15]

At the beginning of the century the press was often seen as more of a nuisance than a conduit for orchestrating public pressure on Congress. Between 1908 and 1912, for example, William Howard Taft largely ignored the press. Even the far more innovative Woodrow Wilson could be—by modern standards—remarkably indifferent to the role of the public in achieving his objectives.[16] Imagine a modern president beginning a press briefing on a piece of legislation as Wilson did in 1915:

> *Mr. President, can you saying anything about the Shipping Bill?*
> *That needn't bother you.*
> *It does.*
> *Well, you must not let it.*
> *It doesn't bother us, Mr. President, we just want to know about it.*
> *It is going through all right.*
> *With some changes, Mr. President?*
> *No changes of any sort that is not consistent with the principle of the bill.*[17]

The presidency today obviously exists in the steady gaze of constant public scrutiny that continues unbroken from campaign to the assumption of leadership. And the institution has responded by keeping many features of the campaign communication apparatus in the move to the White House. Campaign aides frequently join the White House staff as key advisers. Pollsters who tracked issues in the volatile electorate are usually retained to continue to measure public approval ratings. And recent presidents in particular—notably Ronald Reagan and Bill Clinton—have been reluctant to abandon their expressive campaign styles and themes for the more complex and subtle rhetorics of administrative leadership. In 1994, for example, as the Clinton administration floundered in a sea of troubles brought on by an especially ambitious legislative agenda, the president heard repeated warnings from aides to return to the successful "outside game" of the 1992 campaign mode. The "inside game" of dealing with various Washington power brokers, warned adviser James Carville, would draw the president away from the populist impulses that had lead to his election.[18]

We now turn to a more detailed explanation of some of the tools used in the modern campaign-based presidency.

FEATURES OF THE CAMPAIGN-BASED PRESIDENCY

There are six attributes of the modern presidency that owe part of their existence to the campaign model. These attributes are partly the products of the campaigns that preceeded elections, and partly the legacy of press coverage of the modern presidency. Each of the six is worth brief consideration.

Continual Polling by the Parties and the Press

Polls have become the common currency of political power. They value and devalue ideas and individuals. They create headlines, establish artificial benchmarks to assess success or failure, and factor into the political calculations of major or minor figures. Along with all of the other media tools available to the president—access to national television, endless publicity and photo opportunities, an enormous public thirst for humanizing information about the first family—they represent a well-entrenched public relations tool. Pollsters routinely move with a victorious presidential candidate to the White House, continuing to take the pulse of the public on a regular basis. And presidents continue to look at their output. Lyndon Johnson, for instance, was fond of reaching into his pocket to retrieve favorable poll data to impress an oval office visitor. And when the same kind of data suggested that he had lost popular support for American involvement in the Vietnam war, he decided to resign rather than seek a second term.[19]

Key Events in the Development of the Campaign-Oriented Presidency

This brief and selective timeline represents the cumulative introduction of elements common to elections into the processes of governance in the White House.

	Event	*Effects*
1933	Franklin Roosevelt establishes the White House Press Office	Linked the White House to the daily news cycle, contributing to making the president the chief interpreter of national events
1952	Eisenhower's staff embraces television in the presidential campaign; Stevenson attempts to follow	The presidency becomes a familiar part of popular culture
1960	Kennedy begins live TV coverage of press conferences	Contributed to giving the president a public persona, and raising "character" as a presidential feature
1964	Johnson exhibits intense interest in television and news reporting of recent or anticipated actions	Staff sought to dominate reporting on events, and isolate opponents to the president or his initiatives
1968	Nixon establishes the White House Office of Communications	Centralized press, speech-writing, and other communications functions, seeking greater control of daily news agenda
1976	Carter employs many campaign aides in key advisory positions, including his pollster, Pat Caddell; begins campaign-style "town meetings"	Aides brought the campaign perspective to the White House; town meetings gave the president the apparent accessibility of a candidate
1980	Reagan relinquishes day-to-day contact with the press in favor of structured news events, guided by public relations professionals	Hiring of Michael Deaver and others sets the tone for limiting unstructured press conferences

Continued

Continued

1984	Reagan administration uses leased satellite space to address supporters and campaign fund-raisers around the country	Satellites make it possible to extend the perception of contact with the president to a larger number of voters
1992	Clinton brings his use of "informal" candidate forums into the presidency, targeting specific messages to specific audiences	Appearances had the partial effect of lessening the importance of interpretive reporting of the television networks in favor of regionalized coverage of "forums" and local meetings
1994	The Clinton administration establishes a World Wide Web site for the White House, along with Congress, political action committees, and challengers	Presidential statements, campaign materials, and easily searchable databases create a sense of citizen involvement, and provide a link to widely dispersed supporters

In 1992 Clinton pollster Stan Greenberg presented frequent "snapshots" of public attitudes to candidate Bill Clinton. And later in the White House, he continued to advise on policy—especially economic policy—based on poll data and focus groups (small groups of citizens who are asked to respond to a particular concept). His most elaborate effort in 1993 was an extensive citizen survey called the "Presidential Project," which studied how people viewed the Clinton presidency, especially in relation to Congress.[20]

Polls are frequently interpreted by the press as the scorecard that records the success of appeals to the public for support. The news media increasingly generate their own headlines by giving enormous prominence to poll data they have commissioned to track public attitudes. In the last four months of the 1992 presidential campaign alone, over 200 polls were commissioned by news organizations.[21] Even though poll results are usually crude reductions of far more subtle and complex attitudes, a commissioned poll is a "news" event created for and essentially owned by the news outlet. Like carefully tracked ratings for television programs, the fact that they involve questionable methods of construction and tabulation is generally downplayed.[22]

Employment of Public Relations Specialists

It was often the case prior to 1960 that campaign aides tended to move on after a presidential contest. That is now less true. As Larry Sabato notes:

While a consultant's influence undoubtedly is at its peak during the campaign itself, it hardly vanishes after the election. The same tools and experience that make the political professional so necessary to the operation of the modern campaign can be quite useful to a public official as he attempts to influence his constituency and refine his image.[23]

Perhaps the best known of high-level aides in the Reagan White House was Micheal Deaver, who became known as the keeper of the presidential image, a person who excelled at "producing the Presidency for television."[24] Deaver had begun his career doing administrative and public relations work for the GOP in California. He admitted no great interest in politics, but it became apparent to party leaders that he had a flair for helping design campaign events. At the Reagan White House members of the press considered him a master of controlling press access to the president, while at the same time staging events that would appear well on network television. ABC's Sam Donaldson and others complained endlessly to Deaver and others about about limited access to the president. And Deaver complained back that the press was turning the White House and its rituals—including the arrivals of foreign dignitaries—into a circus.[25]

Whatever the truth, Deaver was only a slightly more notorious example of the arrival of scores of communications tacticians from campaigns to important advisory posts within the White House. Some, such as the Kennedy administration's Ted Sorenson and the Reagan-Bush era's Peggy Noonan, made their marks as speechwriters. Others, like the Carter administration's Jody Powell and the Johnson administration's Bill Moyers, were youthful campaign workers groomed by their mentors to eventually assume the vital position of White House Press Secretary. And still others came from professional backgrounds in broadcasting, advertising, or print, for example, former NBC News president Robert Kintner to the Johnson White House; H. R. Haldeman from advertising's J. Walter Thompson to the Nixon administration; and David Gergen from a recent position at *U.S. New and World Report,* to the position of counselor in the Clinton administration.

Dependence on Free Media

Even the most heavily bankrolled campaigns must depend on reaching voters through the "free media," a phrase that covers all of the news and entertainment venues that can provide a forum for the candidate. In a national campaign for president, there is never enough money to buy sufficient "paid media" (advertising, television time, direct mail, and so on). In addition, voters expect to hear about candidates in the more or less neutral settings of news accounts, visits to television talk show hosts, and the like. So every presidential campaign has a virtual army of senior officials and aides to provide for the needs of the news media. These aides must master the logistics of organizing a traveling "road show" that will keep reporters and video crews who are covering the candidate relatively content.[26] At the same time, they must serve the candidate as well, securing the kind of positive press coverage that achieves the objectives of the campaign. It is not an easy balance to maintain, since the press is wary of being exploited, and campaign staffs may come to resent what they see as the unfairness of campaign reporting.

The tools of the trade for developing positive free media coverage are familiar to other aspects of political communication: press releases and video "clips" that indicate what the candidate has said, press advisories about upcoming events with the candidate, and press kits that include extensive background on the candidate and his or her issues. Staffers are assigned various tasks to assure full media coverage, including "advancing" a visit by taking care of the hundreds of details that must be in place for an "event," everything from arranging for public address systems to determining who will be in the accompanying "photo-ops."[27]

At the presidential campaign level, senior staffers are also responsible for building bridges to important members of the national media, including reporters from major newspapers, news magazines, and television networks who are covering the candidate. After a public debate with an opponent, to cite a key moment in any campaign, press secretaries and advisors will circulate among the attending press to "spin" the outcome. Spinning is pushing a point of view or "line" that is complementary to a candidate. Ostensibly, the press ignores the self-serving conclusions these aides pass on.[28] But the unclear nature of most debates, and the urgency to assess their impact, probably means that at least some of these observations filter in to subsequent reporting.

Many of these people and tasks are transferred directly to the public offices that candidates assume after election, though at a more modest level in congressional offices. Consider the communications staffing of the White House after the election of Bill Clinton in 1992. Many of the staffers continued the work they began during the campaign.

- George Stephanopolous, communications director, responsible for coordinating free and paid media with overall strategy set by consultants such as media adviser Mandy Grunwald, campaign adviser James Carville, and pollster Stan Greenberg.
- David Anderson, director of satellite services, responsible for arranging interviews between the president and local television anchors, or special groups such as regional newspaper editors. The scheduling of satellite time—usually billed to the president's party—makes it possible to deliver a message to almost any group at any time. The president can take a relatively small part of his day to tape or deliver a live message from Washington.

- Jeff Eller, director of media affairs, responsible for arranging media coverage in areas other than the traditional White House press. Eller worked with others to make recommendations about using nontraditional settings for presidential appearances, including MTV, and sporting events like the opening day of the baseball season.
- Dee Dee Myers, press secretary, responsible for daily briefings with the White House Press corps, which serves as the most frequently used channel to the public. This position is crucial to any administration, and complicated by the generally robust egos of journalists who have landed this highly visible beat. Like many who have held this post, she moved on before the end of the president's term, a victim of vague but nagging questions about her effectiveness.
- Richard Strauss, director of radio operations, responsible for providing taped "feeds" or "actualities" to stations who request them. Strauss was amazed to find that the old White House system could feed only three stations at a time with taped sound bites. During the campaign he had developed the capacity to relay actualities to 2000 stations.
- Jess Sarmiento, responsible for reaching the more specialized ethnic media and trade press. If governing is frequently about putting together coalitions that support certain common objectives, the value of mobilizing those coalitions with appeals to specific groups is self-evident.[29]

The art of the campaign is the art of attracting positive media attention for a candidate. The task of governing is obviously very different and much more complex. But attention to media coverage that contributed to election must be continually renewed. Presidents know that the news media are the prime agents for constructing our own political realities, and casting them in negative or positive ways.

Thematic Consistency in the Twenty-four-Hour News Cycle

Political campaigns are tuned to the daily routines of news gathering. Increasingly, the presidency follows the same cycle. For chief executives this means keeping press attention on a limited agenda of items.[30] And in the relatively narrow time frame of twenty-four hours, the goal of presidential publicists is to communicate a single message that fits their political needs at that moment. In the simplest campaign terms, advisers encourage candidates not to "step on their own story" by filling the day with too many different and even contradictory themes.[31] At the presidential level, this means planning the daily calender so that members of Congress are reacting to a message that has been delivered once, but multiplied through the media many times.

The Reagan administration was especially effective at coordinating messages that would dominate White House news on any given day. The basic question the senior staff asked each morning at their daily "line of the day" meeting was, "What do we want the press to cover today, and how?" According to investigative journalist Mark Hertsgaard, this question was answered in that meeting, then tied to a consistent news management formula:

- Plan ahead
- Stay on the offensive
- Control the flow of information
- Limit reporters' access to the president
- Talk about the issues you want to talk about
- Speak in one voice
- Repeat the same message many times[32]

One of the reasons the Reagan White House began the modern tradition of fifteen-minute Saturday radio messages is because it presents a chance to control the political news agenda. Saturday is a light news day in Washington, since Congress and the federal agencies are usually closed. The president's message exists through Sunday as something that others in the loop of national politics may need to deal with. The Sunday morning talk shows with small but politically active audiences, for example, often include interviewers who use the president's remarks as a basis for their own questions to congressional and political leaders.

The Shift from Policy to Character

The presidency was transformed by the widespread introduction of television into American homes in the 1950s. In the 1952 and 1956 campaigns, both Dwight Eisenhower and Adlai Stevenson struggled valiantly to adapt to a medium both of them disliked. Both made an effort to adapt their campaigns to what then seemed like the alien world of advertising, producing a number of commercials and brief speeches.[33]

This was the beginning of a transformative period that was largely intensified in the 1960 presidential campaign and was completed when Kennedy was assassinated three years later. The articulate, photogenic John Kennedy seemed a natural for television. The brevity of his remarks and his casual humor suited the medium. He appeared to know that talking to the camera was more like talking to another person than a large audience. Kennedy seemed like someone who belonged to the television age, even when his appearances happened in the context of the entertainers and glib game show hosts of the day. Eisenhower had always looked vaguely out of place: a private man forever uncomfortable with the instant informality of television. But JFK gave the presidency a credible telegenic presence, a rhetorical style that worked on the small screen.

Television changes the way we look at anybody, including political leaders and candidates. As a medium, in Kathleen Hall Jamieson's words, television is *self-disclosive*.[34] It communicates the details and nuances of character, in body language, style of dress, and all the subtle registers of attitude carried in the face. Adlai Stevenson's discomfort in front of the television camera for his 1956 campaign commercials is obvious, eclipsing his considerable rhetorical gifts and intellect. The political skill that is so evident in transcripts of his speeches and writings is invisible in his awkward television persona.[35]

Joshua Meyrowitz makes a related but slightly different point about how television changes how we are perceived. "Highly replicative media" such as television, he notes, tend to "demystify" leaders, stripping them of a dignity of character borne primarily in their ideas, not how they appeared. Jefferson and Lincoln, he notes, are legends in part because of the absence of a media record to document their physical anomalies: the Great Emancipator's thin, high voice and homely face, and Jefferson's problems in articulating certain speech sounds.[36]

> *There is a demand today for two things: fully open, accessible administrations and strong powerful leaders. Rarely do we consider that these two demands may, unfortunately, be incompatible. . . . We cannot have both disclosure and the mystification necessary for an image of greatness. The post-Watergate fascination with uncovering cover-ups has not been accompanied by a sophisticated notion of what will inevitably be found in the closets of all leaders. The familiarity fostered by electronic media all too easily breeds contempt.*[37]

One of the great virtues of print as a medium of political discourse is that it pushes attention toward what should be, arguably, the center of politics: issues and ideas. It does not allow the physical presence a figure to overshadow his or her ideas. When we encounter the historical presidency, for example, we often deal with its figures in terms of what they did and thought. We view them through key historical documents and statements, such as Lincoln's Gettysburg Address or Woodrow Wilson's campaign on behalf of the League of Nations. But when we revisit presidential actions from the recent past—in the rhetoric of Gerald Ford, Ronald Reagan, or George Bush—we do it with only partial reference to their ideas. The contemporary context gives us a televisual point of reference that has transformed our understanding of these men. Sometimes the historical record is enriched. Reagan's widespread popularity in his first term is partly explained by his apparent affability. At other times public understanding seems to be impoverished by the rich textures of appearance, as is evident in some overestimations of John Kennedy's legislative accomplishments.[38]

The counterargument, of course, is that seeing a person in the act of advocacy provides, in prosaic terms, a window into that person's soul. We sometimes assume, for example, that the extreme closeup favored by interviewers on "60 Minutes" and elsewhere is a kind of lie detector. Shifts in the eyes and sweat on the brow are—we assume—valuable cues to the person "behind" the rhetoric. We expect that truth-tellers can look unblinking into the eyes of those from whom they seek trust.

The larger point is that the expressive content of personal presentation can easily overwhelm the more fragile realm of ideas. As Meyrowitz has pointed out, the written transcript of a typical television talk show often makes little sense in informational terms. The reason is that such shows are not really about ideas, but about expression.[39] Perhaps this is why television directors depend so heavily on the "reaction shot"—a picture of someone reacting to what another person is saying. This is a staple of television drama, with a counterpart in news—a "cutaway" shot—featuring an interviewer in rapt attention. Television as a way of knowing puts a premium on feelings about people and ideas, rather than on ideas themselves.

Dominance of "Process" Reporting over "Policy" Reporting

One of the more interesting features of the campaign-based presidency is found in an emerging pattern of reporting about the office that emphasizes strategy and tactics: the "game" rather than the substance of politics.

This emphasis is most easily explained as one that focuses on "process" at the expense of "content." Process reporting emphasizes politics as a series of moves and countermoves designed to gain advantage over a competitor. Using a different metaphor, some critics call this reporting "horse race journalism," focusing on politics rather than policy. In the horse race metaphor, the prime question of journalistic inquiry centers on who are the winners and losers.[40]

Horse race coverage of campaigns is frequently maligned by press critics.[41] Yet it is not unexpected in election reporting, since elections are contests for votes. But its transference to the work of governance has the effect of making news consumers spectators to the sport of power politics more than witnesses to a great debate. Much journalism invites us to become political "insiders," armchair versions of television's political pundits who regularly handicap the key players in national politics based on their finesse and political skill. Consider several examples:

- A June 12, 1995, report on National Public Radio's "Morning Edition" described the joint appearance of House Speaker Newt Gingrich and President Bill Clinton in a forum that had occured in New Hampshire

The Presidency, the Press, and the Rise of "Lifestyle Politics"

Our understanding of the presidency has been primed by a national discourse that has been driven by a heightened orientation to issues of character. Former Republican strategist Roger Ailes, now an executive at cable's CNBC, has identified this trend in the revealing phrase "lifestyle politics."[1]

Lifestyle politics thrives on judgments about the ways people choose to live their lives, even when those choices are frequently out of the range of traditional political issues. As Ailes notes, they are often sustained by radio and television talk show hosts, and they frequently speak to a sense of group-insidedness and moral superiority, as when GOP candidate and CNN commentator Patrick Buchanan sought to portray the Democratic Party in 1992 as an alien force opposed to "American values." In *Newsweek*'s description, Buchanan and other conservative Republicans in that year engaged in a "Jihad, a religious . . . war" where the real state of the nation counted less than "the scarlet sins of liberals, lesbians, gays . . . feminists, Congress, Greens . . . single women who had babies (and) all women who aborted them."[2]

From this perspective, President Clinton's public image during and after the 1992 presidential campaign was partly defined in terms of the questionable choices he had made as a teenager and young man. The GOP—including President Bush—publically worried about what Bill Clinton did when he visited Moscow and other European cities as a Rhodes Scholar. Was he a spy? Did he intend to defect? And why did he protest the war?

And then there were reports of liaisons with different women. When much of the mainstream press found it impossible to ignore the young woman who was paid by a supermarket tabloid to talk about her alleged affair with the Arkansas governor, even ordinary voters had wondered what had happened to the nominal policy orientation of previous political campaigns.

"Character" is an old and familiar realm of political campaigns. But as understood in the context of lifestyle politics, it has been redefined to mean something quite different and much narrower than the public virtue that would have been the measure of previous leaders. There is now a quaintness to presidential analyst Emmet John Hughes's idea—from the early '70s—that the presidency was an office of "mystery" and majesty.[3] In Hughes's day the attention of the mainstream press remained focused on the institutionalized politics of the nation's civil life, with the presidency existing as the apparent source of the nation's prestige and resourcefulness. Now there is less journalistic shame in asking questions about reports of philandering or marital or physical problems.

[1]Nancy Hass, "Embracing the Enemy," *New York Times Magazine,* January 8, 1995, p. 23.
[2]"The Rocky Road to Houston," *Newsweek* Election Issue, December 1992, pp. 68–69.
[3]Emmet John Hughes, *The Living Presidency* (New York: Coward, McCann and Geoghegan, 1972), pp. 54–57.

the previous day. Clinton and Gingrich had very different ideas on how the federal budget should be constructed, where cuts in spending should take place, and so forth. But most of the report—narrated by Cokie Roberts—dealt with the strategic risks taken by the president in sharing a platform with his rival in the Congress. In short, the bulk of the report dealt with the effects of this joint appearance on the two politicians' popularity levels.[42]

- ABC News began one day's coverage of the reelection campaign of George Bush and Dan Quayle with the following story filed from Michigan:

> *Yesterday, at the first hint of winter, the Republican chairman in Battle Creek was putting out signs to welcome Vice President Dan Quayle. Window dressing, really, because he had already told all the local radio and television stations that Quayle was coming. And that's the most important thing he can do—use the local media. At a local high school gym, everything was prepared so that when the Vice President did arrive, there would be a colorful environment for television coverage. Television coverage in all the local markets across the state is what the campaign is after.[43]*

- The response of some news organizations faced with the choice of covering ideas or institutions is to commission polls. A cover story in a June 1993 issue of *Newsweek* about the Clinton administration's early successes and failures featured a Gallup Poll on his popularity, comparing it to that of other presidents in the same first-year period.[44] The pattern is true for most newsmagazine cover stories featuring a president. No question is too trivial to ask and use as the basis of an article, including one put to citizens by *Newsweek* soon after Clinton's inauguration: "Do you approve of the way Bill Clinton has handled his presidential transition?"[45]

Michael Robinson and Margaret Sheehan have noted that "polls tend to be among the least substantive kinds of political journalism."[46] They are symptomatic of a larger trend of covering events as the process of propagandizing the American public. As Matthew Kerbel documents in a recent study, television news is especially awash with such process coverage.[47] We have become frequent but cynical viewers of the staging of politics.

THE PRESIDENCY AND THE PRESS: TWO MODELS

Campaigns for public and congressional support are governed largely by the thick web of relationships any president establishes with the press. And in the last several decades the changing nature of this relationship has given rise to differing views about the nature of presidential leadership. One view attributes enormous power to chief executives in their relations with the news media. The second defines the press as an adversary that weakens and undermines presidential authority. Every presidency is different and inevitably includes both patterns at the same time. But it is useful to look at the components of each model separately.

The News Management Model

When CBS's Robert Pierpoint began covering presidents in 1957, he recalls that the "regulars" in the press room numbered about fifteen.[48] Now about 1700 reporters hold press passes, with perhaps 150 who regularly track the president's words and activities for their organizations. They occupy an area located along a corridor in the west wing, between the living quarters of the White House and the Oval Office.

These members are given one or two daily briefings from the White House press secretary, and sometimes other federal officials, including the president. They have access to an endless supply of press releases, photos from the White House photo office, video and audio copies of statements and ceremonies, and a sizable staff that is available to comment on the thoughts and actions of the administration.[49]

The news management model of press relations flows out of the evident fact that reporters covering one of the most important political offices in the world are also the most isolated. Regulars describe the post as both prestigious and frustrating. In career terms, the presidency is an important assignment. But it is also one that allows very little enterprise (i.e., investigative) reporting. The administration largely sets the agenda of events and ideas to be covered. The press is generally placed in a reactive role: responding to those carefully prepared events with a combination of summaries and skepticism. As veteran reporter Tom Wicker has written, "Everything possible is done to centralize information favorable to the administration in the press office, and to restrict the flow of any other information."[50]

The news management model of presidential power presumes that the White House holds most of the cards in the poker game of seeking favorable coverage. And it often does. Richard Davis cites the factors that strengthen an administration's hand, leaving journalists with the feeling that they are "overfed" but "undernourished":

The White House Press Office blankets them with statements, briefings, and other material, but nevertheless limits their access to the president. They cannot question White House sources at will; they are restricted to the

Keeping the Pressure on: The White House Campaigns for Domestic Legislation During a Foreign Visit

The public relations machinery of the presidency works every day, even when the president is out of the country. The press release below—accessed via the White House World Wide Web site—deals with a domestic initiative favored by President Clinton, and was issued by the White House Press Office while he traveled on a European trip.

THE WHITE HOUSE

Office of the Press Secretary
(London, England)

For Immediate Release   November 29, 1995

STATEMENT BY THE PRESIDENT

I am delighted that Congress has passed lobby reform legislation. This bill will help change the way Washington does business. For too long, Washington's influence industry has operated out of the sunlight of public scrutiny. This new law will require professional lobbyists, for the first time, to fully disclose who they are working for, and what legislation they are trying to pass or kill. Lobby reform will be good for American democracy, and will help restore the trust of the people in their government.

This is precisely the sort of change that the American people have demanded, and that I championed during my campaign for the presidency and as President. I am particularly pleased that a strong bipartisan coalition in both the House and Senate stood firm for reform. I want to especially thank Senator Carl Levin who championed this legislation for many years and the other members for their leadership including Senator Bill Cohen and Representatives Barney Frank, John Bryant and Charles Canady.

Since I took office, I have challenged Congress to enact four significant political reform measures: legislation applying laws to Congress, a ban on gifts to lawmakers, lobby disclosure, and campaign finance reform. The Congress has now acted on the first three of these reform priorities. It is time to finish the job.

press area of the White House, unless otherwise authorized, and even their best sources usually talk only when they want to and not otherwise. . . . The access may be stopped altogether if the reporter is "frozen out" by the White House because of coverage perceived as unfavorable. A succession of critical stories or negative references to the president, White House aides, or the administration generally can result in a denial of access.[51]

In his influential book on the Reagan years, *On Bended Knee: The Press and the Reagan Presidency*, Mark Hertsgaard argues that the news management model reached a new peak in the early 1980s. His criticisms follow a long tradition of charges of news management that began during the Vietnam War, when many in the press came to believe that the administration was "cooking the numbers" regarding enemy and American casualties.[52] These suspicions continuted as the Nixon administration took over management of the war, while at the same time trying to manage public opinion after the revelations of the Watergate affair in 1972 and 1973.[53]

The difference in the Reagan years is that the management of the press was arguably more subtle and benign. The skill of the White House in designing events that could produce only favorable coverage, combined with editorial timidity in major news organizations, produced a bonanza of favorable reporting. The politics of the 1980s, Hertsgaard argues—especially inflated military spending and the so-called Iran-Contra affair involving the illegal sale of weapons to Iran—went largely neglected as subjects of sustained reporting. The "shameful deterioration in the honesty and vitality of the nation's political life" was due in part to masterful manipulation of the press by a cadre of successful public relations specialists, including public relations guru Michael Deaver, campaign advisor James Baker, and press spokesperson Larry Speakes. "Together they sold the official myths of Reagan's presidency to the American public by developing a sophisticated new model for manipulating the press."[54]

Interestingly, Reagan's presidency is the last to be labeled clever and masterful in managing the press, although many observers believe the Clinton-Gore campaign of 1992 came close.[55] Since the election of George Bush in 1988, a second model based on an allegedly enfeebled presidency has gained more attention.

The Attack Press Model

In this perspective the office is portrayed as one that is under siege from a number of quarters, including a revitalized Congress and a public that increasingly sees government as irrelevant or hostile to their interests. The press then feeds on this distrust by unmasking what is often portrayed as the shallow politics of the presidency.

Most recent presidential press secretaries—even those deemed highly successful—have noted that they worked in an atmosphere of seige and combat. In the words of Reagan spokesperson Larry Speakes, "it was Us versus Them. Us was a handful of relatively underpaid but dedicated public servants in the White House press office. Them was the entire White House press corps, dozens strong, many of them Rich and Famous and Powerful."[56]

President Carter's press secretary, Jody Powell, sees the relationship between these factions as fundamentally troubled. Conceding that at times the administrations may wish to manage the news, Powell nonetheless believes that the press overreacts to these instances, creating what is often a poisoned atmosphere of hostility that makes presidential governance enormously difficult. He expressed frustration at the inability of the Carter administration to get the press to focus on presidential policy rather than politics.

> *By the end of four years in the White House, I had reached the conclusion that this relationship between the press and the presidency is seriously flawed. It fails to provide the President with an adequate channel for communicating with, for moving, shaping, and directing the popular will. Perhaps more important, it also fails to provide the nation with the quantity and quality of reasonably accurate information its citizens need to make the decisions necessary for self government.[57]*

One may be tempted to dismiss these observations as self-serving. After all, few Americans would expect to the press to function as slaves to any public information office, even if the office is as important as the chief executive. Even so, there is a growing sense even among many analysts and journalists that coverage of the institution is inadequate.[58]

Larry Sabato's view in his influential 1991 book, *Feeding Frenzy*, is that American politics and especially the presidency suffers under the weight of what he calls "attack journalism":

> *It has become a spectacle without equal in modern American politics: the news media, print and broadcast, go after a wounded politician like sharks in a feeding frenzy. The wounds may have been self-inflicted, and the politician may richly deserve his or her fate, but the journalists now take center stage in the process, creating the news as much as reporting it.[59]*

Writing in 1990, he documents a number of recent cases from the presidency, ranging from press queries about an alleged "secret fund" of Richard Nixon's in 1952 (he was then a vice presidential candidate), to reports that George Bush had a mistress.

Of the latter rumor, which sparked press interest in 1988, Sabato notes that it apparently surfaced from the campaigns of Bob Dole and others seeking to derail Bush's nomination. Some outlets such as ABC were reluctant to report the story, because it seemed to have no basis in fact. But fearing that they would face the same damaging revelations that ended Gary Hart's bid for the presidency in 1987, the Bush campaign issued its own denial, thereby legitimatizing the rumor and triggering a flood of reports.

In the end, it was a classic example of Sabato's point. A story gained widespread circulation in the absence of any merit. And the resulting coverage had consequences. Among other things, the stock market took a 43-point drop in the Dow Jones average, apparently feed by the rumor.[60]

The one factor that makes this and many other instances more than simply a reason to blame the press, however, is the decision of the Bush campaign to respond to the gossip, even before it was reported in the mainstream press. In stories like this the desire by political agents acting on behalf of a figure to manage the news can boomerang into more intensive coverage.

What is perhaps most harmful about the adversarial nature of presidential reporting is not merely press-generated suggestions of presidential incompetence or poor judgment, it is the idea—suggested in Sabato's use of the term *frenzy*—that one story comes to dominate the news agenda at the exclusion of other perspectives. This "pack journalism," long documented in political campaigns,[61] lacks diversity and increases the likelihood that most news outlets will carry the same information and perspective. For example, ABC News executive Hal Bruno called his counterparts at the other networks to verify the Bush mistress story. He thought it was untrue, and had a hunch that no one had any confirming information.[62] Bruno's reluctance to broadcast a rumor was admirable, but his instinct to check a story by finding out what others are reporting leads to news coverage that can be more uniform than it perhaps ought to be.

All of these instances point to a perceptible broadening of the kinds of stories that are thought to be suitable for coverage. Not only is reporting on the president less respectful than it once was, but—as was noted at the outset of this chapter—it is also less likely to exclude what in earlier presidencies would have been private "out of bounds" areas. Relations with spouses, other family members, and youthful activities such Bill Clinton's opposition to the Vietnam War are now more likely to be subjects of public discussion.

In journalism and reporting these are sometimes called character issues. But the idea of character as applied to the presidency of the 1990s is not that of political courage or sense of national destiny that earlier observers associated with strong leaders.[63] Character has now shriveled under the weight of an increasingly inward-looking culture in which every person's experience is reducible to the same proto-psychological frames of references. In this view we are all only slightly different packages of ambition, opportunism, and dysfunction. We are less recognizable for our achievements and thoughts than the traits of our imperfect character. In Robert Hughes's words, we are a "culture of complaint" where the emphasis is on "how we feel about things, rather than what we think or can know."[64] The frequent use of public opinion polls to frame discussion of the president ("How do you feel about the President's decision to. . . ?") and an emphasis on the journalism of personality and celebrity in sources like *People* and *Newsweek* feed this orientation. Reporting emphasizing both of these personalizing levels is likely to weaken both the long-term credibility of individual presidents, and the aura of the presidency itself.

In the end, neither the news management nor the press attack model is adequate by itself. Each needs the balance of the other. Even so, there seems to be an increasing awareness among members of the national press that journalism devoted to the presidency needs to be enriched by more thoughtful reporting on the substance of governing. Whatever the truths about presidential news management, the press attack model is enormously limiting. Tom Rosenstiel's obituary for the 1992 presidential campaign is instructive:

> *For a year, the American press had taken responsibility for its coverage, even if it did so grudgingly. It had conceded that what it published and broadcast had consequences, that the act of observation altered the event— a step toward intellectual honesty. And it was shocked, by a public that it had underestimated, into taking the words and ideas of politics seriously again, a little.[65]*

SUMMARY

The core theme of this chapter is that the presidency has taken on the communication methods and strategies common to political campaigns. Emerging from its past as an office governed by episodic events, the modern chief executive increasingly functions in an environment that is closely tied to the daily news cycle. Presidents and their White House staffs must now consistently play an "outside game" of orchestrating and nurturing public opinion, a marked shift in emphasis from the older "inside game"—common before the 1930s—of dealing primarily with Washington's power brokers. They can no longer afford to wait as well as act. They know they must try and master the increasingly frenetic news media, which casts their fate in terms of constant assessments of the state of their mandate.

The contemporary office draws many of its features from the successful campaign that gave victory to its occupant. Polling experts, press-savvy public relations specialists, and media technicians "produce" the presidency for the American public. They depend on news reports—especially those of the networks and CNN—to communicate with the American public. They generally deal with a press that is sometimes hostile, and geared more to reporting the strategies and processes of winning support than the arguments or reasons behind a presidential decision.

Even with the extensive coverage given the presidency, members of both the press and the White House staff see problems in their relations. In the starkest terms, members of the Fourth Estate often feel like they are used by skillful White House tacticians anxious to press any advantage on behalf of the president. The public relations machine of 1600 Pennsylvania Avenue will sometimes sacrifice information and access, they believe, in the name of protecting the president. For their part, aides within the White House often describe the press as an institution that is out of control, driven by the a need for drama and conflict that has little to do with the details of governing.

NOTES

1. Michael Kelly, "The President's Past," *New York Times Magazine*, July 31, 1994, p. 45.

2. Mary Matalin, quoted in Mary Matalin and James Carville, *All's Fair: Love, War, and Running for President* (New York: Random House, 1994), p. 300.

3. Samuel Kernell, *Going Public: New Strategies of Presidential Leadership* (Washington, DC: Congressional Quarterly, 1986), pp. 9–45.

4. See Godfrey Hodgson, *All Things to All Men.* (New York: Simon and Schuster, 1980), pp. 13–49.

5. Quoted in Bob Woodward, *The Agenda: Inside the Clinton White House.* (New York: Simon and Shuster, 1994), p. 333.

6. The older literature on the office here is revealing. Emmet John Hughes wrote a convicing account of a much more powerful and prestigious office in 1972 (*The Living Presidency* [New York: Coward, McCann and Geoghegan]). In the same period Michael Novak similarly described an office capable of generating awesome moral leadership (*Choosing Our King* [New York: Macmillan, 1974]).

7. In a 1994 television interview, the president of the United States was asked, among other things, what kind of underwear he wore. See Todd S. Purdum, "Moynihan's Mouth and Muscle," *New York Times Magazine*, August 7, 1994, p. 27.

8. Presidential candidate Jimmy Carter created a public stir when he noted in a *Playboy* interview that he had "looked on a lot of women with lust and had committed adultery in my heart many times". He no doubt saw this confession as a simple demonstration of fundamentalist faith, but it became a major event in the 1976 political campaign. See Larry Sabato, *Feeding Frenzy: How Attack Journalism Has Transformed American Politics* (New York: Free Press, 1991), p. 10.

9. Sidney Blumenthal, *The Permanent Campaign: Inside the World of Political Operatives* (Boston: Beacon Press, 1980), p. 7.

10. See Robert M. Entman, *Democracy Without Citizens* (New York: Oxford, 1989), pp. 56–58.

11. See, for example, Theodore L. Glasser and Charles Salmon, eds., *Public Opinion and the Communication of Consent* (New York: Guilford, 1995).

12. Hughes, *The Living Presidency*, p. 69.

13. Elmer Cornwell, *Presidential Leadership of Public Opinion* (Bloomington: Indiana University Press, 1965), pp. 142–161.

14. Jeffrey K. Tulis, *The Rhetorical Presidency*. (Princeton, NJ: Princeton University Press, 1987), pp. 62–87.

15. In terms of expanding the presidency as a forum for public comment, Theodore Roosevelt was significantly ahead of his times. See Willard B. Gatewood, *Theodore Roosevelt and the Art of Controversy* (Baton Rouge: Louisiana State University Press, 1970).

16. Cornwell, *Presidential Leadership*, pp. 26—35.

17. Ibid., p. 40.

18. Quoted in Woodward, *The Agenda*, pp. 178–179.

19. See, for example, Kathleen J. Turner, *Lyndon Johnson's Dual War*, (Chicago: University of Chicago, 1985), pp. 190–199.

20. Woodward, *The Agenda*, pp. 267–269.

21. Tom Rosenstiel, *Strange Bedfellows: How Television and the Presidential Candidates Changed American Politics, 1992* (New York: Hyperion, 1993), p. 329.

22. David Broder, *Behind the Front Page* (New York: Simon and Schuster: 1987), p. 295.

23. Larry J. Sabato, *The Rise of the Political Consultants* (New York: Basic, 1981), p. 41.

24. Jane Mayer and Doyle McCanus, *Landslide: The Unmaking of the President, 1984–1988* (Boston: Houghton Mifflin, 1988), p. 30.

25. Sam Donaldson, *Hold on, Mr President!* (New York: Random House, 1987), pp. 123–126.

26. For a broad overview of these kinds of campaign logistics, see Judith S. Trent and Robert V. Friedenberg, *Political Campaign Communication*, 2d ed., (New York: Praeger, 1991), pp. 265–295.

27. There is no shortage of books documenting campaign–press relations. See, for example, Tim Crouse, *The Boys on the Bus* (New York: Random House, 1972); Roger Simon, *Road Show* (New York: Farrar, Straus and Giroux, 1990), and Paul Taylor, *See How They Run* (New York: Knopf, 1990).

28. Rosenstiel, *Stange Bedfellows*, pp. 307–312.

29. This list is drawn from a summary by Tom Rosenstiel, *The Beat Goes On: President Clinton's First Year with the Media* (New York: Twentieth Century Fund, 1994), pp. 7–16.

30. Hedrick Smith, *The Power Game: How Washington Works* (New York: Random House, 1988) p. 333.

31. Matalin and Carville, *All's Fair* pp. 327–328.

32. Mark Hertsgaard, *On Bended Knee: The Press and the Reagan Presidency* (New York: Schocken, 1988), pp. 34–35.

33. For a history of campaign advertising from this period, see Kathleen Hall Jamieson, *Packaging the Presidency* (New York: Oxford, 1984), pp. 39–121.

34. Kathleen Hall Jamieson, *Eloquence in an Electronic Age* (New York: Oxford, 1988), p. 62.

35. It would be wrong to conclude, however, that television gave the edge to Dwight Eisenhower. He appeared just as awkward but he had the popularity and campaign momentum to win an easy victory.

36. Joshua Meyrowitz, *No Sense of Place* (New York: Oxford, 1985), p. 275.

37. Ibid., p. 276

38. See, for example, Jim F. Heath, *Decade of Disillusionment* (Bloomington: Indiana University Press, 1975), pp. 143–163.

39. Meyrowitz, *No Sense of Place*, pp. 103–104.

40. Rosenstiel, *The Beat Goes On*, pp. 26–27.

41. Many believe, however, that election reporting should be about much more than the strategies of campaigning. See, for example, Thomas E. Patterson, *Out of Order* (New York: Knopf, 1993), pp. 53–93.

42. "Morning Edition," National Public Radio, June 12, 1995.

43. Matthew Robert Kerbel, *Edited for Television; CNN, ABC, and the 1992 Presidential Campaign* (Boulder, CO: Westview, 1994), p. 39.

44. Joe Klein, "What's Wrong?, *Newsweek*, June 7, 1993, p. 16.

45. "Warm up Lessons," *Newsweek*, January 25, 1993, p. 30.

46. Michael Robinson and Margaret Sheehan, *Over the Wire and on TV: CBS and UPI in Campaign '80* (New York: Russell Sage, 1983), p. 252.

47. Kerbel, *Edited for Television*, pp. 28–49.

48. Robert Pierpoint, *At the White House* (New York: Putnam, 1981), p. 32.

49. For a thorough overview of White House press functions, see Michael Grossman and Martha Kumar, *Portraying the President* (Baltimore: Johns Hopkins, 1981), pp. 36–129.

50. Tom Wicker, *On Press* (New York: Viking, 1978), p. 77.

51. Richard Davis, *The Press and American Politics* (New York: Longman, 1992), p. 153.

52. For an analysis of this period, specific to CBS, see David Halberstam, *The Powers That Be* (New York: Knopf, 1979), pp. 487–512.

53. Growing suspicion of the power of the president to mislead is represented in the early work of Theodore H. White. White's series of books on campaigns, all with the title *The Making of the President*, had the effect of dramatizing the presidency for millions of readers. His books remained on best-seller lists for months. But his equally popular *Breach of Faith*, about Watergate "conspiracy" and "manipulation" (New York: Dell, 1975), communicated a sense of presidential betrayal. Watergate seemed to drain his enthusiasm for presidential politics, as it did for most other Americans.

54. Hertsgaard, *On Bended Knee*, pp. 345–346.

55. See, for example, Peter Goldman, et al., *Quest for the Presidency, 1992* (College Station: Texas A and M University, 1994), pp. 483–507.

56. Larry Speakes, *Speaking Out* (New York: Avon, 1988), p. 268.

57. Jody Powell, *The Other Side of the Story* (New York: Morrow, 1984), p. 35.

58. See, for example, Robert E. Denton, Jr., *The Prime Time Presidency of Ronald Reagan* (New York: Praeger, 1988), and Entman, *Democracy Without Citizens*, pp. 17–88.

59. Sabato, *Feeding Frenzy*, p. 1.

60. Ibid., pp. 171–177.

61. See Crouse, *The Boys on the Bus*, pp. 7–8.

62. Sabato, *Feeding Frenzy*, p. 174.

63. "Character" as a feature of a public figure's personality has notably shifted over the years. The shift is illustrated in the differences between the assumptions of John Kennedy's 1960 study of great leaders in the senate, *Profiles in Courage* (New York: Harper and Row/Perennial, 1964), and James Barber's *The Presidential Character: Predicting Performance in the White House* (Englewood Cliffs, NJ: Prentice-Hall, 1972). Each book is very different, but each has the study of character at its core. Kennedy's view is older and more romantic. Character is, among other things, the courage to be different and to stand for principle. Barber's book, on the other hand, is more modern. It psychologizes character as a set of relatively functional or dysfunctional traits of personality.

64. Robert Hughes, *Culture of Complaint* (New York: Oxford, 1993), p. 10.

65. Rosenstiel, *Stange Bedfellows*, p. 346.

5

FOREIGN NEWS, WAR, AND DIPLOMACY

In the last week of the summer Arabic course, Sanaa, the Egyptian teaching aide, told me how much I would love Cairo. "It is so full of vitality—theaters, concerts, new books, all sorts of fun. . . ." Best of all, she pointed out, I could practice reading Arabic every day with the city newspapers.

"Egyptian newspapers are the best in the Arab world, and the Arabs have excellent newspapers, you know. American newspapers are so provincial by comparison."

"How do you mean?"

"Well, the Boston Globe *is all local, all about Boston and New England and America. It really amazes me. An Egyptian newspaper gives you all the news of the world in much more detail. America is very isolated by not paying attention to the world, don't you think?"[1]*

Prior to the battles of the Revolutionary War, immigrants with ties to France, Britain, and Spain had an enormous interest in news beyond America's borders. That interest remains among newer immigrants from Asia, Latin America, and Eastern Europe. But as reflected in our modern news media, most Americans tend to favor domestic over international reporting. This chapter considers this and other features of international news coverage by exploring two broad categories of press coverage. The first is news that provides information about events and developments in other regions of the world. The second is war reporting that develops when American military units are involved in operations on foreign soil.² A prime reference point for this coverage is the 1991 Persian Gulf War. We will look at patterns of news-gathering that are now typical in both of these forms of media, and some of the built-in biases and tendencies reflected in American foreign reporting.

SETTING THE STAGE: PROLOGUE TO THE PERSIAN GULF WAR

It was a period in our national life that historians like to call a "defining moment." In the fall of 1990 the nation's television screens and front pages filled with stories describing yet another Middle Eastern crisis. This time it was Iraq's annexation of its small but oil-rich neighbor to the south. As the Emir and other wealthy Kuwaitis fled to safe havens in London and Cairo, Kuwait was officially designated just another Iraqi province by Saddam Hussein and his military government. President George Bush and other Western leaders increasingly implied that Hussein had made a big mistake. A war to remove his grip on Kuwait and—by implication—on much of the oil-rich Middle East looked increasingly plausible. Daily reports described Hussein's military state and its cruelties with increasing vividness. The detention of foreign workers—many from France, Britain, and the United States—intensified the crisis.

Nothing in this prewar period, however, was as potent as the appearance of a young girl before the Congressional Human Rights Caucus on October 10. Appearing at the apparent request of Chairperson Tom Lantos was a tearful fifteen-year-old Kuwaiti who told a heart-wrenching story about atrocities committed against Kuwaiti babies.

As was the case with this hearing, American public opinion on foreign policy is a battleground of competing interests: corporations, foreign governments, citizens groups, and paid lobbyists. All seek to project their power to Congress, the president, the United Nations, and the American public through the news media. Even the simplest foreign policy issues take on the complex texture of these competing forces, producing news stories that are layered with facts, fictions, and fantasies about other nations and people.

The testimony of Nayirah was such an event. Her last name was concealed, noted Lantos, to protect her relatives still in Kuwait. Nayirah described a scene in a hospital nursery where she witnessed Iraqi soldiers taking babies out of incubators and leaving them to die on the hospital floors. Presumably the soldiers were sacrificing these helpless Kuwaiti children so that the incubators could be taken to hospitals in Iraq. Her story added to other reports that as many as 350 Kuwaiti babies had been killed. Many of these accounts gained credibility as news of beatings and cruelties filtered in from occupied Kuwait.

In ways that were not fully clear then, this moment brought together many of the forces that shape American perceptions of foreign affairs. Nayirah was presented as a foreign citizen testifying before Congress. Her appearance—it was later discovered—was arranged with the help of a man named Gary Hymel, a vice president of the American public relations firm Hill and Knowlton, which was in the midst of a $10 million campaign on behalf of Kuwait, and bankrolled almost entirely by some of its wealthier citizens. Lantos knew, but did not report, that she was actually the daughter of Kuwait's ambassador to Washington. He also neglected to note that he had close ties to the public relations firm, which had—according to John R. MacArthur—contributed over $50,000 to a foundation established by the California Congressman.[3]

Americans were rightly outraged at the Iraqi takeover of Kuwait. But most were unaware of the coordinated campaign undertaken by Hill and Knowlton and others to prepare them for war. Millions of dollars were given to the American firm to influence public opinion, downplaying the questionable human rights record and feudal monarchy of Kuwait while focusing exclusively on Iraqi aggression.

The range of messages produced by the 119 staffers assigned to the Kuwait account was remarkably diverse. They included the sponsorship of a book, *The Rape of Iraq*, the distribution of thousands of video clips to television stations, the printing of thousands of flyers and other materials, the sponsorship of a "Free Kuwait" day, the distribution of books to troops in the Persian Gulf, and the appearance of Nayirah.[4]

Nothing matched the effectiveness of Nayirah. Members of Congress and President Bush made frequent references to the atrocities she alleged as they made the agonizing move toward formal approval of military action against Iraq. Yet her story was, at best, inaccurate, and more likely a cynical attempt to manipulate public opinion. In the months that followed reporters for both ABC and the *New York Times* who interviewed Kuwaiti hospital officials could find no confirmation for Nayirah's story.[5] It is not even certain she was in her home country at the time she alleged.

In reviewing the entire episode, investigative journalist Arthur Rowse wondered why his colleagues hadn't been more skeptical.

> *Why didn't coverage of the heavy propaganda efforts aimed at Congress and the United Nations include the obvious Hill and Knowlton role? And why didn't leading commentators, columnists, and editorial writers discuss the propriety of a private firm's efforts to persuade the nation to go to war?*[6]

A partial answer to Rowse's question lies in the fact that the emerging media narratives that assigned villainy to Iraq and heroism to Kuwait had already been put in motion. The media are storytellers; they sell stories for profit. They need to impose a certain degree of simplicity and coherence to the multifaceted events of real life. In terms of the narrative logic of Persian Gulf crisis, the force of the emerging portrait of crime and punishment would have been complicated by reports of a massive Kuwaiti public relations campaign.

In a more fundamental sense the question Rowse poses is a reminder that there is usually a convergence of public and private interests that play themselves out in most forms of political news. If we are unable to answer the question fully in this chapter, we can at least focus on some of the essential dimensions of public discussion that shape American perceptions of foreign affairs.

We begin with a look at patterns of foreign reporting in the popular (as opposed to specialized) media, including the amount of time and space given for foreign stories, and changing patterns of international newsgathering.[7] In the second section we turn to a discussion of the influence of Washington on the national foreign news agenda. In the third we review the special problems that war and combat impose on political leaders, commanders, and journalists. The chapter concludes with a brief summary of several basic limitations that continue to affect reporting on foreign affairs.

FOREIGN NEWS: RECURRING PATTERNS IN AMERICAN LIFE

Foreign News: Distortion and the Illusion of "Knowing"

It asks a great deal of the citizens of any country to know a great deal about what is going on in other parts of the world. By definition, the mediated realities of journalism are incomplete, and never more so than in the reporting that interprets events in another culture. The nuances of a society are difficult for even a long time visitor to learn. Beyond that, the processes of compressing and decontextualizing that afflict most reporting are even more evident in with foreign news coverage. There are several reasons for this. One is that such reporting often focuses on American foreign policy, a confusing concept at best. That phrase suggests a specific plan of action or set of guidelines applied to another country that have been implemented by the American government. But, as foreign service specialists will often admit, the United States has many foreign policies toward specific nations, often haphazardly instituted and withdrawn, depending on the agencies involved and the political circumstances of the moment. In our recent past, American foreign policy toward Iraq varied distinctly depending on the agency involved. Before the Persian Gulf War the State Department was engaging its government in "constructive dialogue." Meanwhile, the White House was selling it arms, the Central Intelligence Agency was spying on it, and members of Congress were calling for its isolation from the community of "civilized nations."

American relationships with other states are only slightly less variegated. "The fact is," notes a former journalist and White House official, "government is much closer to chaos than most reporters let you know; and they don't let you know because they are part of the process that makes it appear *not* to be the case."[8]

Another effect of decontextualization is a journalistic tendency in much foreign affairs coverage that might be called the impulse to find order. As analysts David Paletz and Robert Entman have noted, in the normal routines of reporting, there is a tendency to downplay the natural chaos of human events in favor of ordered narratives.[9] Reporting organizes reality. It frequently imposes a purpose and thoughtfulness on events that they do not naturally have. Reporters—like the rest of us—must negotiate the fine line that separates the confusions and ambiguities of raw reality with the requirements for coherent narrative that is imposed on them. This is never more apparent than when one is faced with interpreting events in one society to distracted news consumers in another society.

Consider, for example, an account of American acceptance of the death penalty, as offered by a writer for the influential Paris daily *Le Monde*:

> *Opinion polls show that the vast majority of Americans have no real objection to the death penalty. In 1966, 42 percent supported capital punishment and in 1991, 72 percent. There are two explanation for this American phenomenon. . . . First, there is the country's history: The U.S. was founded in violence. [Then there is the] incessant increase of crime in the American cities on a scale unimaginable in Europe. . . . Many Americans no longer discuss the death penalty in terms of the example it sets. They justify the punishment, instead, as vengeance. Thus the greatest power in the world— which talks about the rule of law in international relations—reveals a brutality that can be explained only by fear.*[10]

Most American readers would no doubt view this piece of fact, conjecture, and judgment as entirely too glib, too simple an explanation for a much more complex set of circumstances, attitudes, and state-regulated policies. But such is often the synoptic nature of foreign reporting, which must deal with a world that is more complex than most media outlets can represent, and most news consumers can grasp.

The Scope of Foreign Reporting in American Media

Depending on the source, foreign news generally represents between 15 and 40 percent of the content of general news sources. While subject to variations depending on how foreign news is defined and the length of the period surveyed, American media also spend less time and space on international news items than their counterparts in other Western nations. Between 1972 and 1979, for example, James Larson observed that about 37 percent of the stories developed on the three American television networks at least touched on international events, with nearly half of the items consisting of short pieces of information read to viewers by the anchorpersons.[11]

More recent monitoring in 1989 by Roger Wallis and Stanley Baran indicates a number of interesting patterns. In the nearly twenty days of observation the authors compared the percentages of foreign news presented on American, British, and Swedish broadcast services. They monitored what many news observers consider the most prestigious outlets, including National Public Radio's "All Things Considered" (ATC) and the British Broadcasting Corporation's (BBC) prime evening newscast. As Figure 5-1 indicates, the CBS Evening News devoted 27 percent of its time on foreign news.[12] CNN Headline News, which bills itself as the service that takes its viewers "around the world in 30 minutes" came in with 18 percent of its time devoted to foreign news. Independent Network News (INN)—a division of Fox Broadcasting—had 21 percent. And an independent (non-network) television station in Oakland, California, probably represents many local stations around the country with its comparatively low 9 percent. Among those with significantly higher percentages were Britain and Sweden's highly regarded noncommercial radio and television services.[13]

Major American newspapers are generally more thorough in their coverage of foreign stories. Their greater capacity allows them to develop more of the details relevant to a nation's political affairs, economy, elections, and

Station	Days logged	Items total	Total time seconds	% Foreign (items)	% Foreign (net newstime)
CBS news	16	214	20805	36	27
CNN Head	20	347	24989	22	18
INN news	17	164	17496	31	21
Ch2 KTVU	20	429	48616	13	9
NPR ATC	20	262	65939	30	27
BBC TV	21	259	26373	33	35
BBC Radio	20	423	31459	34	31
Swedish TV	21	292	26883	43	37
Swedish Radio	21	326	23765	46	44

Source: Roger Wallis and Stanley Baran, *The Known World of Broadcast News* (New York: Routledge, 1990), p. 255.

FIGURE 5-1.   Results of Study November 10–November 21, 1986. Nine news programs, six on television and three on radio.

social patterns, though without the obvious impact of "live" video. (Typically, one two-column story in a broadsheet newspaper will contain as much text as that spoken in a full half-hour television newscast.) Wallis and Baran cite a 1985 UNESCO study identifying relatively high percentages of general news space devoted to international news in the *Washington Post* (41 percent), the *New York Times* (39 percent), the Minneapolis *Star and Tribune* (30 percent), and the *Los Angeles Times* (30 percent).[14] It should be noted, though, that these percentages drop dramatically for smaller papers, and many large-city tabloids such as the *New York Daily News*.

In terms of the geography of foreign news reporting, the patterns established by U.S. media show several basic tendencies. It is both obvious and too simple to say that news is "driven by events." In some senses it is. An earthquake with a high number of casualties is going to be news wherever it happens. But beyond such obvious human disasters, American foreign coverage is largely based around the nations of Western Europe, with occasional segments of time devoted to the Middle East and the former Soviet Union. Wallis and Baran, for example, found that CBS coverage in their 1986 sample was extensively focused on noncommunist Europe and some parts of the Middle East, with each region accounting for about 10 percent of all of its domestic and foreign stories.[15]

If it can be said that there are any "black holes" in American coverage, they continue to exist in China, Africa, and Central and South America. These regions represent well over half of the world's total population, but they receive only a tiny fraction of our attention: less than 7 percent for these combined regions, according to Wallis and Baran. Americans know and hear little about Peru, Bolivia, Pakistan, Ethiopia, Guatemala, and Chad, to mention only a few of the nations in these regions.

Part of our national inattention to these areas is due to the difficulties posed to reporters in these regions. The leaders of some African states and China have sometimes been hostile to reporters, seeing their presence as doing little more than building sympathy for their internal opponents. But the larger answer lies in the fact that news from the Third World and the poorer nations of the world generates little audience interest. Their economies are usually relatively small. They are typically not on the major tourist routes. And their cultures seem "foreign" (Moslem, communist, or "primitive"). We frequently see the inhabitants of these states as leading grim and alien lives, a fact that—more than anything else—reflects the very limited disaster or war reporting that comes from their capitals.

The Functions of Foreign News Coverage

Citing the pioneering work on international news by Bernard Cohen,[16] analyst William Adams has identified three basic functions of foreign news in

American life.[17] In its most basic form, print and broadcast coverage of international events allows citizens to function as *observers*. Interest in human events is nearly universal. It does not end arbitrarily at a nation's borders. With every passing year the expansion of satellite and telecommunications services has made it easier to report from even the most remote locations. As a window on the lives of people in other cultures, foreign news is also a frame of reference for our own world as well.[18] In ways that are difficult to quantify but easy to observe, we partially judge our own political and social failures and successes in terms of the information reported to us from other nations. Crime rates in a single American city have been portrayed as larger than the national crime rates in other entire nations. Similarly, we have learned about the United States' surprisingly low child and maternal health-care standards by seeing comparisons with other "developed" counties.[19] We are naturally curious about the ways other nations have responded to problems that do not honor national boundaries, and about the rhythms of their own national life.

A second function of foreign news is as an occasional *participant* in the shaping of foreign policy or short-term governmental responses. Journalists are sometimes agents in the development or resolution of international differences. In 1985, to cite a memorable instance, Lebanese Shi'ites commandered a TWA plane in Athens with 104 Americans on board. In the seventeen days that followed, television vividly recorded the pleas for calm by the pilot, the release of many of the passengers, and the murder of one of them, a member of the Navy. The remaining hostages were eventually released, but not before Nabih Berri, a Lebanese moderate, used the negotiations to dramatize the blight of Shi'ites held in Israeli prisons. As Michael O'Neil notes:

> *For two tumultous weeks . . . Berri and his lieutenants stage-managed the crisis with Madison Avenue skill—arranging photo opportunities, laying on press conferences, supplying hostages for interviews, and hawking tips, inside information and tapes. . . . With full network cooperation, Berri used American television to broadcast his litany of Shi'ite grievances, sent messages to Ronald Reagan and to [Israeli Prime Minister] Shimon Peres, negotiated with Dan Rather of CBS and David Hartman of ABC, chatted with anchormen and other media celebrities and even offered fatherly assurances to the worried wife of [hostage] Allyn Conwell.[20]*

Although professional diplomats in the world's foreign ministries are loath to admit it, the news media sometimes serve as channels of communication between governments and, hence, part of the apparatus that triggers initiatives in foreign policy. The *New York Times* has long been favored by foreign and American leaders, as has television's Cable News Network in recent years. President Bush's press secretary noted that "CNN has opened up a whole new communications system between governments in terms of immediacy and directness. In many cases, it's the first communication we have."[21]

Governments also pay close attention to foreign dispatches from many sources. It is said that in parts of Latin America and Africa, the leaders of troubled governments will use news from the BBC's World Service to assess their chances for maintaining their power. The World Service has enjoyed a long reputation as an impartial observer of events in foreign countries. In the United States, several agencies have developed elaborate and expensive procedures for monitoring what others are writing about them. Composite summaries are published every workday at the White House and the Pentagon. In a 1983 survey, the Pentagon's daily *Current News* included samples of foreign reports from 45 newspapers, all of the major television networks, and 120 magazines.[22] Other summaries, like *Defense Dialog*, provide similar surveys of recent broadcast reports. Not all of this information is treated as reliable. But much of it functions as useful as another source of intelligence that contributes to national security and foreign policy outcomes.

The third function of foreign news is to provide a *catalyst* for political action. At times a series of reports will present such a compelling portrayal of events that they essentially demand a response from officials, opinion leaders, and the general public. In recent years reports of starvation and misery created by civil wars in nations as diverse as Somalia, Ethiopia, and Bosnia have commanded the attention of presidents and world leaders, in part, because of the simultaneous transmission of the same horrific images to millions of their constituents. Media theorist Marshall McLuhan's phrase *global village* may now be too familiar to suggest the irony that it was originally intended to convey. Yet it is worth remembering the intended potency of these words. Distance is no longer an unbridgeable gulf in separating "our" world from the world of the most distant tribe. Such is our fragmented and "mediated" world that riveting images offered by foreign correspondents a continent away can now touch us as thoroughly—involve us as completely—as the news from a neighboring community.

Domestic versus Foreign Content

One of the difficulties researchers have had in assessing the extent to which any nation's news media focuses on international affairs is locating the point that divides foreign from domestic news. A report about American tourists detained in a Latin American country after allegedly purchasing stolen art, for example, is arguably less about another country than about the blight of U.S. citizens traveling abroad. Such a story is, in a word, *ethnocentric*. From an ethnocentric perspective, events have meaning or significance only to the extent that they seem to effect one's own group or culture. In their own

RADIO-TV

DEFENSE DIALOG

WEDNESDAY, July 22, 1992

This publication is prepared by American Forces Information Service (AFIS/OASD-PA) to bring to the attention of key personnel news items of interest to them in their official capacities. It is not intended to substitute for newspapers and periodicals as a means of keeping informed about the meaning and impact of news developments. Use of these articles does not reflect official endorsement. Further reproduction for private use or gain is subject to original copyright restrictions.

CURRENT NEWS
ANALYSIS &
RESEARCH SERVICE

Chief:
Herbert J. Coleman
(703-695-2884)

Deputy Chief:
Walter N. Lang

CURRENT NEWS
BRANCH:

Chief:
Taft Phoebus
(703-697-8765)

Early Bird Editor:
Denise Brown

Writer-Editors:
Elmer Christian
Sharon Foster
Meredith Johnson
Carol Rippe
Lisa Stafford
Carol Summers

RESEARCH BRANCH:

Acting Chief:
Pat Darnell
(703-695-6959)

Writer-Editors:
Alice Boyd
Mary K. O'Donnell

ADMINISTRATION:

Janice Goff
Andre' Caldwell
(703-695-2684)

Radio and TV Reports, Washington, D.C.
Summaries not to be quoted.

(Broadcasts of Tuesday, July 21, 1992)

SUMMARY OF NETWORK NEWS IN THIS EDITION

IRAQ'S DEFIANCE OF U.N.: Iraq continues to deny United Nations inspectors access to its Ministry of Agriculture, and crowds demonstrating against the inspectors are becoming dangerously aggressive. The Pentagon reportedly is reviewing plans for U.S. aircraft to join with allied forces in punitive strikes against Iraq if the U.N. so authorizes. Middle East analysts say Saddam Hussein may feel that the coalition has lost interest in the Iraqi situation and that President Bush is now too politically weak to initiate military action. Reports by Frank Sesno and Wolf Blitzer, CNN; Jim Stewart, CBS.

PREWAR U.S. POLICY TOWARD IRAQ: Representative Henry Gonzalez reportedly is in possession of a document showing that the Bush Administration authorized the shipment of equipment to Iraq that could be used in its nuclear weapons program. Report by Dan Rather, CBS.

V-22 OSPREYS GROUNDED: Following Monday's crash of a V-22 Osprey, the remaining four Ospreys have been grounded. Report by Frank Sesno, CNN.

USS VINCENNES REPORT DENIED: Former Chairman of the Joint Chiefs of Staff Admiral William Crowe has denied a Nightline and Newsweek report that the USS Vincennes was in Iran's territorial waters when it mistakenly shot down an Iranian Airbus four years ago. He also said the charges that the United States was at that time carrying out a secret war against Iran were unfounded. Report by Bob Zelnick, ABC.

SEXUAL HARASSMENT IN MILITARY: Some female military officers are concerned that the increasing number of reports of sexual harassment in the services will cause a presidential commission to recommend against assigning women to combat duty. Report by Fred Francis, NBC.

CLINTON DEFENDS DRAFT RECORD: In response to an attack on his draft record, Governor Clinton said that the Vietnam era records of Dick Cheney, Dan Quayle, and President Bush's sons would also disqualify them from national office. Report by Andrea Mitchell, NBC.

MIDDLE EAST PEACE PROCESS: It is said that the recent movement in the Middle East peace process is largely attributable to President Bush's tough stance with the previous Israeli government. Commentary by John Chancellor, NBC.

PLEASE
RECYCLE

Source: Department of Defense

FIGURE 5-2. A page from *Defense Dialog,* one of several Pentagon publications—including *Current News*—which summarizes media coverage of military affairs. Department of Defense officials use these internally prepared summaries to estimate public opinion and sometimes respond to media "inaccuracies."

study, Wallis and Baran made the useful distinction between "stories reported in wholly international terms" versus "stories reported in terms of home nation involvement." Confirming the work of others, such as Herbert Gans,[23] they found that American outlets (with the exception of the independent TV station in Oakland, California) were more likely to include a foreign news story if it was seen as effecting some dimension of domestic life. "British and Swedish news media," they noted, "while offering almost twice as much foreign news as some of their U.S. counterparts, showed only half as much ethnocentricity."[24]

Some of this effect may be due to sheer size. A small nation like Sweden will more naturally have an enormous stake in the activities and actions of other states, which can drastically effect its exports, imports, security, and so on. But there is some truth to the conclusion that the United States has a greater preoccupation with domestic news. For one thing, there is so much of it, given the size and diversity of a country spread over a continent. In addition, there remains a lingering North American disposition to view foreign relations as the source of too many "entanglements" that drain national resources and sometimes require the sacrifice of American blood. American farmers have learned about the virtues of selling "Chernobyl wheat" to replace the radiation-contaminated grains once grown around the Ukranian city of Kiev. And auto workers in Honda's Tennessee factory have a natural interest in trade barriers and quotas that could effect the import of parts from Japan and the sale of finished automobiles. But Americans—if not their leaders—generally remain reluctant internationalists, preferring a view that sees the nation as largely separate from the regional interdependence that is now increasingly taken for granted in other Western nations.[25]

This general frame of reference on domestic events is evident even in the "elite" media. The television networks now openly admit that they are abandoning their original mission of providing worldwide coverage from their own staffs.[26] And even the prestige print media have smaller foreign news staffs than their counterparts in countries that are only a fraction of the size of the United States. In the mid-1980s, for example, the *Washington Post* had about eighteen correspondents overseas. By contrast, Germany's *Frankfurter Allgemeine Zeitung* and London's *Financial Times* each maintained a foreign staff of over 30. One Japanese newspaper supported the reporting of nearly 40 foreign correspondents.[27]

Interestingly, during the initial invasion of Kuwait by Iraq in 1990—arguably the defining moment of the Bush presidency—there was only one American correspondent stationed within the emirate: the *Post's* Caryle Murphy.[28] Moreover, many American reporters who had to be flown in to Saudi Arabia to cover the military buildup in the Persian Gulf were ill-prepared for the task, speaking neither Arabic nor understanding the very different politics and Moslem culture of the Gulf region.[29]

Praise for Excellence in Foreign Reporting

Each year a range of organizations analyzes the quality of foreign reporting in American newspapers and magazines, identifying particularly effective journalism. Two such organizations include *Forbes Media-Guide 500*, which publishes a critique of journalism of the preceding year, and the Pulitzer Prizes, administered by the Graduate School of Journalism at Columbia University. The following is a sampling of journalists recognized by these two organizations.

Forbes MediaGuide 500

Mark Danner, *New Yorker*, December 6, 1993, "The Truth of El Mozote." Extraordinary and immense, Danner's article on the 1982 massacre of hundreds of Salvadoran peasants in El Mozote by U.S.-trained Salvadoran army units contains a distinct point of view—that the U.S. government unjustly whitewashed the entire affair. From start to finish, this exhaustive piece supports Danner's contention that the handling of the incident reflects the indelicate balance between hard-nosed foreign policy and unpleasant reality during the Reagan Administration.

Tony Horwitz, *Wall Street Journal*, July 6, 1993, "Rise in Kneecappings Shows a Dirty Secret of Long Civil Strife." Through numerous compelling anecdotes from Northern Ireland, Horwitz, portrays the anarchy that results when government institutions collapse. By focusing on the increasingly common and excruciatingly painful practice of "kneecapping"—shooting through the knees or elbows to maim rather than kill—Horwitz describes how vigilante justice quickly turns "habitual and thuggish."

Teresa Watanabe, *Los Angeles Times*, October 30, 1993, "Stacking the Bids in Japan." In this insightful and exhaustively reported piece, Watanabe provides a detailed glimpse of the backroom dealings of the Japanese construction industry and bureaucracy as the two entities engage in a practice called dango—or bid-rigging—which involves payoffs to politicians and cooperation among firms. Emphasizing that the entrenched system will be tough to change, Watanabe employs stunning statistics and connects her story to a larger issue—the penetrability of the Japanese market.[1]

Pulitzer Prizes, 1992

Spot News Reporting: *New York Times* staff for its comprehensive coverage of the bombing of Manhattan's World Trade Center.

International Reporting: *Dallas Morning News* team for its series examining the epidemic of violence against women in many nations.[2]

[1]Terry Eastland, ed., *Forbes MediaGuide 500* (New York: American Heritage, 1994), pp. 28–32.
[2]"Celebrating Excellence in Journalism and the Arts," *Columbia Journalism Review*, May–June 1994, p. 52.

Variations in Assignments: Newsgathering and News Reporting

Reporting on foreign issues originates from many diverse sources. Only the largest news outlets such as wire services, CNN, and a handful of major city newspapers can afford to maintain their own staffs to gather news. Foreign editors rightly feel that no form of newsgathering is superior to having a person on their staff who is permanently assigned to cover a region. More common is the use of wire services, or sometimes "stringers" and free-lancers from remote areas who are on call to file stories as needed. If the *Atlanta Constitution* wants to cover events in Zimbabwe, which is one of the border states near volatile South Africa, it may use the services of an American reporter in Harare, who also supplies stories to the *Dallas Times Herald* and many other newspapers.[30] In the late 1980s United Press International (UPI) used the services of nearly 4000 stringers.

UPI is one of several wire services that represent the most common sources of foreign news used by print and broadcast media. Like the British-owned Reuters or France's Agence France Presse, UPI sells news to outlets who subscribe to the service. Some may also participate in a "barter" (exchange) arrangement with UPI to supply stories for distribution as well.

In recent years UPI has lost ground to its chief American rival, the huge Associated Press, which operates 187 news and photo bureaus in the United States and more than 100 foreign bureaus in over 70 foreign countries.[31] The AP is among the five largest suppliers of print, television, and news photographs, along with Reuters, UPI, Russia's TASS, and Agence France Presse.[32] It is not an unreasonable estimate to assume that 50 percent of all foreign news items selected from a typical range of American newspapers, radio newscasts, and television stations will contain information obtained from the Associated Press.

Print and video news services are invaluable to most newspapers and broadcasters. And they have become increasingly important as basic sources of intelligence to governments seeking to shape and refine their relationships with other states.

Reuters Television—formerly known as Visnews—is an interesting example of a giant in foreign newsgathering that is generally unknown to most viewers. It greatly outdistances the television networks in terms of being a presence in foreign locations. In comparison to CBS's eight foreign bureaus, Reuters maintains thirty-five, selling its video stories to outlets that include NBC, CNN, and assorted European broadcasters.[33] ABC and CBS use a competing service, World Television News (WTN).[34] A WTN or Reuters story may include completely edited and narrated accounts of an event. But the vanity of the American networks usually requires that their raw video from a distant locale will be narrated in New York or London by the more familiar voice of one of its own correspondents. Few viewers of CNN or NBC are probably aware that the stories they are watching may be relaying video footage provided by a multinational news organization.

It makes enormous financial sense to pool video coverage of foreign events. Even the simplest television news bureau may cost well over $300,000 a year to maintain, excluding the costs of satellite links to North America.[35] This trend toward consolidation conceals a deeper revolution in television reporting that has generally gone unnoticed. More and more, the traditional video sources of news in the United States—the networks—are shifting from newsgathering to relaying information from other sources. Because of pressures to cut costs, many networks are content to leave the initial responsibility for basic journalism to the wire services and providers of news footage, such as the Associated Press or Reuters Television. This distinction between gathering and relaying news may seem academic to news consumers, but it carries important implications.

The problem, as some network reporters see it, is the rise of what they call the voice-over story. Television journalist Betsy Aaron, for instance, has risked her life to cover important stories in Eastern Europe, Iran, and Afghanistan. Her on-the-scene reporting of rebel activity during the long and deadly Afghan civil war was a valuable but dangerous attempt to put viewers in the middle of a war in which Afghans fought each other as proxies for the world's two great superpowers. "I know now in my heart and my head that I will never cover stories of that substance again," she noted to a gathering of journalists in 1992. "I don't believe that buying footage and looking at it second-hand is a substitute for going there yourself." In narrating someone else's footage, Aaron notes,

> I am not seeing the story. I'm relying on someone else to gather that story for me. I have no idea what the person's agenda was—and there always is an agenda. And we're putting that on the air with the CBS label or the NBC label or the ABC label and we're doing it in a cavalier fashion that we never would have done twenty years ago or ten years ago or even five years ago.[36]

Ultimately, a shift toward purchasing rather than gathering news means that we may have fewer genuine reporters. If there are fewer observers at a location, the chances decrease that we will see an event through a variety of perspectives.

Whether the decline of the networks as newsgathers will continue remains uncertain. In late 1995 ABC, NBC, and the News Corporation (Fox) announced plans to offer full-time news services in competition to CNN.[37] Presumably they would have to beef up their own news bureaus outside the United States to compete with the well-established Cable News Network. On the other hand, these services scheduled to begin in 1997 could focus predominantly on domestic news, relying on reciprocal arrangements they already have with their two hundred affiliates around the country.

FOREIGN NEWS: DATELINE WASHINGTON

News consumers in most media-saturated Western nations benefit enormously from reporters on the scene of an important interational story. There can be no substitute for reporters like Hedrick Smith and David Shipler, both of whom gave readers fascinating accounts of life in the Soviet Union prior to its collapse in 1991, or CNN's Christiane Amanpour, who reported more recently from Somalia and Bosnia. Dispatches of journalists from the towns and villages of other states help enlarge the sometimes narrow outlook that the American emphasis on domestic news reporting encourages.

Yet it is important to note that much of what we learn about foreign countries does not originate from a correspondent on the scene. The events of other nations are frequently reported through the filtering perspective of national self-interest, as defined by key figures at the White House, Congress, and the Departments of State and Defense.

Covering the "Golden Triangle"

There is some irony to the fact that many stories about the affairs of other countries carry a Washington dateline. But that reality reflects two basic organizational features of foreign news reporting. One is the prevailing view among the nation's editors that important events in other nations should be framed in terms of news of government-to-government contacts. We frequently make our interpretations of life in one country in terms of the quality of official relations that its capital maintains with our own. With some exceptions, patterns of international diplomacy—whether cordial or hostile—tend to extend over into general public perceptions about even the nongovernmental characteristics we attribute to people in other countries. For example, our sometimes uneasy official relations with Japan over trade issues, and with France over differences in security and foreign policy matters, have undoubtedly shaped the collective impressions we have of their cultures. The stormy past that has characterized diplomatic relations with Japan—from Pearl Harbor to American perceptions of their alleged economic protectionism—still serves as the track that guides attitudes about their national life.

The second feature that dictates a Washington dateline for much foreign reporting is the wealth of information that federal agencies accumulate and propagate regarding relations with other nations. Reporters with prestige assignments in the "golden triangle" of the White House, State Department, and Pentagon can depend on at least one briefing a day from press officers. And that is only the beginning. All of these venues are organized to help reporters construct stories on a wide range of subjects, feeding members of the press a vast array of intelligence data on trade and military issues, as well as extensive background information on the political and social conditions that have been relayed to the White House or State Department from foreign service officials. In the press offices of the "golden triangle" there is an endless flow of press releases, congressional reports, and professional journals to be reviewed. Reporters may also want to take advantage of overseas trips with American leaders to observe meetings with their counterparts in other countries, or to see the outcomes of specific federal initiatives.

At their best, the public relations arms of the foreign policy establishment can provide useful background on the political and social changes occurring in a foreign country. In most cases, a reporter may view his or her private sources and general knowledge about a region as miniscule in comparison to the resources of the foreign and military establishments sitting a few miles from each other on separate sides of the Potomac. At their worst, however, governmental press offices contribute to a false sense of uniformity in reporting. Not only are Washington-based correspondents indebted to the agencies they are supposed to be writing about for much of their information, their presence before the same officials at the same locations contributes to a kind of "group-think" or "pack journalism." ABC's Ted Koppel suggested part of the problem in the opening of one of his "Nightline" broadcasts:

> *We are a discouragingly timid lot. By we, I mean most television anchors and reporters and most of our colleagues of the establishment press . . . We tremble between daydreams of scooping all of our competitors and the nightmare of standing alone with our scoop too long . . . People whose job it is to manipulate the media know this about us. They know that . . . many of us are truly only comfortable when we travel in a herd.[38]*

The extent to which much foreign news is the product of official Washington has been extensively documented by many researchers, including Stephen Hess, who has conducted many studies of the routines of Capitol press offices and reporters. Hess found the State Department the least receptive of the three "golden triangle" venues to full press coverage. It was the only beat he surveyed where he found staffers "who came close to challenging the legitimacy of the press."[39] It is the conventional—and largely accurate—wisdom in Washington that the State Department wants to carry on the arts of diplomacy without the glare of publicity. Briefings are frequent, but rigidly controlled by a language of obfuscation and a refusal to amplify conclusions. Most reporters note that the State Department has a semantics of its own. Several former briefers described to Hess how a meeting with foreign leaders might be explained. "You might say the discussions were fruitful. Or you might say that the discussions were frank. 'Frank' means that the discussions got nowhere or were hostile." Similarly, " 'no comment' means 'yes,' while 'can't confirm or deny' doesn't necessarily mean yes."[40]

Reporters covering the State Department soon learn that stories that cite the stale codes of briefings will never win them Pulitzer prizes for enterprising reporting. Television often ignores the department as a source of on-air stories, but still sounds out top-level staffers for background information. Their print colleagues, in turn, use more informal channels and cultivate sources who can fill in the blanks on American responses to events overseas.

Consider, for example, the comparatively "quiet" forty-eight-hour week of rounds logged by the State Department correspondent for a large American newspaper. On three days he attended briefings from the press-relations staff, and routinely scoured wire service reports to see what stories were receiving national attention:

> *Primarily he was "keeping up access with sources" and researching two long articles . . . on "U.S. arms sold abroad" and "basic factors in the Middle East." This meant an estimated ten to fifteen telephone calls daily, and the following face to face interviews: State Department officials on the Israel and Egypt desks; a legal expert on arms transfers; the head of a foreign central bank (breakfast); the president of a national lobbying organization (lunch); a State Department official in the nuclear nonproliferation field; a State Department official knowledgeable in Cambodian and Vietnamese affairs (breakfast); a staff member on the Senate Foreign Relations Committee; an assistant secretary of state (breakfast); a State Department authority on Soviet and Chinese activities in East Asia; the Japan desk officer at the State Department (concerning the forthcoming visit of Prime Minister Fukada); an Asian ambassador (lunch).[41]*

Critics often point out the failures of reporting that is too dependant on official sources in Washington or—by extension—officials in U.S. embassies in other nations.[42] Former CBS diplomatic correspondent Marvin Kalb recalls a time in Moscow in the '50s and '60s when he "generally cooperated with (the) U.S. embassy" and readily accepted "the ambassador's interpretation of Kremlin policy."[43] For Kalb there was ample reason to develop some of his stories with the help of the American embassy staff. Until the late 1980s, much of the Soviet Union was officially off limits to reporters, and the fear of official reprisal made it risky for many citizens to talk to Western reporters.[44] Correspondents needed their American contacts to help get around official obstacles.

Terrorism as Discussed on the "MacNeil/Lehrer Newshour" and "Nightline": An Assessment by Fairness and Accuracy in Reporting

Fair, a media watchdog group, studied the guest lists of ABC's "Nightline" and PBS's "MacNeil/Lehrer Newshour" for a six-month period in 1989. Here are some of their conclusions on how both programs covered terrorism, which at the time included stories about the importation of fruit from Chile that had been injected with toxic chemicals, and the murder of an American colonel in Beirut.

MacNeil/Lehrer and Nightline had remarkably similar coverage of terrorism in the period covered by this study. Both featured six programs on terrorism—the bulk of which were about the "hostage crisis" triggered by the killing of Colonel Higgins, the Beirut hostage.

On MacNeil/Lehrer, 70 percent of the guests were current or former government officials. Ninety-five percent of the guests were white and over 90 percent were men. There were no voices from a critical or alternative perspective. Instead of a spectrum of opinions debating U.S. policy, it was a procession of the same "experts" who always appear on discussions of terrorism: Brian Jenkins of the Rand Corporation; Neil Livingstone of the Institute on Terrorism

and Subnational Conflict; former U.S. government counterterrorist "experts," Noel Koch and L. Paul Bremer; and Edward Luttwak of CSIS (Center for Strategic and International Studies). These men rarely disagree. They all agree, for example, on the importance of reserving the right to "retaliate" militarily, and stress the importance of "counterterrorism." Nowhere in the discussion was there any real questioning of the underpinning of U.S. policies toward terrorism or the Middle East; and nowhere was the military option debated with any seriousness.

Nightline's coverage of terrorism was little different. Two of the terrorism programs focused on the hostages in Lebanon, Two on airport security, one on the political problems hostages present to U.S. presidents. . . . While Nightline may have defined a marginally broader range of issues as terrorism . . . its range of viewpoints was little different from MacNeil/Lehrer's. Seventy-four percent of the guests were current or former government officials and, as with MacNeil/Lehrer, no alternative voices were aired.

Source: William Hoynes and David Croteau, "All the Usual Suspects: MacNeil/Lehrer and Nightline," *Extra!*, Special Winter Issue, 1990, p. 11.

In less exotic locales reporters who rely on American sources may do so for other reasons. Either their editors may only want to offer their readers "the American perspective" on a region, or the reporter may be looking for a shortcut to filing a quota of stories, using views from American foreign service personnel in place of the more bothersome task of taking an independent look at the nation's national affairs.[45]

The Need to Manage Public Opinion

It would be difficult to underestimate the importance that American defense and diplomatic staff attach to the press as a conduit for shaping public opinion on foreign affairs. Public perceptions about American relations with other states are almost totally in control of the foreign policy establishment, and the journalists who cover it. A former staff aide to Secretary of State Alexander Haig noted that as much as 90 percent of staff time was spent "worrying about the press."[46] Even though public attention to foreign policy is sporadic, it can flare up quickly if events are mismanaged. In an increasingly interdependent world, presidents and legislative leaders can pay a high domestic price if they miscalculate voter acceptance of specific policies regarding trade status, foreign aid, arms sales, human rights, and immigration. If many citizens plead ignorance to the fine points of foreign policy, they nonetheless expect that their government will act from strength, and with some regard for the national principles that are urged upon "less developed" nations.

The inevitable internal struggles that exist in Washington also give individual agencies an additional incentive to project their unique perspectives in the press. It would be a serious mistake to see Washington as monolithic, or the president as the undisputed leader of foreign affairs.[47] Because so many different agencies are involved in advocating and shaping policy, the reporting of journalists at the White House, State Department, and Pentagon frequently reflects an ongoing tug-of-war for the support of the American public, and sometimes the president.

It is a matter of Washington folklore that secretaries of state and defense, along with White House national security advisers, will often have different views on foreign policy. Former Defense Secretary Caspar Weinberger was barely on speaking terms with State Department head George Schultz in the early years of the Reagan presidency, so intense were their differences on approaches to the Middle East and arms-control policy.[48] The conflict common to the agencies (and sometimes within them) helps create ample opportunities for reporters to develop a story. The very size of the Department of Defense, for example, works to the benefit of reporters from the national media and specialized publications who cover it on a full-time basis. As the *New York Time*'s Richard Halloran observes, "If someone is promoting the M-1 tank, there are plenty of people around who will tell you what's wrong with the M-1."[49]

As global economic competition replaced the Cold War in the early 1990s, feuds between various Washington agencies have become even more multisided. Anticommunism was a simple organizing principle for foreign policy. Its eclipse by far more difficult trade and industrial issues left the Bush and Clinton administrations open to criticism that they had no national policy for dealing with the economic powerhouses of Japan and the European Economic Community. "I was on the Japan Desk 20 years ago," noted a former State Department official, "and in those days Japan policy was essentially run by State, the Pentagon and the National Security Council." "Now," he notes, "you have so many more players—State Treasury, Commerce, the Trade Representative, Pentagon, Justice, (and the) Council of Economic Advisers." They represent groups who "do not want to consult each other and who hold radically different views about how to deal with Japan."[50] These interagency rivalries drive a good deal of Washington journalism. Stories are naturally fueled by the dialectic of competing advocates. Conflicts over how to deal with a foreign friend or adversary encourage the principals of various agencies to use journalists to carry their views to the nation. For their part, journalists have several incentives for reporting the details of such disputes. Not only do they illuminate the immediate issues at stake, but reports of conflict among the mighty help assure that the story (and the journalist) will not be consigned to obscurity. Disputes over the leadership of foreign affairs is a form of political theater that is as old as Shakespeare's *Julius Caesar* and as recent as yesterday's headlines.

Thus, as we have seen, the White House, the State Department, and the Pentagon each have a stake in positively representing its interests to the American public. In major and minor ways, each influences the agenda and contents of foreign news reporting.

WAR AND THE MEDIA

No reporting has more urgency than war coverage. In this final section of the chapter we will explore the nature of war reporting, and the uneasy rivalry that pits the Pentagon (and sometimes the American public) against the basic instincts of an adversarial press.

In his landmark study of war reporting from the Civil War to Vietnam, Phillip Knightley provides a vivid picture of journalists who sought to bring the terror of battle to readers and viewers. Every age has identified with some of these colorful figures: photographer Mathew Brady with the Union Armies at Bull Run and Gettysburg, Ernest Hemingway seeking out stories from the battle lines in the Spanish Civil War, Ernie Pyle with infantry units in the Second World War, and CBS's Jack Laurence covering an ambush and firefight in Vietnam.[51] Such front-line correspondents have always provided the most vivid images of war. In unexpected ways they put a human face on the most inhuman of all activities. By describing the ugly and often senseless consequences of war, they provide a valuable check on the lofty political rhetoric that often justifies it.

Additional coverage of war is provided by journalists who specialize in the strategies and technologies available to military commanders. For these journalists war is a chessboard full of dangerous and decisive options. Covering the military through the Cold War has created a small core of specialists who have been able to describe complicated weapons systems, intramilitary frictions, the views of Pentagon officials and dissidents, and the biases of particular commanders or congressional power brokers. In recent years the emphasis of journalists such as Drew Middleton of the *New York Times*, Charles Corddry of the *Baltimore Sun*, and Fred Francis of NBC has been less on eyewitness reporting from military hotspots than on explaining the behavior of those who make key military decisions. In peacetime they have been aided by a Pentagon that is often more open and receptive to press coverage than even the State Department. But "hot" wars severely strain the relationship. For reasons that are both obvious and subtle, the history of press coverage of military activity is full of suspicions, charges, and counter-charges.

Military News Management, Then and Now

Since World War I few journalists have bothered to argue with what has become a standard list of restrictions regarding military actions. These prohibitions have included detailed information on the location of troops or weapons; discussions of planned tactics; the location of missing troops, planes, or ships still subject to possible rescue; and news about operational weaknesses that could be used by the enemy. But with the partial exception of the Vietnam War, there has been little agreement between commanders and reporters on less strategic types of information.

Edward R. Murrow's experiences with Britain's Ministry of Information in 1940 is illustrative. The popular journalist sought permission to do several live broadcasts to his huge CBS radio audiences in the United States during the massive German air attacks on London. Permission was initially declined. It is difficult to figure out what kind of news might have been broadcast that would have compromised British secrecy; the devastation of the nighttime raids on central London's docks and homes would have been obvious to German air crews. More likely, the Ministry was bothered by the prospect of the world witnessing the nightly pounding that the capital city was taking from the Luftwaffe's five-hundred-pound incendiary bombs. Murrow kept asking, and agreed to record his reports in a number of practice runs, attempting to prove to the ministry that he would not expose vital military secrets.[52] The ministry finally relented, slow to realize that his accounts of the stoic resolve of the city's residents would help achieve Winston Churchill's objective of motivating Americans to come to Britain's aid.

Murrow and other reporters were often less successful in getting stories cleared through British and American military censors. Drew Middleton recalls that "total censorship prevailed. Everything written, photographed, or broadcast was scrutinized by censors. Anything that did not meet the high command's considerations of security was deleted."[53] In the Pacific Theater, for example, Americans were not initially told of the heavy damage to the Navy inflicted by Japan at Pearl Harbor. Even at the end of the war information about the desperate Kamikaze attacks of the Japanese air force against American ships was largely kept out of the American press by military censors.[54]

In spite of strict censorship rules in World War II, the press generally gave the military and its planners high marks. Several factors explain why. One reason is that the skeptical adversary model that is so common today was less clearly a part of the journalistic *ethos*. Members of the press suffered less from the antipolitical bias that is now a fixture in contemporary American life. In addition, most reporters were personally committed to the broad political objectives of the allies, and they were routinely allowed to join specific units, talk to their members, and fly on bombing and supply missions. Key commanders from Dwight Eisenhower to George C. Marshall were willing to provide thorough briefings "off the record" on the effects of particular campaigns. Control over what was reported usually came after reporters had been given extensive information. Then censors restricted what they allowed journalists to reveal in news reports and newsreels. As in World War I, correspondents soon learned to engage in self-censorship to avoid the delays that rewriting stories sometimes entailed.[55]

The stalemated and deadly "police action" in Korea signaled a gradual shift away from this pattern of broad access but strong official censorship, a pattern that would be complete by the time the Vietnam War had escalated into a major conflict. Partially because Vietnam was an undeclared war, journalists had a freer rein in determining for themselves what they would file to their editors and producers.

Vietnam has been called the "uncensored war," a label that is technically accurate but also misleading. In the last half of the 1960s correspondents in Vietnam found that they had wide access to individual units in the field. Many became effective chroniclers of the peculiar hell that results when the "enemy" becomes indistinguishable from the inhabitants of jungle villages. UPI's Neil Sheehan, the AP's John Wheeler, NBC's Greg Harris, and many others captured in words and images much of the incredible horror of the Vietnam conflict, usually shipping their reports back to their offices without prior military screening. The continuous intensity of this reporting—most dramatically, on the network's evening newscasts—left Americans with few illusions about the high costs and muddled objectives of the war.

But the absence of military censorship of outgoing dispatches and film stories conceals what Drew Middleton describes as the common practice of "censorship at the source."[56] Especially in the case of Vietnam, an enormous credibility gap developed that increasingly pitted journalists—and soon, a sizable portion of the American public—against the president and military commanders in Saigon. The gap was created by the enormous discrepancies between what reporters were seeing and relaying to Americans from the villages in the countryside and what briefers were more optimistically describing in Saigon and Washington. The daily afternoon sessions between correspondents and representatives of the Joint U.S. Public Affairs Office became for many Americans a notorious symbol of purposeful equivocation. What was dubbed "the five-o'clock follies" provided abundant evidence that the bureaucracy was intentionally attempting to manage news about the overall scope of the conflict, often by claiming that information was not available, or by inflated estimates such as the number of enemy soldiers killed in combat. After 1968 it was obvious that optimistic estimates about South Vietnamese control over its own regions did not square with what front-line journalists were seeing and reporting.

The later years of the Vietnam conflict saw an unprecedented degree of stunningly vivid combat reporting. If the graphic imagery was not matched by a clarity about the United States' objectives and policy, it was perhaps the first and last time Americans would confront the gritty realities of combat as they unfolded.[57] One reason was that many officers in the field welcomed reporters as potential allies. Many wanted the American public to see the difficulties and daily frustrations of combat against an enemy of uncertain origins in obscure locations. The press was also able to develop its coverage because of the extended period of time it had to organize its own infrastructure.

In deploying resources in Vietnam for long-term coverage, journalism organizations were able to overcome one of their major liabilities: the fact that the press is naturally a *reactive* institution. As the Nieman Foundation's Bill Kovach has observed, the press typically responds only after other organizations have already put their plans in motion.[58] At least in the short term, the press is easily lead. It has a strong tendency to cover an event initially from the perspective of those who have orchestrated it. Only because the

Vietnam conflict grew incrementally over a decade did the press have the capacity to establish an independent presence in the region.

It was ironically a small operation on the island of Grenada in 1983 that would signal the weakness of the media to cover short-term military actions, a weakness that could be exploited by defense planners.

Grenada: A Time for Press–Military Negotiation

The Grenada invasion was a quick military strike—what then White House Chief of Staff James Baker accurately described as a commando raid—centered on the airport of that small Caribbean island. Its primary objective was the rescue of American students thought to be held by a government friendly to Cuba. The invasion occurred without the press, and was virtually over before any were able to fly to the island. Although there were strong objections from news organizations, most had no choice but to grudgingly provide after-the-fact accounts of the invasion provided by the Pentagon and the White House.[59] Even the Pentagon's public affairs spokesperson, Pete Williams, later conceded that it was a "journalistic disaster."[60]

The political consequences of the Grenada invasion may have been as important as its strategic value. It pushed the military into meetings with news executives and reporters about how to arrange coverage of the smaller combat operations that were now predicted in a world no longer dominated by East–West tensions. The primary result of these meetings was the so-called Sidle Commission Report, named after retired army general Winant Sidle, who oversaw the deliberations. Sidle worked with retired military officers and journalists to establish a set of recommendations governing press-military planning in future operations. The most basic included the following:

- That public affairs planning for military operations be conducted concurrently with operational planning. . . .
- When it becomes apparent during military operational planning that news media pooling provides the only feasible means of furnishing the media with early access to an operation, planning should provide for the largest possible *press pool* . . . and minimize the length of time the pool would be necessary. . . .
- That a basic tenet governing media access to military operations should be voluntary compliance by the media with security guidelines or groundrules established and issued by the military. These rules should be as few as possible. . . .
- Public affairs planning for military operations should include sufficient equipment and qualified military personnel whose function is to assist correspondents in covering the operation adequately.[61]

Testing the "Pool" System in the Middle East

The first combat test of the guidelines proposed by the panel was in 1987, after the United States agreed to escort merchant ships through the Persian Gulf. Iran—then nearly at the end of its long and deadly war with Iraq—had threatened to attack commercial vessels in the region that it deemed to be a threat. Several *press pools* were placed on navy destroyers that would escort Kuwaiti tankers that had recently been reregistered under the American flag. For example, joining the escort on the USS *Fox* were several print reporters, a radio journalist, and a *Time* photographer. Most of their reports made during their time aboard the *Fox* were approved for release, although with some delays. But after one of the tankers ran into a mine, *Time's* photographer was denied permission to use a photo that clearly showed that the navy ships were behind the wounded tanker they were supposedly escorting.[62]

The same general guidelines remained in effect for the American invasion of Panama in December of 1990, and the Persian Gulf War the following year.

As the invasion to capture and disarm General Manual Noriega and his soldiers began, the military agreed to fly a large pool of sixteen reporters to the scene. But members reported that they were consistently delayed from covering the fighting. Incongruously, during the early hours of what was officially dubbed "Operation Just Cause," the pool was escorted first to a room to watch CNN's television coverage of the conflict, and then on to a lecture by the U.S. charge d'affaires on the history of Panama. Over the four days that followed, they were generally kept at some distance from the fighting in Panama City, and only escorted into an area after combat had mostly ceased. One disgruntled member of a pool under military escort came up with his own motto: "Semper Tardis" (Always late).[63]

For their part, the few journalists who were already in Panama before the invasion found it difficult to do much more than provide phone reports from a Marriott hotel that was periodically raided by Noriega loyalists. Several were taken as hostages, and one was killed. But in contrast to official reports announcing the end of the conflict from the military's southern command, they continued to send a less simplified picture that included evidence of new fighting and massive looting of businesses in the city.[64]

Military News Management: The Persian Gulf War

"With an arrogance foreign to the democratic system," CBS's venerable Walter Cronkite told readers of *Newsweek* magazine, "the U.S. military in Saudi Arabia is trampling on the American people's right to know."[65] What he and other journalists objected to was a series of specific guidelines laid down to the approximately 1000 accredited reporters and technicians who covered the 1991 war from Saudi Arabia. Of this number no more than 126 were ever assigned to pools for coverage of the half-million Americans in the area during the five-week air war. During the three days of ground combat that began on February 24 approximately 250 journalists were allowed to join combat pools.[66]

Built on the Sidle Commission model, the military's rules in the Middle East put heavy and burdensome restrictions on members of the press. To be sure, they were less onerous than the strict Iraqi censorship imposed on reporters in Baghdad and Tel Aviv, but in some cases not by much. Even before the massive air offensive began, Pentagon rules issued to the Washington bureaus of news organizations required that all reports not disclose sensitive military information, that access to combat units would be limited to preselected pools of reporters, and that reports from members within a pool would have to be submitted to "security review." The Pentagon's Pete Williams wrote to the press corps on January 14 reminding them that tight rules "intended to meet the specific operational environment of the Persian Gulf" would be enforced by public affairs officers working in Riyadh and Dhahran.

The small number of reporters who ignored the Pentagon's guidelines in the weeks that followed discovered that they sometimes gained protection from commanders who were sympathetic to their desire to break free of Pentagon restrictions. At other times, however, these so-called unilaterals were rounded up by military MPs and detained in rear-staging areas.[67] The most unlucky of the unilaterals were CBS's Bob Simon and his crew, who were captured by Iraqi troops and held until the end of the war.

The two-page list of restrictions that would be placed on the press included the obvious and traditional limits on coverage. Reporters were reminded to restrict the use of lights at night. They were told that they would have to carry their own gear, and were cautioned against giving out information regarding the names of casualties and the movements of troops, and specific information on individuals or aircraft down behind enemy lines. The more troublesome restrictions involved the requirement to travel in military-escorted pools, and the indication that some materials might be reviewed by military censors.

The idea of using a representative group of journalists in a specific setting is not new. In some cases the sheer number of accredited reporters in a given location makes it impossible for press offices to arrange access for all who with it. The White House, presidential campaigns, NASA, and other agencies have often put limits on coverage by selecting a limited number of reporters to relay impressions to others. Those who are selected relinquish the right to claim an "exclusive" on the events they witness. Much like wire-service reporters, their job is to provide a factual running narrative of what took place. In the early days of the air war less then ten pools were initially

These controversial rules for journalists were issued to the press by the Pentagon in January of 1991, defining a long list of conditions for press reporting on military activities during the air and ground war with Iraq.

ASSISTANT SECRETARY OF DEFENSE

WASHINGTON, D.C. 20301-1400

PUBLIC AFFAIRS

January 15, 1991

MEMORANDUM FOR WASHINGTON BUREAU CHIEFS OF THE PENTAGON PRESS
CORPS

SUBJ: Ground rules and guidelines for correspondents in the
        event of hostilities in the Persian Gulf

Last Monday, I sent you copies of our revised ground rules
for press coverage of combat operations and guidelines for correspondents that are intended to meet the specific operational
environment of the Persian Gulf. I appreciate the comments I
have received from some of you and understand your concerns,
particularly with respect to security review and pooling in
general. I also was pleased by the general consensus that the
one-page version of the ground rules was an improvement.

The ground rules have been reviewed and approved with no
major changes. They became effective today.

The guidelines were revised to comply with operational concerns in Saudi Arabia. We added a provision that media representatives will not be permitted to carry weapons, clarified the
escort requirement, added a sentence giving medical personnel the
authority to determine media guidelines at medical facilities,
and deleted the sentence saying the JIB in Dhahran would verify
next of kin notification on casualties. We also added a section,
in response to many questions, which clarifies our policy on
unilateral media coverage of the forward areas during the period
when the pools are operational.

Last Saturday, I conducted a conference call with the majority of the CENTCOM public affairs officers, who were gathered in
Riyadh and Dhahran, and discussed the ground rules and guidelines
to ensure that the intent and purpose of the ground rules is
clearly understood.

I appreciate your counsel and remain ready to discuss any
problems or questions you may have.

Pete Williams
Assistant Secretary of Defense
(Public Affairs)

**FIGURE 5-3.   Department of Defense Rules for Members of the
Press Covering the Persian Gulf War.**

OPERATION DESERT SHIELD
GROUND RULES

The following information should not be reported because its publication or broadcast could jeopardize operations and endanger lives:

(1) For U.S. or coalition units, specific numerical information on troop strength, aircraft, weapons systems, on-hand equipment, or supplies (e.g., artillery, tanks, radars, missiles, trucks, water), including amounts of ammunition or fuel moved by or on hand in support and combat units. Unit size may be described in general terms such as "company-size," multibattalion," "multidivision," "naval task force," and "carrier battle group." Number or amount of equipment and supplies may be described in general terms such as 'large,' "small," or "many."

(2) Any information that reveals details of future plans, operations, or strikes, including postponed or cancelled operations.

(3) Information, photography, and imagery that would reveal the specific location of military forces or show the level of security at military installations or encampments. Locations may be described as follows: all Navy embark stories can identify the ship upon which embarked as a dateline and will state that the report is coming from the "Persian Gulf," "Red Sea," or "North Arabian Sea." Stories written in Saudi Arabia may be date-lined "Eastern Saudi Arabia," "Near the Kuwaiti border," etc. For specific countries outside Saudi Arabia, stories will state that the report is coming from the Persian Gulf region unless that country has acknowledged its participation.

(4) Rules of engagement details.

(5) Information on intelligence collection activities, including targets, methods, and results.

(6) During an operation, specific information on friendly force troop movements, tactical deployments, and dispositions that would jeopardize operational security or lives. This would include unit designations, names of operations, and size of friendly forces involved, until released by CENTCOM.

(7) Identification of mission aircraft points of origin, other than as land- or carrier-based.

(8) Information on the effectiveness or ineffectiveness of enemy camouflage, cover, deception, targeting, direct and indirect fire, intelligence collection, or security measures.

(9) Specific identifying information on missing or downed aircraft or ships while search and rescue operations are planned or underway.

(10) Special operations forces' methods, unique equipment or tactics.

(11) Specific operating methods and tactics, (e,g., air angles of attack or speeds, or naval tactics and evasive maneuvers). General terms such as "low" or "fast" may be used.

(12) Information on operational or support vulnerabilities that could be used against U.S. forces, such as details of major battle damage or major personnel losses of specific U.S. or coalition units, until that information no longer provides tactical advantage to the enemy and is, therefore, released by CENTCOM. Damage and casualties may be described as "light," "moderate," or "heavy."

FIGURE 5-3. *Continued*

GUIDLINES FOR NEWS MEDIA

News media personnel must carry and support any personal and professional gear they take with them, including protective cases for professional equipment, batteries, cables, converters, etc.

Night Operations — Light discipline restrictions will be followed. The only approved light source is a flashlight with a red lens. No visible light source, including flash or television lights, will be used when operating with forces at night unless specifically approved by the on-scene commander.

Because of host-nation requirements, you must stay with your public affairs escort, while on Saudi bases. At other U.S. tactical or field locations and encampments, a public affairs escort may be required because of security, safety, and mission requirements as determined by the host commander.

Casualty information, because of concern of the notification of the next of kin, is extremely sensitive. By executive directive, next of kin of all military fatalities must be notified in person by a uniformed member of the appropriate service. There have been instances in which the next of kin have first learned of the death or wounding of a loved one through the news media. The problem is particularly difficult for visual media. Casualty photographs showing a recognizable face, name tag, or other identifying feature or item should not be used before the next of kin have been notified. The anguish that sudden recognition at home can cause far outweighs the news value of the photograph, film or videotape. News coverage of casualties in medical centers will be in strict compliance with the instructions of doctors and medical officials.

To the extent that individuals in the news media seek access to the U.S. area of operation, the following rule applies: Prior to or upon commencement of hostilities, media pools will be established to provide initial combat coverage of U.S. forces. U.S. news media personnel present in Saudi Arabia will be given the opportunity to join CENTCOM media pools, providing they agree to pool their products. News media personnel who are not members of the official CENTCOM media pools will not be permitted into forward areas. Reporters are strongly discouraged from attempting to link up on their own with combat units. U.S. commanders will maintain extremely tight security throughout the operational area and will exclude from the area of operation all unauthorized individuals.

For news media personnel participating in designated CENTCOM Media Pools:

(1) Upon registering with the JIB, news media should contact their respective pool coordinator for an explanation of pool operations.

(2) In the event of hostilities, pool products will be the subject to review before release to determine if they contain sensitive information about military plans, capabilities, operations, or vulnerabilities (see attached ground rules) that would jeopardize the outcome of an operation or the safety of U.S. or coalition forces. Material will be examined solely for its conformance to the attached ground rules, not for its potential to express criticism or cause embarrassment. The public affairs escort officer on scene will review pool reports, discuss ground rule problems with the reporter, and in the limited circumstances when no agreement can be reached with a reporter about disputed materials, immediately send the disputed materials to JIB Dhahran for review by the JIB Director and the appropriate news media representative. If no agreement can be reached, the issue will be immediately forwarded to OASD(PA) for review with the appropriate bureau chief. The ultimate decision on publication will be made by the originating reporter's news organization.

(3) Correspondents may not carry a personal weapon.

Source: Department of Defense

FIGURE 5-3. *Continued*

established, with sizes ranging from seven to eighteen members. The largest pools were assigned to the Army and Marines. Smaller groups were established to cover the Air Force, the Navy, the military hospitals, and any unexpected events. Even so, large gaps remained. According to the *New York Time*'s R. W. Apple, out of a total of eight Army or Marine divisions numbering over a hundred thousand men and women on the ground near Kuwait, only thirty spots existed for the press.[68] Most of the approximately one thousand journalists who wanted to cover the war in the Persian Gulf were left at the Dhahran International Hotel or the Riyadh Hyatt, able only to receive pool reports and the daily military briefings issued by the Joint Command.[69]

The use of pools as a way to manage press coverage was especially evident in efforts by the Pentagon to keep pilots and members of the press apart. Members of a pool hoping to interview or fly with the crews of the massive B-52 bombers that contributed to the seventy-two thousand air sorties during the war were instead given ground interviews with Air Force commanders or a single preselected pilot. At one point they ended up interviewing drivers in a motor pool, where the commander suggested stories about the "unsung" role of military truck drivers. Apparently only one reporter—ABC's Forest Sawyer—actually flew on a bombing mission, even though many forms of aircraft had ample space.[70]

In practice, the pool/escort system sometimes did work. No reporter could easily defend the premise that in a military campaign all members of the press should be accommodated in specific locations. Some escorts were helpful in getting reporters to key locations and helping them see particular aspects of Operation Desert Storm, especially in its early phases. A few reporters described helpful escorts and sympathetic field commanders.[71] Others viewed the system as an efficient filter that worked against the press and in favor of the ostensible news management objectives of the military.

Even worse, for many reporters, was the stipulation by the Pentagon that "in the event of hostilities, pool products will be subject to review before release to determine if they contain sensitive information about military plans, capabilities, operations, or vulnerabilities." (See Operation Desert Shield Ground Rules, Figure 5-3.) To a person, members of the press resent the implication that they might pass on information that would either jeopardize the lives of Americans involved in combat or give useful information to the enemy. Review of copy prior to publication goes against the notion of a free press, even though successful combat may require secrecy and a degree of surprise. Most journalists attribute demands for advance clearance to the desire of political and military leaders to screen potentially embarrassing copy. For their part, commanders are fearful they will lose the element of surprise—and possibly put their troops at risk—if information about their locations and probable plans are reported. In wartime, as Stephen Hess notes, the military equates "secrets with national security" and loses its "tolerance for the press's role as critic."[72]

Whatever the political consequences of the short war against Iraq, it is increasingly clear that it confirmed the military's hold on news management that began in the Panama invasion. In a future where superpower confrontations will be replaced by rapid and intense skirmishes, the press is at an enormous disadvantage. In short wars it has less time to establish an independent presence in a region. Perhaps they had no choice, but it is apparent that the nation's editors and reporters have acquiesced to the military's insistence that it will set the terms and conditions that govern press access to combat.[73]

SUMMARY

As we have seen, foreign news is one of the thoroughfares of American life that carries a steady flow of important traffic. The longstanding American wish to exist on a continent separated from the feuds and discontents of other nations has been steadily eroded by a combination of factors. Since World War II we have exercised a strong desire to project American power beyond our borders. We have entered into wars—both "hot" and "cold"—that have generated enormous interest in the well-being of Americans stationed in military posts overseas. And, like much of the world, we are the victims and beneficiaries both of an interdependent world economy and of new communications technologies that make insistent demands on our attention.

Layered over this need for news from other nations lies an equally strong interest by the agencies of American government to manage American public opinion. Democracies require the support of their citizens in wartime. Sporadic acts of terrorism against American interests invites the assignment of villains and blame. Even the routine processes of diplomacy need to be portrayed as consistent with the basic principles of the nation and its economic interests. Congress, the White House, the State Department, and the Department of Defense all have enormous interests in the successful leadership of public opinion on foreign policy issues.

Overall, the response of media and governmental forces to the globalization of politics and information has been enormously varied, but includes several conclusions reached in this chapter:

- A tendency by media organizations to focus more on domestic rather than international affairs
- A pattern of foreign reporting that emphasizes an American angle to foreign stories

- A reduction of "in-house" foreign newsgathering by the broadcast networks, in favor of greater use of international video news services
- A reliance on government sources to set the context for foreign reporting
- Increasing confusion by the public and news organizations about the role of the press in wartime

To be sure, the task facing correspondents who deal with foreign affairs is enormous. They must deal with editors and producers who are reluctant to commit large amounts of time or space to the coverage of foreign news, especially if it is not given an ethnocentric frame of reference in concurrent American events. And they must attempt to interest an American public that—in the mass—lacks a deep interest or knowledge of even the most elemental issues effecting other societies. Given the limitations of space and the enormity of the task, journalism is left with the need to reduce the very complex to something that is far more simple.

NOTES

1. Peter Theroux, *Sandstorms: Days and Nights in Arabia* (New York: Norton, 1990), p. 39.

2. Sections of this chapter dealing with the Persian Gulf War have been adapted from Gary C. Woodward, "The Rules of the Game: The Military and the Press in the Persian Gulf," in Robert E. Denton, Jr., ed., *Mass Media and the Persian Gulf War* (New York: Praeger, 1993). Used by permission.

3. John R. MacArthur, "Remember Nayirah, Witness for Kuwait?," *New York Times,* January 6, 1992, p. A17.

4. Arthur E. Rowse, "Flacking for the Emir," *Progressive,* May, 1991, pp. 20–23.

5. Ibid., p. 21.

6. Ibid., p. 20.

7. "Popular media" here means the mass audience television networks (including CNN), news wire services, and general print media, including newspapers and newsmagazines. It is important to note, however, that a vast array of trade and specialized publications also closely follow foreign affairs. Among specialized publications that regularly assign reporters to the Pentagon, for example, are *Armed Forces Journal, Aerospace Daily, Aviation Week,* and *Air Force Magazine.*

8. Hodding Carter, quoted in David Rubin and Ann Marie Cunningham, eds., *War, Peace, and the News Media* (New York: New York University, 1983), p. 196.

9. David Paletz and Robert Entman, *Media Power Politics* (New York: Free Press, 1981), pp. 151–154.

10. *Le Monde,* quoted in *World Press Review,* July 1992, p. 8.

11. James F. Larson, "International Affairs Coverage on US Evening Network News, 1972–1979," in William C. Adams, ed. *Television Coverage of International Affairs* (Norwood, NJ: Ablex, 1982), pp. 22–25.

12. Roger Wallis and Stanley Baran, *The Known World of Broadcast News* (New York: Routledge, 1990), pp. 172–173.

13. Ibid.

14. Ibid., p. 11.

15. Ibid., p. 256.

16. Bernard Cohen, *The Press and Foreign Policy* (Princeton, NJ: Princeton, 1963).

17. William C. Adams, "Covering the World in Ten Minutes: Network News and International Affairs" in Adams, *Television Coverage*, p. 18.

18. For a useful discussion of various perspectives taken by newsgatherers as they look at other cultures, see John C. Pollock, "An Anthropological Approach to Mass Communication Research: The U.S. Press and Political Change in Latin America," *Latin American Research Review*, 1978, pp. 158–162.

19. Philip J. Hilts, "In a Ranking of Maternal Health, U.S. Trails Most Developed Nations," *New York Times*, July 26, 1995, p. C8.

20. Michael O'Neil, quoted in Robert J. Donovan and Ray Scherer, *Unsilent Revolution: Television News and American Public Life* (New York: Cambridge University Press, 1992), p. 210.

21. Marlin Fitzwater, quoted in ibid., p. 211.

22. Stephen Hess, "The Golden Triangle: Press Relations at the White House, State Department and Department of Defense," in Rubin and Cunningham, *War, Peace*, p. 154.

23. Herbert J. Gans, *Deciding What's News* (New York: Vintage, 1980), pp. 31–38.

24. Ibid., pp. 174–179.

25. See, for example, Eugene R. Wittkopf, *Faces of Internationalism: Public Opinion and American Foreign Policy* (Durham, NC: Duke University, 1990), pp. 214–221.

26. Bill Carter, "Networks Cutting Back on Foreign Coverage," *New York Times*, June 10, 1992, p. C18.

27. Walter Laqueur, "Foreign News Coverage: From Bad to Worse," *Washington Journalism Review*, June 1983, p. 33.

28. Jude Wanniski, *1991 Media Guide* (Morristown, NJ: Polyconomics, Inc., 1991), p. 55.

29. See, for example, Chris Hedges, "The Unilaterals," *Columbia Journalism Review*, May–June 1991, pp. 27–29.

30. Dan Baum, "On the Job: How to Make It on Your Own as a Foreign Correspondent," *Columbia Journalism Review*, July–August 1988, pp. 48–49.

31. Melvin DeFleur and Everette Dennis, *Understanding Mass Communication*, 4th ed. (Boston: Houghton Mifflin, 1991), p. 419.

32. Howard H. Frederick, *Global Communication and International Relations* (Belmont, CA: Wadsworth, 1993), p. 108.

33. Teresa L. Waite, "As Networks Stay Home, Two Agencies Roam the World," *New York Times*, March 8, 1992, p. F5.

34. "WTN Signs $10 Million Deal with CBS," *Broadcasting and Cable*, September 19, 1994, p. 42.

35. Ibid.

36. Tal Sanit, "The New Unreality: When TV Reporters Don't Report," *Columbia Journalism Review*, May–June 1992, p. 18.

37. Bill Carter, "ABC and NBC Look Ahead to Rival All-News Channels," *New York Times*, December 6, 1995, p. D5.

38. Ted Koppel, quoted in Martin A. Lee and Norman Solomon, *Unreliable Sources: A Guide to Detecting Bias in News Media* (New York: Lyle Stuart, 1991), p. 337.

39. Hess, "Golden Triangle," p. 149.

40. Ibid., p. 150.

41. Stephen Hess, *The Washington Reporters* (Washington, DC: Brookings, 1981), p. 57.

42. See, for example, Lee and Solomon, *Unreliable Sources*, pp. 15–32; and Paletz and Entman, *Media Power Politics*, pp. 213–233.

43. Marvin Kalb, preface to *The Media and Foreign Policy*, ed. Simon Sefaty (New York: Macmillan, 1990), p. xvi.

44. See, for example, Hedrick Smith's descriptions of his first days in Moscow as the *New York Time*'s bureau chief in *The Russians* (New York: Ballantine, 1977), pp. 1–28.

45. For more discussion of this point, see John C. Pollock, *The Politics of Crisis Reporting* (New York: Praeger, 1981), pp. 85–102.

46. Kalb, preface to *The Media*, p. xiv.

47. See, for example, Leon T. Hadar, "Covering the New World Disorder, *Columbia Journalism Review*, July–August 1994, pp. 26–29.

48. Hedrick Smith, *The Power Game: How Washington Works* (New York: Random House, 1988), pp. 579–584.

49. Hess, "Golden Triangle," p. 153.

50. Thomas L. Friedman, "America's Japan Policy: Fractured Vision," *New York Times Magazine*, June 28, 1992, p. 24.

51. Phillip Knightley, *The First Casualty* (New York: Harcourt, Brace Jovanovich, 1975).

52. A. M. Sperber, *Murrow: His Life and Times* (New York: Freundlich, 1986), pp. 161–174.

53. Drew Middleton, "Barring Reporters from the Battlefield," *New York Times Magazine*, February 5, 1984, p. 37.

54. Knightley, *First Casualty*, pp. 273–274, 297.

55. Richard W. Steele, "News of the 'Good War': World War II News Management," *Journalism Quarterly*, Winter 1985, pp. 707–783.

56. Middleton, "Barring Reporters," p. 61.

57. See, for example, Peter Braestrup, *Big Story*, vol. 1 (Boulder, CO: Westview, 1977), pp. 156–160, and Michael Arlen, *Living Room War* (New York: Viking, 1969), pp. 6–9.

58. Bill Kovach, Speech to the Cambridge Forum, National Public Radio, July 26, 1991.

59. Mark Hertsgaard, *On Bended Knee: The Press and the Reagan Presidency* (New York: Schocken, 1989), pp. 205–237.

60. Pete Williams, "Statement before the Committee on Governmental Affairs, Washington, United States Senate," February 20, 1991. Photocopy.

61. Winant Sidle, Report by CJCS Media-Military Relations Panel, appendix in Peter Braestrup, *Battle Lines: Report of the Twentieth Century Fund Task Force on the Military and the Media* (New York: Priority Press, 1985), pp. 161–178.

62. Mark Thompson, "With the Press in the Persian Gulf," *Columbia Journalism Review*, November–December 1987, pp. 40–45.

63. Gilbert Cranberg, "A Flimsy Story and a Compliant Press," *Washington Journalism Review*, March 1990, p. 49.

64. Juan Vasquez, "Panama: Live From the Marriott!" *Washington Journalism Review*, March 1990, pp. 44–47.

65. Walter Cronkite, "What Is There to Hide?" *Newsweek*, February 25, 1991, p. 43.

66. David Lamb, "Pentagon Hardball," *Washington Journalism Review*, April, 1991, pp. 33–36.

67. Hedges, "The Unilaterals," pp. 27–29.

68. R. W. Apple, "Correspondents Protest Pool System," *New York Times*, February 12, 1991, p. A14.

69. Lamb, "Pentagon Hardball," p. 34.

70. Jason DeParle, "Keeping the News in Step: Are the Pentagon's Gulf War Rules Here to Stay?" *New York Times*, May 6, 1991, p. A9.

71. Lamb, "Pentagon Hardball," p. 33; Michael Massing, "Another Front," *Columbia Journalism Review*, June 1991, pp. 23–24.

72. Hess, "The Golden Triangle," p. 155.

73. For details of this argument, see John R. MacArthur, *Second Front: Censorship and Propaganda in the Gulf War* (New York: Hill and Wang, 1992).

6

WITNESSING JUSTICE: PRESS COVERAGE OF THE COURTS

Trials make dramas of our social texts.[1]

Dramas of crime and punishment represent one of the most basic and compelling forms of public discourse. In many ways the United States is a nation obsessed with issues of justice. Graphic discriptions of criminal acts often dominate the headlines and the prime-time television schedule. Trials condense in one place and one cast of characters many of the social tensions that permeate our culture. And yet our fascination is hardly unique. Shakespeare's plays regularly gave its often impoverished audiences vivid glimpses of justice served on the powerful and mighty. Even as King Lear and Macbeth vainly attempted to remake human law in their own image, Shakespeare was quick to reassure his audiences by Act III that the higher laws of God and nature would still hold them accountable.

There is irony in our fascination with crime. Violence and harm inflicted by one person on another presents the world as we do not want to see it: dangerous, unpredictable, and potentially life-threatening. And yet this same news is also a source of reassurance. The social payback for the lawbreaking of a villain is our faith that the state will ultimately hold that person accountable. Popular media in the form of television news, crime novels, and courtroom dramas give us what Shakespeare portrayed in his plays: portrayals of justice confirmed or denied. If the truth is rarely so simple, and the requirements of justice not so easy to define,[2] we are still drawn to the idea of perfect justice visited upon those who have made it an imperfect world.[3]

This chapter treats crime and trial reporting as a form of media-supported public discussion. Crime news is "political" for several reasons. It shapes public opinion and sometimes sheds light on social ills in need of legislative remedies. Presidents, for example, regularly offer up crime bills for public and legislative consideration in what are clearly responses to widespread perceptions that we live in a dangerous culture. In New York City, Joan Didion writes, crime is the "city's endorphin," a constant source of intense examination about the social ills that tear at the fabric of civilized life.[4] In addition, crime is intimately tied to the third branch of government, the courts. Legal bodies from the Supreme Court to the local magistrate enforce what legislatures enact. In the criminal process court dockets are largely determined by prosecutors who understand the effects of their actions on the public and political institutions. And there is frequent movement of people between these two spheres.[5]

Civil and criminal cases also touch on sensitive issues addressed in the larger political arena. For instance, to view the trial of former football star O. J. Simpson as simply the outcome of a double-murder case misses the larger political dynamic of his arrest and trial. Among other things, the entire episode was also about the identity politics of race, and the apparent racism of some elements of American law enforcement. One only had to look at the stark differences of opinion along racial lines about his alleged guilt to see how deep the potential meanings of the trial were.[6]

This chapter offers several sections that account for the importance of the criminal justice process as a major political arena. The first part reviews the extent to which the stories of crime and punishment appear in the popular media, with special attention to news reporting and the highly visible "mega-trial." The second describes a societal cause for this interest in an underlying cultural bias that gives special status to the idea of victimage. A third section proceeds with a review of some of the major issues effecting how trials can be covered in the United States. And the chapter closes with an overview of civil litigation as a strategy intended to promote media coverage.

Because of the complexity and many dimensions of the legal process, this survey is necessarily selective rather than exhaustive. Even so, the broad theme developed here is essential to understanding one of the important sources of contemporary political discourse. As this chapter argues, the national political landscape has been significantly altered by intense news coverage of issues of crime and justice.

THE PERVASIVE DEPICTION
OF CRIME AND PUNISHMENT

By nearly any measure, crime and its effects remain high on the list of topics that command widespread attention. In early 1993, for example, all of

the American television networks devoted an evening's prime-time programming to the retelling of the same tawdry "real life" story about a Long
Island teenager who shot the wife of her middle-aged lover. The three separately produced television films contained little of any social or legal significance, but all promised stories based loosely on headlines emphasizing
bizarre behavior and lurid sex. Viewers in more than half of all American
households tuned in to at least one of the movies.[7] And many others saw
related news programs, ranging from the tabloid "Hard Copy" to the more
mainstream "CBS This Morning," which devoted long segments to interviews of the participants about the original shooting, the subsequent plea
bargaining, and the portrayals of the participants in the "Amy Fisher
Story." Only two days later, CBS followed this familiar path of finding
large audiences in the degrading details of crime by re-creating the plot
line of the successful, Oscar-winning film *Silence of the Lambs*. Like the 1991
film, their own version exploited the peculiar eroticism of a plot built
around a young female police officer's attempt to capture a sadistic serial
killer.

Media Attention to Crime and Justice

News of the mayhem that humans inflict on each other is constant, but it is
also highly skewed. In a 1979 study monitoring local television and newspapers, Doris Graber reported that between one-fifth and one-quarter of all
news dealt with topics of crime and justice.[8] Other similar content analyses
indicate that approximately 30 percent of newspaper space and 20 percent of
available time in local television newscasts is devoted to the same themes.[9]
But even given this extraordinary amount of attention, mass media coverage
of crime is highly selective and unrepresentative. In monitoring undertaken
by Graber in 1990 and 1991, for example, she notes:

> *64 percent of the crime stories reported in the* Chicago Tribune *dealt with
> murder in a year when murder made up three-tenths of one percent of the
> actual crimes in the city. By contrast, white collar crime, which is widely
> prevalent and often threatens public health and safety, received little cover-
> age, concealing its seriousness as a social problem.*[10]

Graber also points out that other likely-to-be-reported instances of crime are
among the least representative types of law-breaking. Sexual assaults, for example, represented barely 1 percent of the official police crime reports, but
gained over 8 percent of the crime coverage in the *Tribune*. Conversely, various forms of theft, which make up 85 percent of all crimes in Chicago, gained
only 23 percent of the newspaper's crime coverage.[11]

Table 6-1   Police versus Newspaper Crime Reports, Chicago, 1991:
A Comparison of Police Reports to stories in the *Chicago*
Tribune

Crime	Police reports of Chicago crime		*Tribune* reports of Chicago crime	
Murder	925	0.3%	180	64.0%
Sexual assault	3,575	1.1	23	8.2
Assault	42,237	13.1	14	5.0
Theft/Robbery/Burglary	275,101	85.4	65	23.0
Total	321,838	99.9%	282	100.2%

Compiled from police crime reports and newspaper index.
[a]Murder includes attempted murder and manslaughter, sexual assault includes rape; theft includes auto thefts.
Source: Doris A. Graber, *Mass Media and American Politics,* 4th ed. (Washington DC: Congressional Quarterly, 1993), p.119.

Clearly, a murder or rape is more serious than a robbery. And "news" is, after all, the unusual and the unexpected. Even so, the fact that there is a negative relationship between the likelihood of a crime occurring and the likelihood of it being reported distorts public perceptions. Individuals generally assess the relative safety of their communities in terms of the very selective news accounts they see and hear, rather than by more objective measures, such as uniform crime statistics for their region. Not surprisingly, heavy news consumers thus tend to overestimate the extent and seriousness of crime in their own communities.[12]

The Attraction of the Unusual: Three Reasons

In addition to the obvious news value of particularly brutal or sadistic acts, three essential factors account for this tendency to emphasize the least likely kinds of criminal behavior. One is our voyeuristic fascination with reports and portrayals of human violence. We might want to exempt ourselves from this dark impulse, but the fact is that there is a kind natural fascination with the details of crime. As the durability of crime dramas and tabloid newspapers suggests, there is entertainment value in narrations about the misdeeds of others. These stories interest and entertain us, even while we protest our distaste and outrage. We describe crime as one of the nation's most serious problems; but we use its basic elements to fabricate our most profitable forms of entertainment.

In a broad sense, art has always had an uneasy but profitable alliance with its audiences when it comes to portraying murder, rape, and other forms of brutality. Public discourse that documents in words or images the "inhuman" acts of others helps moralize us. We are drawn in by the artist or author who provides graphic evidence of our own failings. Stunning images of the rape and murder of the mythical Sabines of ancient Italy, for example, have been repeatedly captured by artists and sculptors. Nicolas Poussin's famous version in New York's Metropolitan Museum is both romantic and horrific, beautiful and violent. The picture is an allegory about power and subjugation, but it is also a vivid depiction of victimage in the face of unbridled power. Its attraction in some senses mirrors the stories captured in the violent *film noir* murder mysteries produced in great numbers by Warner Brothers in the 1940s, and in Alfred Hitchcock's 1960 classic *Psycho*. Nearly every form of media—news, the feature film, and the novel—keeps entertaining us with similar images adapted to their particular contexts: as "high" art such as a David Mamet play about campus sexual harassment,[13] or in the lower arts of commercial film genres.

A second factor contributing to high interest in crime reporting is the emotional reward of a "just" verdict. As we have noted, the legal process mirrors the very human tendency to identify and label victims and villains. The public sanctions of a trial and the sense of closure that it offers provides an important kind of social glue. Even trials with inconclusive cases end in conclusive outcomes, officially designating the innocent and the guilty. They benefit from a sense of legitimacy that a state-sanctioned trial confers.

To be sure, there can be exceptions. When four Los Angeles police officers were acquitted of charges in the 1991 beating of motorist Rodney King, the resulting public disbelief contributed to rioting that took nearly fifty lives and destroyed property worth over $1 billion.[14] The eighty-one-second tape of the beating made by a bystander had created widespread expectations that the police would be found guilty of using excessive force.

A third and potent political role performed by the legal process involves the tendency of individuals to interpret mass media accounts of crimes and trials in terms of class and social tensions. Layers of class fantasies and resentments that may lie dormant can suddenly surface in a high-visibility trial. Participants in a proceeding may come to stand in as convenient symbols of races and classes of people. The trial itself may be transformed. The state will not only decide on the guilt or innocence of particular parties, but the status of an entire class who have come to identify with victims or defendants.

These defendants become what Murray Edelman called "condensation symbols"[15] and Kenneth Burke described as "synechdoches."[16] They are stand-ins for many others who see the case as a mirror of their own injuries or social grievances. Those represented by these symbols come to stand for an entire issue, and often for the group they have sometimes involuntarily come to represent. In the context of recent headlines, "they" may include a young woman seeking admission to an all-male college, a member of the Senate facing expulsion over the charges of sexual harassment or misuse of funds, a "law-abiding" subway rider who shoots several youths who ask for money, or Moslems assumed to be involved in the bombing of a federal facility. As condensation symbols they become identified—however accurately or inaccurately—with certain identifiable traits of heroism or villainy. As synecdoches, they enter the long process of crime and punishment as singular representations of what is "right" or "wrong," "just" or "unjust" in the society.

A classic case of an event producing a synecdochal figure was the assault of a jogger in New York's Central Park in 1989. The young woman—white, well-educated, and a bright executive for a Wall Street investment firm—was found barely alive. She had been raped and repeatedly assaulted. Doctors wondered whether she would survive a crushed skull and severe internal injuries. The news media regularly pointed out that her assailants were African American: six boys between the ages of fourteen and sixteen, some of whom confessed to the assault. The headlines of the New York tabloids took little space to set the tone of the story:

"Central Park Horror,"
"Wolf Pack's Prey,"
"Female Jogger Near Death After Savage Attack by Roving Gang,"
"Rape Suspect: 'It Was Fun.' "[17]

Given the polarized racial tensions of the city, the case had become something more than the wheels of justice dealing with yet another grizzly assault. Trials can be seen by the public as tests of their own social subgroup's political strength. The case of the jogger had taken on the role of a moral drama, carrying out the fantasies and fears of many New Yorkers for whom one's skin color was perceived to be a significant marker in defining loyalties and enemies. Its various participants came to be seen by many as synechdoches in a larger war. As Joan Didion described it, the prosecution of the defendants in the trial became a way for many blacks and whites to identify with two very different visions of social relations in New York:

One vision, shared by those who had seized upon the attack on the jogger as an exact representation of what was wrong with the city, was of a city systematically ruined, violated, raped by its underclass. The opposing vision, shared by those who had seized upon the arrest of the de-

*fendants as an exact representation of their own victimization, was of a
city in which the powerless had been systematically "ruined, violated,
raped by the powerful."[18]*

Trials thus draw our attention because of our basic fascination with
crime and our desire to identify villains and victims, and because they sometimes represent larger differences of class and status across the society.

The Reemergence of the Mega-Trial

A related phenomenon that helps keep crime news near the top of the national agenda is the court trial that has enormous media coverage. These trials are not particularly new to American life. The 1935 trial of Bruno Richard
Hauptmann for the kidnapping of the child of Charles Lindburgh contained
excesses of reporting and publicity-seeking that transformed the sleepy town
of Flemington, New Jersey, into a national media circus.[19] Yet in recent years
television has given these kinds of trials new immediacy and visibility.
Aided by the judiciary's increasing willingness to allow cameras in the courtroom, and by the enormous amounts of time now available to television programmers on Cable News Network (CNN) and the Court TV, live trial
coverage can now approximate what had been available only to spectators
on the scene. Consider the following cases:

- A 1984 trial of six Portuguese immigrants accused of the gang rape of a
  women in a New Bedford, Massachusetts, bar was carried live by CNN
  for several hours a day. CNN sometimes cut away for other news segments, but was usually careful to return to live coverage when the testimony was particularly lurid. Noted one of the network's writers, "Let's
  face it, they are running the trial because of its sexy nature. I do not think
  any of us is so naive to believe that ratings are not a factor. And ratings
  are up."[20]
- The retrial of the Rhode Island socialite Claus von Bulow for the attempted murder of his wealthy wife achieved something of the status of
  a national obsession in the last half of the 1980s, producing not only a
  string of steady news stories, but a best-selling book by one of the attorneys and a popular film based on it. As Susan Drucker and Janice
  Hunold have noted, the trial and its players became household names.
  "There was continuing comprehensive coverage in *Newsweek* and *Time*.
  Daily coverage on national network and local news reflected the presence of more than two hundred media people. Cable News Network
  (CNN) broadcast the proceedings. There were nationally televised interviews. The stepchildren, Alex and Ala, appeared on '60 minutes' to label

von Bulow a liar. The defendant himself told Barbara Walters on ABC's '20/20' that he loved his wife. A heated debate on ABC's 'Nightline' addressed the contention that 'money available on both sides may have distorted justice.' "[21]

- The trial of O. J. Simpson for the double murder of his wife and her friend saturated the American consciousness for nearly a year. No criminal trial had ever recieved so much live television coverage and accompanying media speculation. At various points the networks, CNN, E-Entertainment television, and Court TV covered the proceedings, with especially extensive coverage from the cable networks. Over the enormous period of the trial the interest of the public sometimes waivered, but not before the networks saw a precipitous decline in daytime ratings. Television industry observers attributed that downturn to the decision of CNN and E-Entertainment to stay with long-term coverage of the trial, which significantly boosted their ratings and advertising revenues.[22] The effects of this coverage were uncertain. The proceedings probably offered the first opportunity for many to see the rituals and procedures of a criminal trial. For others, witnessing long stretches of complicated argument involving DNA analysis of blood at the scene, and the maneuvers of the prosecution and defense were probably confusing and annoying. Few, however, could have missed the obvious and unsettling conclusion of the long and expensive trial. In the United States there are vast differences between the legal resources available to the poor and to the wealthy.

THE CHANGING NATIONAL PERSONA: "VICTIMS" IN SEARCH OF JUSTICE?

Over the last two decades a number of social critics and observers have claimed that, while some American values have remained relatively constant, others have undergone a gradual change. It is still our "moral" tendency to seek justice—frequently punishment—for those who have violated important codes of conduct. We also seek vindication for individuals and groups who have been unfairly victimized, and with whom we indentify. What *has* seemed to shift over the last several decades are our ideas about personal responsibility. More and more, note writers such as Christopher Lasch and Thomas Szasz,[23] we are defining various forms of dysfunctional behavior in terms of the failures of someone or something else. It is increasingly part of our culture to see ourselves as the products of other people's actions or influences.

The extent to which we view ourselves as free agents responsible for our own successes and failures is partly a matter of personal philosophy. But in the recent past the idea of individual responsibility has been eroded by the view held by many in the social sciences that there are many social and biological influences on behavior. There is also some psychological comfort in seeing ourselves as victims or beneficiaries of someone else's actions, or—at the very least—of chemical or physical predispositions that are beyond our own control. This may seem an abstract and somewhat philosophical point, but it helps explain the increasing prevalence and importance of litigation in American life.

Psychiatrist Thomas Szasz was among the first to develop the argument that the social sciences in particular have explained away the idea of human choice, replacing it with scores of bogus "illnesses" or biological tendencies that are beyond the control of the individual. In a battle that still rages, to cite one instance, Szasz takes the view that alcoholism is not a medical condition but a habit. He argues that to label someone's drinking behavior as a "disease"—as does the self-help group Alcoholics Anonymous—allows them to escape personal and moral responsibility for their actions. In his view, by renaming defects of character as illnesses, the individuals can shift the burden of responsibility to others.[24]

More broadly, John Taylor has identified the phenomenal growth of a mindset he describes as our "culture of victimization," noting that we now share a general attitude that if something bad happens to a person, someone else is probably responsible:

> It's a strange phenomenon, this growing compulsion of Americans of all creeds, colors, and incomes, of the young and the old, the infirm and the robust, the guilty as well as the innocent, to ascribe to themselves the status of victims to try to find someone or something else to blame for whatever is wrong or incomplete or just plain unpleasant about their lives.[25]

Taylor notes that "victim status not only confers the moral superiority of innocence. It enables people to avoid taking responsibility for their own behavior."[26] Thus, where members of previous generations may have been willing to accept the consequences of their life choices—compounded with the uneven access we all have to certain "givens," such as one's own family history—their offspring are more apt to attribute their success or failure to others. They may come to see themselves as the victims of problems largely determined by institutional, parental, or even genetic forces. Taylor cites several features of the culture of victimization.

Psychic Exhibitionism

It is increasingly acceptable to discuss the crises in one's personal life in terms of its emotional effects and possible external causes. Television and radio talk shows are now often constructed around a panel of guests sharing intimate details about their afflictions. The dominant themes of most television talk shows—"Geraldo," "Oprah," "Sally Jessy Raphael"—are those involving personal traumas or dysfunctional behavior. These popular shows are just the most visible part of a larger pattern in American life that has seen a shift in interest away from the formal and public roles of people and in favor of what is often an intense preoccupation with private issues.[27]

In a society that fosters psychic exhibitionism, embarrassment gives way to a sense of entitlement. Whatever failures are identified with the guests on television and radio talk shows—wife beating, child abandonment, excessive gambling, and so on—are understood to be partly mitigated by extenuating circumstances that deserve understanding rather than criticism. These panelists are often presented and defended as individuals with life histories or personal circumstances that "explain" their actions. And television talk show hosts such as Phil Donahue and Oprah Winfrey usually add a thin veneer of therapeutic rhetoric to the discussion, increasing our sense that the confessor is really a victim, entitled to our sympathy rather than rebukes.

Old-fashioned shame, with its corollary of personal responsibility and guilt, has been replaced by a sense of justified blame. In Taylor's prosaic words, "The United States is becoming a nation of belligerent shirkers, of pouting, mewling finger-pointing crybabies."[28]

Litigation as a Panacea

The courts have increasingly become an outlet for individuals who feel that they have been victimized by others. Taylor recalls the widely reported case of a New Jersey woman who sued several tabacco companies after she had contracted lung cancer.

> *After smoking a pack and a half of cigarettes a day for 40 years, she didn't blame herself for stupidly ignoring the warning labels on cigarette packs, as well as the American Cancer Society's ubiquitous ads decrying the hazards of smoking and the continual barrage of reports on television and in the papers linking it to death. She didn't accept, with a shrug, the fact that she had gambled with her health and lost.*[29]

The last several decades have seen an explosion of civil and criminal suits brought against institutions and organizations alleging a host of imagined and sometimes real forms of victimage: racial or sexual discrimination, sexual harassment, causing an accident, inadequate medical care, faulty maintenance of facilities, giving bad advice, making allegedly defective products, creating unsafe work environments, and so on. Certainly not all such cases are frivolous. But many are. And the now common structure of contingency fees used by attorneys specializing in class action or personal injury cases (collecting a portion of a cash settlement in lieu of a fee) encourages and legitimizes some types of "speculative" litigation.[30]

It would be a mistake to assume that all of this is more legal than political. As Robert Hughes has noted, "a polity obsessed with therapies and filled with distrust of formal politics" is bound to produce a dishonest political language.[31] Collective action, the basis of useful political discourse, is hindered by psychologies of victimage that legitimize scenarios of persecution and victimage. The long-term effect of this tendency is polarizing and alienating, putting the individual or the group ahead of the polity. As Hughes observes, Thomas Jefferson or other icons of our political past would be unelectable today; their faith in a public rhetoric that embraces "the legitimate interests of others" would be replaced with a search for scapegoats. "When political utterance descends to such levels, fanatics enlist in the crusade, but sensible people tend to wash their hands of it."[32] The public forum withers under the weight of a society that has fragmented into self-absorbed individuals.

MAKING NEWS AND SHAPING OPINIONS: ISSUES OF TRIAL REPORTING

Extensive mass media coverage of crime news has led some—including a recent Supreme Court Chief Justice—to urge that press access to trials should be curbed.[33] In recent years concerns have increased over the rights of the accused, the victims of crimes, and those ordinary citizens who are asked to testify or sit in judgment. There can be little doubt that the Sixth Amendment's mandate to conduct a speedy and impartial trial is sometimes made more difficult under the intense scrutiny of the press. But the same amendment also calls for a "public" trial, creating the kind of constitutional paradox that often accompanies discussion of the media's roles in American life. Sorting out these issues of media access to legal proceedings—ranging from requests to televise arguments given before the Supreme Court, to the withholding of names of rape victims in the news media—now represents a major legal specialization.[34] What follows is a summary of several important issues of media access that have been in dispute.

Issues of Privacy

Although its constitutional origins are less certain than those of other protected rights, most legal theorists and most Americans believe in an individual's right to privacy. We believe we have a right to be left alone, to carry out aspects of our private lives without intense public scrutiny. There may be times, however, when the threshold that separates private information from legitimate "news" can be difficult to define. Consider, for example, the following newsgathering instances:

- A newspaper reports that a popular sports celebrity has disclosed to family and close friends that he is HIV-Positive. The celebrity later confirms the story, but expresses resentment that the press did not "protect my privacy or the privacy of my family."
- A tabloid pays free-lance journalists to go through the garbage of a famous person, and to photograph that celebrity while he is on vacation.
- A newspaper prints the name of a thirteen-year-old girl who was the victim of a brutal assault and rape.
- A television station routinely uses video footage of wives, husbands, and parents at the moment they receive police notification of the death of a family member.
- A paper reprints conversations overheard on a cellular phone frequency that imply that a member of Congress is a "party animal" and a "recreational" cocaine user.
- A television station asks permission to photograph the execution of a prisoner convicted of a capital crime.
- A judge grants permission to a local television station to carry live coverage of a highly publicized murder trial.

Each of these instances is based on an actual case. And while each involves different legal and moral issues, all of them raise the same basic issue of privacy.

Concerns over privacy raise a fundamental question: At what point does the freedom of the press guaranteed by the First Amendment, as well as our collective need to know about the major events of the day, conflict with the desire of individuals to live through moments of their lives with a certain degree of privacy? Are there ever compelling reasons to "muzzle" a free press?

There are no easy answers to these questions, although the courts and countless codes of professional conduct have routinely considered similiar situations in which privacy is at stake.[35] Many Americans are clearly uncomfortable with the aggressive and sometimes thoughtless and cruel intrusions of newsgatherers into the lives of ordinary people.[36] And yet we generally endorse the idea that information is a valuable commodity, and accurate information-gathering is a worthy enterprise. In addition, among the strongest ideals of open, democratic societies are the twin conditions of freedom of expression and the right to know. As First Amendment scholar Rodney Smolla notes:

> *Free expression serves the collective search for truth through the market-place of ideas, and the needs of the polity in facilitating democratic self-government. Free expression also, however, serves needs unrelated to the collective good; it is an end itself, an end intimately intertwined with human autonomy and dignity.*[37]

In this simple statement Smolla makes both the easy and the more difficult case for unfettered expression. The easy claim is that a society needs to have complete information in order to make intelligent judgments about their ideas. The tougher claim is that free expression is itself an absolute good: "an end itself." And while he opts for a some restrictions on the kinds of personal information that should be published,[38] it is by no means certain who should enforce such a ban.

It is important here to make a distinction between accurate and inaccurate information. There seems to be no justifiable defense for distributing inaccurate information, even government-sanctioned "disinformation" intended to mislead an enemy. Libel laws offer some redress to individuals ("ordinary" citizens more than public figures) who believe their reputations have been harmed by press reports that are grossly inaccurate.[39] But it is far more difficult—as it probably ought to be—to gag the press as it engages in the process of newsgathering.

The nation's courts have generally opted for a wide interpretation of the First Amendment by limiting the power of individuals to seek legal redress for invasion of privacy, especially if the work of these individuals invites public attention, or if they have become part of a legal proceeding such as a trial. In practical terms, for example, actors and other celebrities lose part of their claims to privacy by the public nature of their work, as do persons— even young victims and offenders—identified in the normal process of a courtroom trial.[40]

On a day-to-day basis, the right to privacy is often considered as one of only several factors that weigh in on how a news story will be presented. Most journalists want to be fair and may have at least a practical sense of journalistic ethics. But they also live in a business climate where the decisions of the competition and the need for higher circulation numbers may shape their news judgment.

Imagine a story providing information about the suicide of a popular civic and business leader. How much detail about his death is needed to tell the story? Are pictures from the scene—or of family members stricken with grief—essential to the narrative? In a child-custody case involving another local political leader and his estranged wife, how much of the per-

sonal information about his income, living arrangements, and sexual orientation are relevant to the story? Does it matter that his own testimony
indicates that he is not on speaking terms with his parents, or that he has
accumulated an enormous amount of debt? Each separate outlet tends to
define its journalistic limits, ranging from the tabloid television show that
will use nearly any photo or piece of information to attract an audience,
to more circumspect members of the press who are likely to make decisions on what to publish based on determinations of what the public needs
(rather than wants) to know.

CNN, for example, used a blue dot to cover the face of a Palm Beach,
Florida, woman who had charged William Kennedy Smith with rape. They
also sought to protect her privacy by momentarily deleting their audio feed
when her name was mentioned. Yet it seems apparent that the news network extensively covered the 1991 trial largely because the subject was
rape and the defendant was a member of a prominent political family.[41]
CNN was among more than three hundred reporters assigned to the trial,
and not all of them honored the practice of concealing the identity of the
alleged victim.

There is a great deal of public disapproval directed to what many see as
the intrusive media.[42] Yet, as we have already noted in this chapter, there is
also an enormous public appetite for the private details of people living mar-
ginal or dysfunctional lives.

Pretrial Publicity

It is important to keep the criminal process in some perspective. In the
United States, abouty 90 percent of all cases involving crimes against persons
and property are plea-bargained. That is, there is no trial and no jury verdict.
In place of a trial there is an agreement that is reached between the prosecution, the defense, and the court. This agreement usually involves a guilty
plea that is offered by the defense in exchange for a reduced sentence.[43] The
relatively small number of cases that do actually go to trial in the United
States do so against a backdrop of low public awareness. Jurors are easily
found who know nothing about the case, and can—at least in theory—hear
the evidence unprejudiced by prior press coverage.

In a significant but very small number of cases such as "mega-trials" the
need to find a panel of impartial jurors is made more difficult by the advance
publicity that has preceded it. In the first trial to prosecute the four Los
Angeles police officers in the beating of motorist Rodney King, for example,
it fell to the court to find jurors who could convince the prosecution and the
defense that they had not been influenced by the publicity of the case, especially the widely shown-amateur video of the officers subduing and beating

King. By nearly any measure, the pretrial publicity surrounding the event was intense.

Of course, trial lawyers cannot control early reporting about a criminal case. But the courts often caution their clients from talking to the press. The very malleable ethical guidelines set down by the American Bar Association leave plenty of room for different interpretations about how much publicity is too much. The ABA notes:

> *A lawyer shall not make an extra-judicial statement that a reasonable person would expect to be disseminated by means of public communication if the lawyer knows or reasonably should know it will have a substantial likelihood of materially prejudicing an adjudicative proceeding.*[44]

The conventional wisdom about pretrial publicity is that the press sometimes "tries and convicts" a defendant before he or she has had his or her day in court, and courts work mightily to curb such publicity. But neither view is fully accurate. There is no question that pretrial publicity *can* effect a legal outcome. What is less known is that attorneys sometimes employ public relations techniques and experts to win sympathy for their clients. San Fransicso's flamboyant Melvin Beli has remarked that pretrial communication with the press is "an opening statement before the [trial's] opening statement."[45] Many celebrity attorneys like Beli believe that prosecutors frequently use their offices as publicity machines, holding dramatic press conferences and releasing details about evidence that leave defendants at a public relations disadvantage. Judges admonish lawyers on both sides to curb their statements to the press.[46] But the practice of attempting to influence public opinion in advance of a trial goes on in high-visibility cases.

Lawyers representing William Kennedy Smith, for example, hired Washington publicist Barbara Gamarekian to handle press requests for interviews and statements. Among her most successful efforts prior to the rape trial was a flattering profile of defense lawyer Roy Black, and photo opportunities with Smith showing his "human" side. One such photo of the defendent with his new labrador puppy was picked up by the Associated Press and published in hundreds of newspapers.[47]

Confidentiality of Sources

One of the most interesting First Amendment issues involves a journalist's right to keep his or her sources confidential. The issue does not arise often, but when it does, it dramatically pits a whole cluster of constitutional and moral principles against one another. It is not unusual for a journalist to explore issues of crime and corruption by promising anonymity to sources who can provide useful information. Members of street gangs, drug users, and others engaged in illegal activities will sometimes consent to tell what they know on the condition that their names will not be used. At other times investigative work may uncover wrongdoing, but a promise of confidentiality may be necessary to gain access to relevant evidence.

Guarantees of anonymity put journalists in a quandry. Defenders of confidentiality note that one of their most important functions is to cast light on some of the darker aspects of American life. They argue that the individuals who are closest to the edges of social disintegration are a useful resource in correcting the problems that they represent. That information is lost if the press is required to act as extensions of the evidence-gathering apparatus of the police. They see an implied right of "journalistic privilege" in the First Amendment's guarantees of an unencumbered and free press.

The courts often view the issue of confidentiality differently. Citing Sixth Amendment assurances that those charged with a crime have the right to require witnesses to testify to what they know, judges and grand juries often do not accept any absolute right of immunity for the press. Journalists who have information relevant to a criminal or civil case are sometimes sought out—usually through subpoenas that require them to appear—if the officials in the criminal justice process believe that they have collected information useful in solving a crime. Beyond the appearance of the journalist, subpoenas may also include requests for notes or video or film "outtakes" of material not shown on the air.

In 1987, for example, a Detroit television reporter was issued a subpoena for himself and video outtakes from a series he produced on the city's street gangs. Brad Stone's interviews with a number of gang members had been an eye-opening experience for many of the city's television viewers. But he had gained their confidence only on the condition of guaranteeing their anonymity. The police believed that one of the members interviewed was connected to a murder, hence the subpoena of unused video footage that could have helped the witnesses make a positive identification. Stone refused to appear, and was placed in contempt and ordered to jail. Appeals to higher courts failed to reverse the contempt decision. As one appeals judge noted, "The Constitution does not, as it never has, exempt the newsman from performing the citizen's normal duty of appearing and furnishing information relevant to the grand jury's task."[48]

Other journalists using privileged information have fared better. About half of the states now have shield laws that offer some protection against demands for notes and other forms of information.[49] To various degrees, shield laws exist to discourage juries and attorneys from seeking evidence from journalists, usually citing the need to have a vigorous and independent press that can explore issues without being used as extensions of the courts. Requests to testify are still issued in many of those states, but these laws generally prolong the process of gaining access to reporters, making them less attractive as targets for subpoenas.

Another bright spot for the press is the 1980 Privacy Protection Act, which was passed by Congress and signed by Jimmy Carter after a series of police searches of newsrooms for evidence in criminal cases. Prior to the act, the Supreme Court had upheld the right of the police to search the offices of news organizations. The specific case involved a search of the offices of Stanford University's student newspaper. The police hoped to find photos of people who had temporarily occupied that institution's hospital. The law now makes it more difficult for law enforcement agencies to gain search warrants to go through the archives of news organizations.[50]

Television in the Courtroom

In spite of constitutional guarantees assuring the public's right to witness courtroom proceedings, many federal and state courts have been reluctant to grant full access to still cameras and television equipment. Before his death in 1995, former Supreme Court Chief Justice Warren Burger was among the most outspoken critics of cameras in the courtroom. He felt that cameras endangered the judicial process, citing several reasons:

> *(1) That the televising of trials diverts the trial from its proper purpose in that it has an inevitable impact on all the trial participants; (2) that it gives the public the wrong impression about the purpose of trials, thereby detracting from the dignity of court proceedings and lessening the reliability of trials, and (3) that it singles out certain defendants and subjects them to trials under prejudicial conditions not experienced by others.[51]*

In at least a superficial sense, Burger's claims would seem to be without merit. In fact and custom television *is* part of "the press," and thus deserving of First Amendment and Sixth Amendment protection. But few would argue that television is simply the equal of other forms of the press. It obviously carries more influence, both because of the potential size of its audiences, and because—unlike print—it reaches its viewers without the requirement that they exert some effort to understand its content.[52] But Burger's objection is even more succinct. Television's representatives, he notes, "have only the rights of the general public, namely, to be present, to observe the proceedings, and thereafter, if they choose, to report them."[53]

Prior to the trial of O. J. Simpson in 1995, opposition to cameras had been eroding, even while the legal establishment—notably, the higher levels of the federal judiciary and the American Bar Association—remained very cautious. At present forty-seven states allow coverage by cameras.[54] Some federal courts had also allowed cameras, but surprised observers by

Ways to Avoid Contempt Problems

Subpeonas directing reporters to appear in court are usually unwelcome. A *subpeona* is a court order requiring a person to appear as a witness. Failure to have the subpoena "quashed," or dismissed, may result in a court ruling of contempt, which can result in fines and jail terms. Reporters generally do not want to function as witnesses, especially when they have promised anonymity to sources. The following advice from Ronald Lovell suggests courses of action for journalists in response to court requests for information.

Subpoena, Request to Testify

1. Never appear voluntarily as a witness.
2. Be careful in disclosing any information about a story to an attorney even in an informal way.
3. Notify your editor immediately if you get a subpoena, but do not contact the attorney involved; the newspaper's attorney should make the contact to find out the nature of the proceeding and the testimony sought.
4. Do not agree to produce material before any court appearance.

Subpoena, Factual Testimony

1. Seek to have the newspaper's attorney petition the court to quash the subpoena because it would jeopardize the reporter's future work and relationship with sources.
2. Go to court—if you have to go—with an attorney.

Subpoena, Source Names and Notes

1. Notify your editor and the newspaper's attorney as quickly as possible.
2. File any petition to quash the subpoena immediately.
3. Do not discuss anything about the case with anyone, especially the attorney issuing the subpoena.

Search Warrant

1. Assert First Amendment rights to the officers arriving to search the offices of the news organization.
2. Step aside and allow them to search without necessarily volunteering to show them the location of what they want.
3. Make a list of any items taken by police in their search.

From: Ronald P. Lovell, *Reporting Public Affairs* (Belmont, CA: Wadsworth, 1983), pp. 376–377.

announcing that they would discontinue the practice in the fall of 1994, after a three-year experiment.[55] In the states that allow coverage, the presiding judge in a case has discretion to determine what may be presented. In some instances, just the opening and closing statements of attorneys may be allowed. In other instances the wishes of the attorneys and principals in a proceeding are taken into account. And many judges attempt to assess whether the subject matter of the trial will be too explicit or graphic for a general television audience.

To date, New York State has developed the most elaborate procedures for experimenting with television coverage of criminal trials. With generally positive reviews,[56] the courts have permitted greatly expanded broadcasts of trials, even those dealing with murder and rape.

In establishing guidelines, the state sought to avoid some of the major arguments against television coverage, specifically: (1) that testifiers would be intimidated, lessening the chances of a defendant to gain access to all of the evidence in their defense, (2) that the work and identities of undercover police would be compromised, (3) that jurors could be distracted, and (4) that the privacy of individuals required to discuss the personal aspects of their lives would be compromised. Some of the rules proposed by Chief Administrative Judge Albert Rosenthal sought to address some of these issues, and many others. For example:

(a) *No audio pickup or audio broadcast of conferences that occur in a court facility between attorneys and their clients . . . shall be permitted . . . without the prior consent of all the participants. . . .*

(b) *No conference in chambers shall be subject to coverage.*

(c) *No coverage of the selection of the prospective jury . . . shall be permitted.*

(d) *No coverage of the jury, or of any juror or alternate juror, while in the jury box . . . or while going to or from the deliberation room at any time, shall be permitted.*

(e) *No coverage shall be permitted of a witness, who as a peace officer or police officer acted in a covert or undercover capacity in connection with the proceedings being covered, without the prior written consent of such witness.*

(f) *No coverage shall be permitted of a witness, who as a peace officer or police officer is currently engaged in a covert or undercover capacity, without the prior written consent of such witness.*

(g) *No coverage shall be permitted of the victim in a prosecution for rape, sodomy, sexual abuse, or other sex offense. . . .*

(h) *No coverage of any participant shall be permitted if the presiding trial judge finds that such coverage is liable to endanger the safety of any person.*[57]

(i) *Witnesses and defendants can exercise the right to have their images electronically blotted out, as in the William Kennedy Smith trial.*[58]

The effect of extensive and sometimes obsessive coverage of O. J. Simpson led many judges and attorneys to rethink their support for televison. That the trial as presented on CNN and elsewhere had become a national obsession is obvious. The day the not-guilty verdict was announced

Americans watched in numbers massive enough to affect patterns of national phone and utility consumption and airline usage.[59] Near the end of the case some reporters noted an increased willingness of judges around the country to ban cameras,[60] notably in the last stages of the trial of Susan Smith for the murder-by-drowning of her two children, and the retrial of Erik and Lyle Menendez for the murder of their parents.[61] Many observers accept some of Chief Justice Burger's reservations, particularly with regard to the trivializing effect of haphazard video coverage of what is a long and sometimes subtle process.[62] Others add their own judgment that—at least in the short term—cameras put additional pressures on lawyers to be glib and pointlessly repetitive.[63]

In the future cameras will probably continue to appear in some highly newsworthy trials at the state level. However, judges will undoubtedly consider the Simpson trial and similar cases in deciding whether their proceedings can be photographed. No doubt they will also consider how much freedom will be given to defense and prosecution teams who may be tempted to expand and extend their cases for the cameras.

CIVIL LAW: LITIGATION AS PUBLIC RELATIONS

In the last quarter century the United States has seen a dramatic rise in the number of lawsuits brought against manufacturers, doctors, government agencies, and the providers of many kinds of services. Typically, these are not criminal cases, but cases involving tort law, which covers the liabilities of corporations, institutions, or individuals based on their alleged negligence. Damages awarded in such suits typically involve money and/or promises to end certain kinds of practices.

There is almost no end to the range of suits that are filed in federal and state courts, ranging from class action suits against car makers alleging faulty design, to efforts to seek damages from school officials over the broken fingers and arms of high school athletes.[64] The sheer number of these cases has contributed to the widely held view that the legal profession has abused the original intentions of laws covering, among other things, product liability and medical malpractice.[65] In 1995 it became one of the most contentious issues in Congress, with the Republican majority pushing reform to limit what its leadership called "abusive lawsuits."[66]

What is sometimes less evident in this explosion of litigation is the increasing participation of social reformers and political activists in the use of the legal system as a force for publicity. Advocates for social and political reform sometimes rely on highly visible lawsuits to raise the consciousness of citizens on matters as diverse as civil rights and environmental issues.

Even against the rising tide of American hostility to the explosion in the number of practicing attorneys and various forms of "junk litigation," defenders of the lawsuit argue that it allows an important kind of redress. Longtime consumer activists Ralph Nader and Joan Claybrook, for example, strike a notably old-fashioned note in arguing that litigation is a fundamental tool in agitating for increased accountability of corporate and political institutions.[67] Nader has became a national force with his highly visible attempts to gain accountability from General Motors, the United States Congress, and many other groups.[68]

Earlier agitators for social reform often came from the fields of medicine, academe, and the political parties. But these traditional sources of change have been partially eclipsed by not-for-profit groups and their activist legal staffs.[69] These organizations exist primarily on the contributions of citizens who are active in the social movement that the group represents. Among the better known have been the Environmental Defense Fund, Center for Auto Safety, Common Cause, the Project for Corporate Responsibility, and the Center for Responsive Law. Since the 1950s, these groups and others like them have had a significant impact in taking the courts into policy areas traditionally left to legislators. By using lawsuits to mandate court enforcment of the increasingly complex web of state and federal laws protecting individual and community rights, they have pushed the judiciary into territory it has been reluctant to claim. Judges and juries frequently must now decide how institutions will be administered, and how broad policies—school busing to desegregate the races, for example—will actually be implemented. This gradual but important shift has not been lost on members of the news media, who now cover the courts not just as deliverers of verdicts defining responsibility or guilt, but as de facto legislators defining the specific responsibilities of agencies and organizations.

The strategy of publicity through litigation is one important component of public interest law. Aside from their legal merits—which may be considerable—suits brought against manufacturers, polluters, and government agencies have intrinsic news value. They are typically not the kinds of actions that corporations or governmental agencies want to debate in the court of public opinion, even though they may well win. A long and drawn-out civil suit accusing a corporation of neglecting its public responsibilities is inevitably going to harm its image, possibly triggering a further litigation or punitive legislative action. On the governmental side, the desire to avoid negative publicity is much the same. What state agency, for example, would want to defend itself against a suit charging it with allowing a hospital to decay into a chaotic and filthy warehouse for children? New York faced that question with regard to its poorly managed Willowbrook Hospital. The persistent reporting of a young ABC television reporter named Geraldo Rivera added to the negative publicity about its conditions.[70] Likewise, few corporations want to engage in a protracted trial over their business or manufacturing practices.

A class action suit against Alcoa Aluminum, for example, had partially achieved the purpose of its Australian initiators, even though they eventually lost in court. The 1981 suit alleged that the American company had expanded its bauxite mining in Western Australia without suitable safeguards to protect the local environment. The fact that citizens of another country had sought redress in an American court gave force to the charge that other forms of advocacy probably could not match. In the end, Alcoa paid a price for appearing not to be a very good corporate citizen, and the environmental leaders who brought the suit increased their clout and visibility.[71]

A similar battle waged by the Environmental Defense Fund (EDF) against the use of the pesticide DDT resulted in both the manifest objective of controlling the chemical's use and increasing the fund's status and ability to influence the public agenda. As Joel Handler notes, the DDT litigation was always viewed as serving these multiple ends. "From the very start, EDF used the litigation to dramatize the dangers of environmental degradation and to launch a massive, and successful, fund-raising drive."[72]

In the immediate future the most visible cases of litigation against an industry group will probably include those targeted at large American tobacco companies. A number of states and groups involved in class action suits undoubtedly have multiple aims in these cases; and some probably include the demonization of the tobacco industry, a process that has already characterized some press coverage and public-service ad campaigns in recent years.[73] For their part, these corporations are finding it increasingly difficult to use legal maneuvers to avoid these high-profile suits.[74] They have also been hurt by damaging publicity that has suggested that a few companies manipulated levels of nicotine to maintain levels of addictive potency.[75]

The industry has tried to counter these cases with a litigation strategy of its own, aggressively pursuing media outlets that quote former employees who have signed agreements of nondisclosure about their work. A host of news organizations have been subpoenaed for documents used in stories about the tobacco industry, including CBS, the *Washington Post*, the *New York Times*, National Public Radio, and *USA Today*.[76] On other occasions outlets such as CBS and ABC have apparently retreated from stories out of fear that they will end up with costly lawsuits initiated by the tobacco industry.[77]

SUMMARY

The American criminal and legal structure represents a variety of processes that fall under the attention of the media, as well as the executive and legislative branches of government. Even though simple flow charts would seem to suggest that the legal process is largely beyond the pressures experienced by other political bodies, the truth is far more complex. At particular moments the courts and their officers can emerge as active agents in the shaping of the American news agenda. In very diverse ways, significant moments of civil and criminal proceedings are offered to the American public as partial answers to the oldest and most basic of all queries in the information age: "How safe am I, and how safe is my world?"

In this chapter we have noted that popular accounts of crimes and trials can represent an important kind of political spectacle. Crime news represents a sizable segment of the daily output of print and broadcast journalism. It is also an agenda-setting issue that feeds on an unquenchable national appetite for reports detailing how victims were violated, and how the state will judge those who are held responsible.

Several reasons account for the durability of crime and litigation journalism. Reports of trials represent an ancient kind of public ritual that allows members of a culture to share in the psychologically satisfying process of retribution. Whatever gaps exist between the ideal and the reality, we want to see the "justice" of state-enforced sanctions given to the guilty. This need is even more intense when a highly visible trial involves individuals who have become social symbols, carrying either the hopes or the enmity of groups energized by racial or social conflict.

Trials also follow a logic that has found a place in the changing American character. Legal proceedings depend on the idea of victimage: the view that a person's or a group's fate has been unfairly limited by the actions of others. This tendency to mitigate our own failures by assigning responsibility or blame to others is evident in much of the therapeutic rhetoric of the television talk show and the self-help manual. It is also a rationale for using litigation as an attempt to formally assign blame. In public interest law, for example, litigation is used to hold government, corporations, and institutions responsible for various kinds of community or personal conditions. A potent feature of some of this litigation is that it is undertaken in part for its publicity value.

Television and other forms of mass communication responded to the heightened profile of criminal and civil litigation by seeking ways to increase their overall access. Many states now have shield laws that make it more difficult for the courts to see notes or learn the names of confidential sources who may be called in a legal proceeding. Others are experimenting with partial or full broadcast coverage of trials. This access has intensified concern over the loss of privacy for those victims and witnesses who are sometimes unwilling participants. It has also raised concerns about how pretrial publicity and extended television coverage—typified in the prosecution of O. J. Simpson—will affect public attitudes, as well as the performance of jurors, lawyers, defendants, and judges.

NOTES

1. William F. Lewis, "Power, Knowledge, and Insanity: The Trial of John W. Hinkley, Jr." in *Popular Trials: Rhetoric, Mass Media, and the Law*, ed. Robert Hariman (Tuscaloosa: University of Alabama Press, 1990), p. 132.

2. See, for example, Chaim Perelman, *The Idea of Justice and the Problems of Argument*, trans. John Petrie (London: Humanities, 1963).

3. For a general discussion on the nature of the political symbolism and its "hyperreal" place in popular discourse, see Murray Edelman, *Constructing the Political Spectacle* (Chicago: University of Chicago Press, 1988) pp. 1–11.

4. Joan Didion, *After Henry* (New York: Simon and Schuster, 1992), p. 284.

5. In 1995, for example, former prosecutor Ed Rendel of Philadelphia won a second term as mayor, following the path of one of the state's senators, Arlen Spector. Many federal and state elected officials come with similar experience as prosecutors, attorneys, or attorneys general.

6. Martin Gottlieb, "Racial Split at the End, as at the Start," *New York Times*, October 4, 1995, pp. A1, A12.

7. Bill Carter, "Amy Fisher Story a Surprise Smash in 3 TV Movies," *New York Times*, January 5, 1993, p. C11.

8. Doris Graber, "Is Crime News Coverage Excessive?" *Journal of Communication*, Summer 1979, pp. 83–85.

9. Janice Schuetz, "Narrative Montage: Press Coverage of the Jean Harris Trial," *Journal of the American Forensic Association*, Fall 1988, p. 65.

10. Doris Graber, *Mass Media and American Politics*, 4th ed. (Washington, DC: Congressional Quarterly Press, 1993), p. 332.

11. Ibid., p. 119.

12. Walter B. Jaehing, David H. Weaver, and Frederick Fico, "Reporting Crime and Fearing Crime in Three Communities," *Journal of Communication*, Winter 1981, pp. 95–96.

13. The play is entitled "Oleanna." For a discussion of its themes of sexual harassment, see "He Said . . . She Said . . . Who Did What?" *New York Times*, November 15, 1992, p. H6.

14. Seth Mydans, "Tape May Help U.S. Prosecute Police Beating," *New York Times*, January 25, 1993, p. A12.

15. Murry Edelman, *The Symbolic Uses of Politics* (Urbana: University of Illinois, 1967), pp. 1–13.

16. Kenneth Burke, *A Grammer of Motives* (New York: Prentice-Hall, 1954), p. 503.

17. Didion, *After Henry*, p. 255.

18. Ibid., p. 300.

19. See, for example, Carol Wilkie, "The Scapegoating of Bruno Richard Hauptmann: The Rhetorical Process in Prejudicial Publicity," *Central States Speech Journal*, Summer 1981, pp. 101–110.

20. William A. Henry III, "When News Becomes Voyeurism," *Time*, March 26, 1984, p. 64.

21. Susan Drucker and Janice Hunold, "The Claus von Bulow Retrial: Lights, Camera, Genre?," in Hariman, *Popular Trials*, p. 135.

22. David Tobenkin, "Reality Programs Cut Back O. J. Intake," *Broadcasting and Cable*, May 22, 1995, p. 24.

23. See Christopher Lasch, *The Culture of Narcissism* (New York: Norton, 1979), pp. 3–30, and Thomas Szasz, *The Myth of Mental Illness: Foundations of a Theory of Personal Conduct* (New York: Hoeber-Harper, 1961).

24. Richard E. Vatz and Lee S. Weinberg, *Thomas Szasz: Primary Values and Major Contentions* (Buffalo, NY: Prometheus Books, 1983), pp. 126–127.

25. John Taylor, "Don't Blame Me," *New York Magazine*, June 3, 1991, p. 28.

26. Ibid.

27. For explorations of this trend, see Richard Sennett, *The Fall of Public Man* (New York: Vintage, 1978), pp. 269–268.

28. Taylor, "Don't Blame Me," p. 28.

29. Ibid., p. 26.

30. Walter K. Olson, *The Litigation Explosion* (New York: Plume, 1991), pp. 247–270.

31. Robert Hughes, *Culture of Complaint* (New York: Oxford, 1993), p. 4.

32. Ibid., p. 31.

33. Bob Woodward and Scott Armstrong, *The Brethren: Inside the Supreme Court* (New York: Simon and Schuster, 1979), p. 421.

34. For a thorough overview of this field, see Ralph L. Holsinger, *Media Law*, 2d ed. (New York: McGraw Hill, 1991).

35. See, for example, Richard L. Johannesen, *Ethics in Human Communication, 2d ed.* (Prospect Heights, IL: Waveland, 1987), pp. 147–148.

36. Peter Stoler, *The War Against the Press* (New York: Dodd and Mead, 1986), p. 186.

37. Rodney A. Smolla, *Free Speech in an Open Society* (New York: Knopf, 1992), p. 119.

38. See ibid., pp. 119–150.

39. In most states libel laws seek to protect individuals whose character has been wrongly defamed or severely harmed in the press. These laws typically do not define criminal behavior, but the right of the libeled to win damages. In theory, these laws do not protect individuals who have been the subject of embarrasing but true reports. Nor do libel cases typically move to a successful conclusion if a public figure has been attacked simply with flamboyant or exaggerated criticism. In most cases public figures who sue for damages must prove that the claims made about them are not only not true, but were published with actual malice. That is, the plaintiff must prove that the publisher knew that they were not true, or had a total disregard for their accuracy. Although there have been several spectacular victories against the press in the last few years, the standard of proving actual malice has long given the press an edge in defeating libel suits. For general background, see Holsinger, *Media Law*, pp. 90–126. For a review of successful suits against CBS and *Time* magazine, see Renata Adler, *Reckless Disregard* (New York: Knopf, 1986).

40. Holsinger, *Media Law*, pp. 195, 209–244.

41. David A. Kaplan, "Remove That Blue Dot," *Newsweek*, December 16, 1991, p. 26.

42. See, for example, Clifford G. Christians, Kim B. Rotzoll, and Mark Fackler, *Media Ethics*, 2d ed. (New York: Longman, 1987), pp. 109–123.

43. Howard Abakinsky, *Discretionary Justice: An Introduction to Discretion in Criminal Justice* (Springfield, IL: Charles C. Thomas, 1984), p. 68.

44. Quoted in Timothy Harper, "When Your Case Hits the Front Page," *American Bar Association Journal*, July 1984, p. 82.

45. Quoted in ibid., p. 79.

46. Jan Hoffman, "May It Please the Public," *New York Times*, April 22, 1994, pp. B1, B7.

47. Susanne Roschwalb and Richard Stack, "Litigation Public Relations," *Communications and the Law*, December 1992, p. 21.

48. Quoted in Holsinger, *Media Law*, pp. 311–312.

49. Thomas Tedford, *Freedom of Speech in the United States*, 2d ed. (New York: McGraw Hill, 1993), pp. 248–249.

50. See Holsinger, *Media Law*, pp. 322–336.

51. Quoted in Warren Freedman, *Press and Media Access to the Criminal Courtroom* (New York: Quorum Books, 1988), p. 52.

52. Media theorist Joshua Meyrowitz notes that television, unlike print, lacks any limiting "access code." Individuals have to attain a certain degree of ability and maturity to make sense of the printed page. Television, he argues, makes no such demand. See Meyrowitz, *No Sense of Place* (New York: Oxford, 1985), pp. 74–97.

53. Quoted in Freedman, *Press and Media Access*, p. 52.

54. Paul Thaler, *The Watchful Eye: American Justice in the Age of the Television Trial* (New York: Praeger, 1994), p. xx.

55. The future of federal court limits is unclear. For a recent overview of the issues, see Lyle Denniston, "A Reversal on Cameras in Federal Courts," *American Journalism Review*, May 1995, p. 50.

56. See, for example, David A. Kaplan, "The Camera Is Proving Its Case in the Courtroom," *New York Times*, December 18, 1988, p. 37; Floyd Abrams, "Watching Steinberg," *New York Times*, January 4, 1989, p. A21; and Dennis Hevesi, "Cameras in the Courtroom: Assessing the Role of the Image on the Screen," *New York Times*, May 24, 1992, p. 40.

57. Quoted in Freedman, *Press and Media Access*, pp. 57–58.

58. Thaler, *The Watchful Eye*, pp. 78–79.

59. N. R. Kleinfield, "A Day (10 Minutes of It) the Country Stood Still, *New York Times*, October 4, 1995, pp. A1, A12.

60. Associated Press, "Simpson Case Backlash Keeps Cameras Out of Other Courtrooms," *New York Times*, September 17, 1995, p. 35.

61. See Kenneth B. Noble, "Why Judge Might have Banned Cameras from Prominent Trial," *New York Times*, October 8, 1995, p. A31.

62. For a representative North American view, see George Bain, "The Criminal Trial as Sport Spectacle," *Macleans*, February 20, 1995.

63. David Stout, "The Jury Is Still out on the Effects of Long Televised Trials," *New York Times*, August 4, 1995, p. B18.

64. See Jethro K. Lieberman, *The Litigious Society* (New York: Basic, 1981), pp. 4–5.

65. See, for example, Lawrence Tribe, "Too Much Law, Too Little Justice," *Atlantic*, July 1979, pp. 25–30; Jeffrey O'Connell, *The Lawsuit Lottery: Only the Lawyers Win* (New York: Free Press, 1979); and "The Rights Explosion: Splintering America?" *U.S. News and World Report*, October 31, 1977, p. 29.

66. Katharine Seelye, "Agendas Clash in Bid to Alter Law on Product Liability," *New York Times*, March 8, 1995, p. A16.

67. Ralph Nader and Joan Claybrook, "Preserving a Pillar of Our Democracy," *Trial*, December 1991, pp. 45–49.

68. Joel F. Handler, *Social Movements and the Legal System: A Theory of Law Reform and Social Change* (New York: Academic Press, 1978), pp. 73–75.

69. Ibid., pp. 1–34.

70. See David J. Rothman and Sheila M. Rothman, *The Willowbrook Wars* (New York: Harper and Row, 1984), pp. 15–65.

71. S. E. Rada, "A Class Action Suit as Public Relations," *Journalism Quarterly*, Spring 1985, pp. 150–154.

72. Handler, *Social Movements*, p. 216.

73. California has been especially aggressive in sponsoring antismoking ads, including one that portrays industry figures as schemers intent on luring new smokers to a lifetime of addiction. See B. Drummond Ayres, Jr., "Phillip Morris on Offensive in California," *New York Times*, May 16, 1994, pp. A1, A12; and Bradley Johnson, "Anti-Smoke Torch Flickers," *Advertising Age*, April 16, 1990, p. 66.

74. Andrew Skolnick, "Spate of Lawsuits," *Journal of the American Medical Association*, April 12, 1995, pp. 1080–1081.

75. John Slade et. al., "Nicotine and Addiction: The Brown and Williamson Documents, *Journal of the American Medical Association*, July 19, 1995, pp. 225–233.

76. Debra Hernandez, "Tobacco Company Subpoenas Several News Organizations," *Editor and Publisher*, June 18, 1994, p. 18.

77. See, for example, Christopher Stern, "ABC Would Rather Not Fight," *Broadcasting and Cable*, August 28, 1995, p. 18.

7

ART, POPULAR ENTERTAINMENT, AND POLITICS

> *If you can write a nation's stories, you needn't worry about who makes its laws.*[1]

Art and politics have never been comfortable companions. We usually assume that the fine arts of the museum and the theater—even the commercial arts of the novel and television—speak to higher values than is found in political discourse. But the political and artistic impulses within the creative communities of any society are not easily separated. Beethoven is reported to have torn up the dedication page of his Third Symphony after hearing that Napoleon Bonaparte had declared himself emperor of the French. Apparently nothing of the grandeur of what is now called the *Eroica* was to be tainted by association with the "new tyrant."[2] Similarly, Diego Rivera came under the wrath of John D. Rockefeller, who commissioned the great Mexican fresco painter to decorate the public entrances of the New York office complex bearing his name. This captain of American industry was willing to condone Rivera's sympathetic murals of toiling workers, but not when one of them included Vladimir Lenin, the founder of the modern Soviet state.[3] Rockefeller had that particular panel destroyed.

Art and politics intersect at one of the busiest thoroughfares of American culture. A society is justifiably defined by the traffic of ideas and values that flows through its art, both "high" and "low." Vice President Dan Quayle was widely criticized in the 1992 presidential campaign for attacking situation-comedy character Murphy Brown. The television newswoman played by Candice Bergen had decided to have a child outside of marriage. But if the vice president's aim was off, his assumptions about the importance of television's icons were probably right. The low arts of mass-produced popular culture especially carry their own messages of praise and blame. Characters are heroes or fools. They make good choices or bad ones. Some live enviable lives that feed on our fantasies of success. Others survive nightmares that dramatize the nightly horrors of the evening news.

The commercial arts of novels, films, and television help establish the frames of reference against which the issues that we have in common as a nation are discussed or ignored. If they are trivial or questionable as art, their wide exposure still makes them important forms of national dialogue. As we consume them—mostly by gazing into our television screens—they represent some of the most vivid sources of our national consciousness. As film critic Richard Schickel has noted, when he was asked why he took the output of the Disney studios seriously:

> *To me it seems clear that the destruction of our old sense of community, the irrational unrationalized growth of our "electronic" culture, the familiar modern diseases of fragmentation and alienation, are in large measure the results of the failure of the intellectual community to deal realistically—and on the basis of solid, even practical knowledge—with the purveyors of popular culture.*[4]

This chapter examines both the assumptions and the concrete effects of viewing the popular arts as extensions of the political media. We start by identifying art as one of the basic tools by which a society views itself. The section that follows explores four basic methods for assessing political meaning in art and popular culture. Using some of these methods, we then turn to the subject of locating levels of political meaning in ostensibly nonpolitical forms of communication, such as the popular film or a television situation comedy. In this section we also look at the uniquely American tendency to see the popular arts as vehicles for the alleged "subversion" of American values. The chapter concludes with a look at the emerging "culture wars" that have placed art and popular culture at the center of some of the most heated political battles.

As is implied in the above examples, "art" is defined here very broadly. The reason is simple. Our concern is less aesthetic than political. Plays, films, music, and photography of vastly different quality can share the common thread of potent description. A symphony by a great composer is unquestionably a "higher" and more enduring form of art than a television show that thrives because it has captured the fleeting approval of advertisers and audiences. But, as the next section amplifies, both may have the same abilities to communicate negative or positive judgments about our national life.[5]

ART AS NARRATION AND PORTRAITURE

Art—much of it anyway—tells stories and paints pictures. Part of the rhetoric of art lies in our use of it to compress and heighten experience. Those large segments that are representational (as opposed to purely abstract) define and communicate a wealth of judgments about the human and institutional relationships that make up the fabric of our common culture. *To a large extent we judge art by judging how efficiently it functions as a commentary on these relationships.*

Rivera's Rockefeller Center murals communicated the dignity of people engaged in ordinary work. Even with the sly addition of a Soviet leader, the murals were generally meant to confer honor on its patron and pride in their viewers. In more recent times Robert Mapplethorpe's much-discussed "X Portfolio" of photographs depicting various homosexual sex fantasies offers a very different message.

Mapplethorpe's photography severely tests our views about creativity as the expression of a nation's collective soul. It is an understatement of enormous proportions to say that his images flaunted social conventions. Before he died of AIDS, he surely knew that his homoeroticism would incite the very kind of gay-bashing he opposed. The commentary in the photographs of the "X Portfolio" was ironic, gross, and confrontational.

When the photos were scheduled for a 1988 show at Washington's Corcoran Gallery (*Robert Maplethorpe: The Perfect Moment*), objections sprang from the important assumption that art has the power to legitimatize its subjects.[6] The photographer's work offended not only Senator Jesse Helms, Pat Robertson's Christian Coalition, and others, but—more importantly—the generalized assumption that the artistic products of a culture should represent its highest achievements. The prestigious gallery had entered the political realm by giving a flamboyant homosexual perspective the imprimatur of a national forum.

As a nation, we generally believe that art should be celebratory, even inspirational. It should create the myths we want to validate and endorse.[7] In the words of the writer and art critic Robert Hughes, American art institutions operate under the mistaken belief that they are "good for us." We expect that their work will be "therapeutic."[8]

Never mind that Hughes and other surveyors of the cultural scene are eager to deflate this view.[9] The fact that this expectation remains widespread helps to explain why dissonant messages such as those communicated by Mapplethorpe can generate political controversy.

METHODOLOGICAL POINTS: THE LIMITS OF "UNMASKING" ART FOR "POLITICAL" MEANING

Before we proceed to explore how important national issues and attitudes gain expression in the popular and entertainment media, four methodological points should be kept in mind as tools for exploring political meaning in artistic content.

Political Meaning Is Not Communicated Uniformly

First, art is complex communication. Like the messy discourse of everyday life, it communicates diverse messages at the same time, partly because we as individuals "read" content so differently. The routes to the politicizing of content always pass through the context of individual experience. Perhaps—but only perhaps—Beethoven's Third or Ninth Symphonies communicate political attitudes to modern audiences. Different listeners will hear different motivations reflected in scores and texts. Listeners who own the recording of conductor Leonard Bernstein's famous Berlin concert celebrating the end of a divided Germany may consider the famous "Ode to Joy" conclusion of the Ninth Symphony as Bernstein intended it, and as Beethoven perhaps intended the Third: as a celebration of human freedom. But in music, as in other cultural forms, audiences construct rather than simply discover meaning.

Consider another example of how content can be interpreted in several different ways. In their own study of political films, analysts Michael Ryan and Douglas Kellner describe the message of the 1979 Academy Award Winner, *Kramer vs. Kramer*, as one where "feminism is put in its place."[10] They see this film in which a mother leaves her son and husband as a defiant statement against women. But the story can be "read" somewhat differently.

It portrays the bonding of a son and father after the breakup of a marriage, a focus that is established in the first few minutes. Suffering from stress and an almost complete inability to cope with her life, Joanna (Meryl Streep) leaves Ted (Dustin Hoffman) and their six-year-old son. She is not featured again until near the end of the film, when she appears with an attorney in a courtroom to make a case for sole custody. In the meantime, the bulk of the story allows us to witness Ted's heroic attempt to gain control over his unraveling life. He is initially unprepared to be a single parent, but he gains a new sense of equilibrium as the months pass. His commitment to his son deepens, and they begin to function as a team. He also scales back his career goals in order to have more time to spend with his son.

In many ways, *Kramer vs. Kramer* stacks the deck. The sacrifices and adjustments that Ted makes to accommodate the demands of parenting make us want him to succeed. We come to see Ted as the parent better able to provide for the child, even as the court exercises what was then the almost inevitable—if heartrending—decision to award custody to the mother.

This modest story of the dissolution of a marriage communicated the progressive point that the courts need to consider custody issues on their merits, not on tradition. It is no attack on feminist values to note that in some instances, a male may better serve as the primary parent. How this film is "read" indicates that there is an enormous diversity in the ways the artifacts of the popular media can be understood.

Art and Entertainment Need to Be Assessed for Their Manifest and Latent Content

Media content can make sense on two very different levels. There are *manifest* or obvious primary meanings in discourse. A film has a plot and characters that are clearly intended and equally well understood. But there is often a more subtle level of meaning as well. By both accident and design art also works on us at a *latent* or *subtextual* level. The very evident realities of a film or any entertainment can be easily extended into symbolically rich layers of meaning that comment on other times, people, and places. *The Wizard of Oz*, for example, was first written as a cautionary tale about the inaction of President William McKinley. We no longer pick up that latent message, but we still enjoy its simple message of determination in the face of the unknown. In the context of the times, messages gain weight and importance because their allegorical aspects resonate with audiences. Thus, film goers have found in Lawrence Kasdin's films *The Big Chill* (1983) and *Grand Canyon* (1991) not just stories about the ebb and flow of friendships. Both also communicate a subtext of societal and cultural failures. They are small morality plays about his generation's alienation from the sense of political participation they felt in their youth.

Even the ostensibly nonpolitical content of prime-time television carries important messages at the latent level. The characters that populate prime-time's family situation comedies generally do not express their political views or identify party loyalties. They are usually not involved in political causes, nor social action groups engaged in battles for American public opinion. Yet most programs carry an attitude—a quiet judgment—about the state of the nation's civil affairs, even if the writers' intention is to leave their characters untouched by the starker realities of modern American life.

Events on the very popular "Cosby Show" proceeded in such a pattern. The Huxtables of Brooklyn, New York, lived an idyllic life, as they continue to do in reruns. Neither the internal stresses felt by many families nor the crime and racial problems plaguing the nation's largest city were allowed to intrude. As Mark Miller points out, the exclusion of some of these problems perhaps carried its own message. The show, he notes, was a denial of harsher truths about race relations, and perhaps served as a symbol of reassurance to a racially polarized America.[11] Black Americans, one could deduce from the show, need only work hard to achieve the American dream.

The subtext in television's "Roseanne" was altogether different a few years later. The Conners of Langford, Illinois, never directly discussed their political views during the 1992 presidential campaign. But in many episodes they seemed to be living out the angst felt by millions of middle-income Americans attempting to stave off the effects of job losses and mounting financial problems. In ways that were never explicit, the encroaching poverty of the Conners was a subtext that made the prospect of "Four More Years" of the Bush administration seem as unwelcome as a bounced check.

The Stories a Nation Tells about Itself Are Sometimes Best Understood by Looking for What Is Missing

Seasoned observers and researchers on the content of prime-time television have often discovered that what is excluded from programming is often more revealing than what is present. The *omission* of certain points of view, types of characters, themes, or lifestyles can function as its own form of powerful social commentary.

Beth Austin, for example, has taken on the makers of modern "emotional blockbuster" pictures such as *When Harry Met Sally* and *Defending Your Life* for being too socially insular. Austin argues that many older films managed to tell interesting stories about people who had well-developed senses of public responsibility in addition to private lives. In *On the Waterfront, High Noon*, and *To Kill a Mockingbird* the central characters were not only governed by their personal desires and needs, but by duties to the communities they were a part of. "A little looking out for the next fella," she writes, "is precisely what filmmakers are leaving out of their family pictures—a dangerous signal to be transmitting to our kids."[12]

Others have pointed out the absence of serious portrayals of differences of class in American films,[13] the neglect of fully developed portrayals of older Americans, mature women, homosexuals, and many categories of people in prime-time television.[14] Part of the significant content of all communication is what its designers have decided to exclude.

Messages Are Sometimes No More than They Seem

A final methodological guideline for understanding political content is perhaps obvious, but important to remember. Some communication must simply be accepted on its own terms. There is little point in searching for significant political content in every cultural artifact. There is probably little meaningful political content in the music of Vivaldi or Little Richard, the paintings of Jean Renoir or Claude Monet, Shakespeare's *Much Ado About Nothing*, or a representative episode of television's "Seinfeld." We doubt that much can be said about the political content of such celluloid epics as *Airplane!* or *Father of the Bride*, or film adaptations of *Little Women* or *Jurassic Park*. Sometimes the best methodological approach to a message is to accept it at face value.

WHEN IS ART POLITICAL?: THREE LEVELS OF MEANING

There is no simple line separating art from politics, or entertainment from political persuasion. But it is useful to look at three levels of political meaning that can exist in the products of the artistic and entertainment industries. First, content may directly advocate a political position, as in the feature documentary, *The War Room*, which presents an endearing portrait of those who ran Bill Clinton's 1992 presidential campaign. Second, it may reconstruct an event from the political past with a certain emphasis or perspective, such as in films like *Quiz Show* and *All the President's Men*, both of which look at episodes of organizational or political corruption. Third and most subtle, the content may indirectly endorse or devalue certain groups—women, homosexuals, military leaders, ethnic groups, and others—who share political objectives or attitudes effecting groups with real political agendas. It is useful to look briefly at each one.

Content as Direct Political Advocacy

Art sometimes becomes part of the ongoing discourse of a period. Rap music, performance art, political cartoons, and popular satire are often the first media forms to carry public controversy beyond the predictable contexts of news shows and legislative debate. Gary Trudeau's president-watching in "Doonesbury," "Tonight Show" monologues, topical novels, television movies, and even song lyrics often accompany the first wave of public discussion of surrounding high-visibility issues. Other different forms of discussion may later emerge in films, art exhibitions, and plays.

Art is frequently used to identify the political villains of a society. In 1937, for example, Germany's Nazi Party held official exhibitions of allegedly "degenerate art," including the works of Paul Gauguin and Vincent van Gogh. Their work was thought to be danger to the public and a threat to the glory of the Third Reich.[15]

More common is the justifiable instinct among members of every creative community to embody their own convictions into their work. Gay activist Randy Shilts, for example, was encouraged to speed up the writing and release of his book defending homosexuals in the military in order to take advantage of the public debate that emerged on that issue in the early months of the Clinton administration. *Conduct Unbecoming: Lesbians and Gays in the Military* eventually became an important reference point on that issue.[16] Filmmaker Michael Moore's attack on General Motors in his 1989 documentary, *Roger and Me*, merges humor and outrage directed to another American institution, General Motors. Moore's deceptively modest search for the chairman of GM only partly conceals his biting indictment of the auto giant, and its alleged broken promises to the residents of Flint, Michigan.

The great Russian symphonist Dimitri Shostakovich deserves credit for using political advocacy in an especially creative way. His stormy Fifth Symphony speaks to its listeners in an ironic subtextual code. Under pressure from the political and music bureaucracies that dominated Soviet arts in the 1930s, the composer apparently used this symphony as a response to criticism that his music was too dour and "modern." Much of the work develops a deliberately forced optimism that brilliantly mocks the music his critics wished he would write. Marches that aren't quite heroic and "pretty" themes that sound vaguely dissonant seem to communicate the pain of an artist whose freedom has been compromised.[17]

Content as the Reconstruction of the Political Past

Another kind of political content flows from the work of artists and writers intent on recreating a past event with political significance. Painters, illustrators, and even stained-glass artisans working in the great medieval cathedrals of Europe were perhaps the first narrators of events deemed important to a community. Their goals—frequently determined by official benefactors—were often propagandistic and generally supportive of a certain perspective. Similarly, huge paintings in the Capitol Rotunda in Washington present scenes depicting the colonization of the United States in idyllic images. In John Trumbull's massive paintings in this ceremonial space the Indians are noble and agreeable; the settlers are respectful and peaceful. This art simplifies and purifies a much more complex political past.

Artist Emanuel Leutze's well-known painting *Washington Crossing the Delaware* is an especially interesting case. The painter's rendering of Washington moments before a crucial Christmas Eve battle gives the colonial leader a dignity and resolve that fits the mythical image. The picture is probably less significant as art than as a national icon. And like much narration with a political view to sell, the rules of successful storytelling may sometimes overtake the truth. Leutze never visited the site north of Trenton, New Jersey, where the crossing from Pennsylvania took place. He also painted the picture in Germany, a fact that may explain why Washington seems to be going the wrong way, and carrying an American flag that was not in common use at the time. It is also doubtful whether so savvy a general would have chosen to stand up in a Durham Boat made unsteady by a swollen, ice-filled river. Such is the nature of historical re-creation. It can feed (and dissident art can sometimes undermine) the myths that may be central a culture's understanding of what it is or wants to be.

On a more elaborate scale, director Oliver Stone's controversial 1991 film, *JFK*, constructs a paranoid narrative of high-level government involvement in the assassination of President Kennedy. It is obviously political because it attributes roles—rather sleazy ones—to institutions charged with acting in the interests of the public. Stone's unbelievable conspiracy theory of the assassination notwithstanding,[18] the film fits into a long history of narratives about our political past, ranging from D. W. Griffith's *Birth of a Nation* (1915) to Tim Robbins's savage 1992 portrayal of a right-wing psuedo-populist in *Bob Roberts* (1992).[19]

Both direct advocacy and historical re-creation represent the easiest kind of political content to observe. But there is a third category that is of special importance when looking at the products of popular culture.

FIGURE 7-1. Emanuel Leutze's painting *Washington Crossing the Delaware* depicts the general on his way to battle British forces on Christmas Night, 1776. The huge canvas (21 feet wide) was painted in Germany in 1851, and is now in the collection of the Metropolitan Museum of Art, New York.

Content Portraying the Just and Unjust Distribution of Power

From Karl Marx to contemporary writers like Robert Bellah,[20] politics makes sense largely in terms of the quality of the relationships that exist between members of a society. Marx, for example, was preoccupied with the abuse of power reflected in uneven and exploitative hierarchical relationships.[21] Such power may be financial, involving an organization's or individual's ability to influence the actions of others. It may also be legal, as when judges, legislators, the police, and many others are invested with power that is constitutionally defined and enforced by entrenched governmental units. Or prestige may flow to some groups and away from others in the ways traditions and core values of the culture are represented. Films or novels that define individuals as existing (and even prospering) in dominant and subordinate positions communicate a great deal—at least at the latent level—about the social distribution of power.

The legitimating effects of narration are easily seen in the observation of feminist writers and others who note that portrayals of women in film represent a reasonable—if sometimes disturbing—indication of how women are valued or devalued across the culture.

Consider the cultural and political meanings imbedded in the simple story of a prostitute portrayed by actress Julia Roberts in Garry Marshall's popular 1990 film, *Pretty Woman*. One of the fascinating truths of popular culture is that political themes have a way of surfacing in unexpected places. The story is deceptively simple. Richard Gere plays a millionaire who specializes in corporate takeovers. By an accident of chance he asks directions of a young woman named Vivian, who is standing on a corner of Hollywood Boulevard. On a fluke, he "hires" her for a week, and becomes more human and caring in the process. As a Hollywood vehicle, *Pretty Woman* is a variation on a very old theme: the prostitute with the heart of gold who is—as one critic pointed out—part Cinderella and part Pygmalion.[22] The manifest plot is predictable. She teaches him how to see the consequences of his quest for more corporate power. And along the way she teaches stuffy store clerks on Rodeo Drive that the prostitute they previously kicked out of their stores will have the last laugh.

Marshall is not a political filmmaker, nor is this talented writer and director a misogynist. Yet *Pretty Woman* has what is a remarkably retrograde subtext. It recreates the sexual politics of an earlier and less sophisticated time. It plays like a male fantasy film of the 1950s, when women were not infrequently portrayed as objects to be captured by strong protecting men. Gere's powerful businessman gives this prostitute dignity and a redeeming identity. The film wants its audience to cheer for her salvation by winning the affection of the attractive and savvy businessman. Hollywood actresses who made their careers playing tough-minded women in the 1940s (Katherine Hepburn, Barbara Stanwyck, Carole Lombard, and others) would have cringed at the empty vessel that Roberts's character represents.[23]

In such media forms, which are ostensibly not about political issues, revealing glimpses of a nation's priorities can still be persuasively defined. The conferring of power or powerlessness in many forms of art can thus be a potent kind of political advocacy.

THE POTENCY OF NARRATIVE RE-CREATION: BATTLES AND CASES

We learn a good deal about the importance of "reading" political content in the media by sampling some of the battles that have been waged by those within the entertainment industries. The often quoted maxim of Samuel Goldwyn that "Messages are for Western Union" has been repeated by many producers and writers who want to emphasize entertainment as their solitary goal.[24] But even a fast take on key moments in the history of the film industry raises suspicions that Goldwyn was expressing a wish more than a fact. Among other things, as a Jew and as one of the pivotal figures of early Hollywood, he had reasons to be concerned about rising suspicions that popular film entertainment was the perfect environment for planting the seeds of "alien" beliefs.

We begin this section with a brief look at several effects of "nativist" thinking on the film industry through its first fifty years, roughly 1905–1955. Then, the prime targets of suspicion were Jews and political liberals. That is less true today, though concerns about the liberal entertainment axis centered on each coast remains, as does the persistent fears about the ripeness of the media for indoctrination. If communist domination no longer seems possible, there are still many who believe that popular entertainment is hopelessly infected with subtle secular advocacy that erodes the sacred values and traditions. In the last half of this section we examine recent battles in the so-called culture wars that have sprung up from this concern.

Hollywood in the 1930s and '40s: Making Movies Safe from Jews, Communists, and "Subliminal" Persuasion

Americans have always had a love–hate relationship with Hollywood, even in the heyday of the large studios when the moviegoing habit was more ingrained. The film industry was then what the many facets of the television industry have since become: the prime shapers of our most evocative national fantasies. The old cliché still seems valid: Hollywood was the national dream factory. How men and women wanted to look, how they wanted to act around each other, and what they wanted to do with their lives was defined and embellished on the large screen.

The irony in this simple fact, as Neal Gabler has pointed out, is that many of those who gave the nation its most vivid glimpses of the American dream were—in the tradition-bound standards of the 1920s and '30s—quintessential outsiders. The creative entrepreneurs who developed many of the early studios were Jews of recent European ancestry. Louis B. Mayer (MGM), William Fox (20th Century Fox), Carl Laemmle (Universal), and Adolph Zukor (Paramount) were only the most visible early pioneers.[25] They shared backgrounds that excluded them and their families from the best American country clubs, the most prestigious city leagues, and the most sought-out private schools and universities.

Even while the film industry was being invented by these figures, the rest of the nation remained largely comfortable with a streak of anti-Semitism that, although less ominous than the scapegoating sweeping Germany and much of Europe, was still potent. In the 1930s some religious and civic groups at the time spoke openly about "the Jewish advantage" in the film industry, and—to quote an oxymoron straining to be an indictment—the "dangers" posed by "500 un-Christian Jews" doing the devil's work in the film industry.[26]

Part of the effect of this anti-Semitism was that it forced these enterprising men to compensate for the cloud of suspicion they lived under as non-Christian immigrants. As Gabler notes, they went out of their way to reassure the rest of the nation by providing it with flattering fantasies of largely nativist, non-European, American life. "By making a 'shadow' America . . . which idealized every old bromide about the country, the Hollywood Jews created a powerful cluster of images and ideas—so powerful that, in a sense, they colonized the American imagination."[27] They compensated for their vulnerabilities by producing a celluloid America that was politically reassuring: with some notable exceptions, their body of work was more conservative than liberal (in contrast to most Jewish citizens) and more upbeat in its themes than the original print sources from which the films were adapted, with the filmmakers themselves generally reluctant to take on major institutions, including their own board of censorship, known as the Hays Office.[28]

Perhaps what is most interesting about the anti-Semitism to which these men were forced to respond was the underlying mythology of subversion that supported it for decades. From the birth of the film industry in the early 1900s, and well into the 1950s, there was a pervasive sense that entertainment could be a vehicle for indoctrination. This fear surfaced frequently in various segments of the population, and was regularly fanned by worriers in Congress, the church, and anyone else with claims to the protection of American values. The focus in Hollywood was originally on the hidden or subliminal messages that might be communicated by Jews and immigrants.

Movie Censorship: A Case Study from the Files of the Hays Office

Between 1934 and 1968 Hollywood set up its own board of censors, named after its director, Will Hays. One significant purpose of the office was to head off direct sanctions of the studios by Congress, the Catholic Church, and others who were fearful of Hollywood's permissiveness. The Hays office reviewed scripts and routinely asked directors to alter their films in accordance to their own sense of public decency. Suicide was often a taboo, as was the portrayal of unmarried men and women in sexual situations, and clergy engaged in unseemly activity.

By all accounts one of the most beloved films ever made by director Frank Capra was *Mr. Smith Goes to Washington*. In the 1939 film, adapted from a novel called *The Gentleman from Montana*, Jimmy Stewart plays an ordinary citizen appointed to fill a Senate seat left vacant by a deceased Montana politician. Smith is generally horrified by the corruption and cynicism he finds in the work of the Senate. In some ways it was the first in a long line of stories—most recently, in Eddie Murphy's 1992 *The Distinguished Gentleman*—about craft, corruption, and the failure of professional politicians to remember their own constituents.

The Hays Office's Joe Breen discouraged Columbia Pictures and its president, Harry Cohn, from making the film:

The difficulties we sense in this story fall under the following general headings:

The United States Senate is a body of politicians who, if not deliberately crooked, are completely controlled by lobbyists. . . .

The unflattering portrayal of several senators from various specific states create the indication that a large number of senators are willing to barter their votes for tickets to the World Series.

The generally unflattering portrayal of our system of government, which might well lead to the picture being considered, both here and particularly abroad, as a covert attack on the democratic form of government.

For the above reasons, we most earnestly ask that you take serious counsel, before embarking on a production of any motion picture based on this story. . . . It looks to us like it might be loaded with dynamite.[1]

Columbia persisted and made the film. And its final scenes of Smith shaming his colleagues into reforming their own ethics remains an effective (if implausible) film moment. But the studios paid a political price from an angry Congress. Soon after the release of the film, Congress imposed harsh penalties on movie studios who bargained with theater owners by offering the "carrot" of one film to encourage bidding on more sought-after films.

[1]Gerald Gardner, *The Censorship Papers: Movie Censorship Letters from the Hays Office, 1934 to 1968* (New York: Dodd and Mead, 1987), p. 101.

Later, immediately after World War II, the nation's attention shifted to "leftist" writers, directors, and actors. This myth had its most vivid example in fears of subversion from Hollywood's creative community, especially its writers, but it has always had a life of its own.

Those who were immune to the truth and the almost desperate patriotism of the industry managed to find Russians behind most liberal political activism. Fantasies of thought control are paradoxically fed by the absence of hard evidence. The sinister works best as an unseen, subliminal force. It somehow made sense that foreigners could be intent on turning Los Angeles into Moscow on the Pacific.[29] Former Screen Actor's Guild President Ronald Reagan was certain of a Soviet plot to dominate labor unions in the film industry. Relying in part on the dubious work of the California Senate's Committee on Un-American Activities, he noted in 1965:

> *The Communists . . . used minor jurisdictional disputes as excuses for their scheme. Their aim was to gain economic control of the motion picture industry in order to finance their activities and subvert the screen for their propaganda.*[30]

At least on the surface, there is something to be said for the possibility that propaganda perhaps never works more effectively than when it appears in the benign costume of "entertainment." When we think that we are "just" being entertained, our defenses and critical judgments are probably less alert. The rhythm of television's unceasing commercial interruptions, for example, allows us to raise our defenses: one reason, no doubt, why advertisers have sought out opportunities to place their products in the context of feature films, sporting events, and other locations that perhaps disarm our natural doubts.[31]

But as a nation we tend to overstate the effects of persuasive messages, and the arsenals of those who seek our agreement. The ideas of "brainwashing" or "subliminal" (subconscious) persuasion, for example, appeal to us as the likely outcomes of expensive market research. We tend to assume that the accumulated wisdom of psychology and the social sciences has provided ways to short-circuit what are in reality the surprisingly resilient defenses that exist within us. These views of easy manipulation of the masses are aided by self-help industries and advertising agencies, who have a professional interest in presenting themselves as efficient and effective persuaders who are worthy of their high fees.

The reality, however, is far more complex. In very simple terms, attitude change is difficult to achieve, even in very well-crafted messages, and regardless of whether the appeals are rational, stunningly emotional, or both.[32] The "minimal effects" outcomes found in most persuasion research suggests that individuals do not easily change. There can be no doubt that any message or medium that is a constant part of someone's life can produce new or altered attitudes. But human attitudes are remarkably resilient in the face of external pressures for change. Anyone who has tried to talk a friend out of smoking or some other self-evidently harmful behavior knows that symbolic appeals can be effectively ignored.

Confirmation of this theory of minimal influence can be seen in the precipitous collapse of the Soviet Union. The demise of the political structure of the union was a complex and evolving phenomenon. Even so, this author and probably many others expected the elaborate state-supported system of youth groups, patriotic organizations, propaganda media, and "official art" to prop up the old power structure better than it did. The relatively rapid rise of regional loyalties in Georgia, Ukraine, the Baltic states, and elsewhere was dramatic evidence that long-standing attempts to nurture a love of the Soviet state did not easily take.

The point here is not to dismiss the idea that "political" content can be effectively communicated or advocated in the media. But it is worthwhile to remember that the fear of conversion to radical causes that existed behind concerns about Hollywood's power probably owes more to science fiction than to hard fact.

The Culture Wars: Current Battles over the "Politicalization" of the Arts

As a nation we have fallen into the grip of what James Davison Hunter has aptly described as a "culture war" to define America.[33] A major cause of this "war" is the recognition that the organs of popular culture and the mass media have the power to define what kind of society we are or want to be. In this view, consciousness *is* reality, and the media hold most of the cards in offering views we are likely to internalize. To simplify, conservatives on what Davison calls the "orthodox" side of this conflict are largely energized by the belief that media outlets should project positive, prosocial, "mainstream" values emphasizing personal responsibility, respect for the traditional, and Judeo-Christian beliefs. The liberal counterweight is a modernist impulse to embrace secularism and experimentation in the arts and media, as well as a general tolerance for social diversity.

These two views represent nothing less than different cultural worlds: different assumptions about what constitutes moral authority in society. In the orthodox view, one's character is capable of being assessed and judged, because it either conforms to, or fails to meet, the essences of what it means to live a virtuous life. By contrast, secular progressives are likely to accept variations of conduct as merely human extensions of the natural pluralism that one expects to find in a complex world.[34]

Hunter's scheme oversimplifies, but it points to the reasons the entertainment media have become so controversial as vehicles of public discourse.

Minimal Effects Theory: The Limits of Media Power

We commonly assign enormous power to the mass media in influencing attitudes and behaviors. For instance, a 1995 Time/CNN poll indicated that roughly 75 percent of Americans surveyed believed that the depiction of violence in television shows, movies, and music "inspires young people to violence."[1] Generally speaking, however, social science research on persuasion and attitude change does not support the idea that individuals are easily persuaded to alter their behavior based on exposure to single or even multiple messages. *Minimal effects theory* is the name given to the general conclusion that individual attitudes are generally resistant to change.

The theory has grown out of a number of studies from World War II to the present. What most have found is that there is significant variation in what individuals learn as a result of repeated persuasive attempts. Melvin DeFleur and Everette Dennis summarize the conclusions of this attitude-influence research:

1. People in contemporary society are characterized by psychological diversity, due to learned individual differences in their psychological makeup.

2. People are also members of a variety of social categories, based on such factors as income level, religion, age, gender, and so on. Such categories are characterized by subcultures of shared beliefs, attitudes, and values.

3. People in contemporary society are not isolated but are bound together in webs of social relationships based on family, neighborhood ties, and work relationships.

4. People's individual differences, social category, subcultures, and patterns of social relationships lead to them to be interested in, select, attend to, and interpret the content of mass communications in very selective ways.

5. Thus, because exposure to media messages is highly selective and interpretation of content varies greatly from person to person, any specific mass-communicated message will have only limited effects on the public.[2]

[1]Richard Lacayo, "Violent Reaction," *Time,* June 12, 1995, p. 25.
[2]Melvin DeFluer and Everette Dennis, *Understanding Mass Communication*, 5th ed. (Boston: Houghton Mifflin, 1994), p. 557.

As he notes, the instruments of popular culture—film, television, music, and all the rest—"define reality."

This means that the battle over this symbolic territory has practically taken shape as a struggle to influence or even dominate the businesses and indus-

tries of public information, art, and entertainment—from the major television and radio networks to the national Endowment for the Arts."[35]

We close this chapter with an extended look at the increasingly visible clash of factions over the alleged responsibilities of entertainment and arts organizations, as well as the federal government as an underwriter of some of their work. The sections that follow offer glimpses of several areas of controversy, including tax support for arts organizations, "antisocial" content in popular entertainment, and charges of regional and ideological bias in the narrative media of film and television.

Federal Funding for the Arts and Television

The year 1989 turned out to be pivotal in the long-simmering public debate about the role of federal and state governments in the funding of art and popular entertainment. More than anything else, one piece of art had triggered a public brawl about the increasing use of tax dollars to support artists, galleries, orchestras, single performers, and public television programming. However atypical it was, the focus was on a photograph by Andres Serrano called *Piss Christ*, featuring the image of a dime-store plastic crucifix in a glass container of the artist's urine. As art critic Robert Hughes notes, it represented a fairly long-established tradition in modern art of using blasphemy to comment on the cheapening of sacred icons.[36] Serrano had received a $15,000 grant from a regional group, the Southwestern Center for Contemporary Art, which had itself acquired partial funding from the National Endowment for the Arts (NEA).

When the photo traveled to Richmond, Virginia, along with other winners selected by the regional association, it attracted the attention of a self-styled lobbyist for more "wholesome" media, the Reverend Donald Wildmon. Wildmon's American Family Association had already defined itself as one of the keepers of the nation's moral values. The organization had received notoriety for its partly successful attempts to boycott the sponsors of television programs thought to contain more sex or violence than was good for the American public. It took little time to establish a letter-writing campaign to the media, other conservative religious organizations, and Congress.

In the Senate Jesse Helms took up the issue. With a recent history of controversy against funding exhibits that encompassed "degenerate works"—including Mapplethorpe's masochistic photographs—Helms neary succeeded in winning support for a congressional mandate against federal funding of "obscene" material that "denigrates, debases, or reviles a person."[37]

The presence of Serrano's and Mapplethorpe's photos served as a flashpoint in the culture war. However isolated they were from the hundreds of community organizations quietly receiving support for children's television programs, dance, classical and jazz performances, and more traditional art, they came to represent for many conservatives the corruption of culture through by a federally supported elite. "Is this how you want your tax dollars spent?" asked the American Family Association in full-page newspaper ads.

Public financing for diverse forms of culture came slowly to the United States, years after it had been a common feature in most European nations. The Corporation for Public Broadcasting (CPB), for example, was established by the Johnson administration in 1967 to foster arts and public affairs programming that the commercial networks did not want to produce. Today, along with corporate and foundation contributions, CPB is part of a crazy quilt of funding to support program production carried by PBS, the Public Broadcasting Service. Affiliated stations get most of their operating funds from state and federal taxes and viewer contributions. They may also receive CPB money for programming they originate that has been picked up by other public stations. But with so much funding from tax and corporate sources, there has been no shortage of controversy over PBS's programming, especially when it focuses on journalism out of the American mainstream.[38]

Similarly, the NEA was brought into existence in 1965 with a modest $8-million allocation from the federal budget. By 1991 that sum had swelled to $175 million, dispersed throughout the United States to support national and regional efforts in music, dance, art, and drama. Though attacks by Helms and Wildmon made it seem otherwise, the NEA followed a generally safe pattern similar to what had been done at the CPB, focusing its support on enterprises that would generally not challenge conventional sensibilities.

In many ways, the NEA and the CPB exist on an unstable bed of quicksand. Americans have a tradition of thinking of art as a distinct arena that should be separate from politics. For those on the orthodox side of the cultural divide, less government and lower taxation are always preferable to the reverse. And there is an ingrained suspicion of government as a tool of "progressive" social engineering.

Moreover, the arts in America have never had particularly close connections to local or national governments. There is no deep history of public patronage for the arts, as there has been in many countries in Europe. French and Italian opera audiences expect state and regional support for major companies; leaders can get themselves into serious trouble over the appointments and funding decisions they make to performing groups. But in the United States federal support to various individuals and organizations is a source of continuing discomfort, as least for a vocal minority. The response of arts administrators—and the organizations that depend on their funding—is often defensive and reassuring, resulting in a search for the high ground of safe and respectable programming.

Life for those who must search for funding of the higher "arts" is made even tougher when federal money functions to "seed" but not fully support exhibits and programs. Public money frequently pays for part of the costs of mounting performances, exhibits, and broadcasts. But the private sector remains an important—if generally a conservative—influence on much content. As Hughes notes:

> *Corporate underwriting has produced some magnificent results for American libraries, museums, ballets, theaters and orchestras. . . . But . . . Corporations' underwriting money comes out of their promotion budgets and—not unreasonably, since their goal is to make money—they want to be associated with popular, prestigious events. It's no trick to get Universal Widget to underwrite a Renoir show, or one of the PBS nature series (six hours of granola TV, with bugs copulating to Mozart). But try them with newer, more controversial, or demanding work and watch the faces in the boardroom drop.[39]*

Increasing Frustration with Hollywood's "Antisocial" Art

Since the mid-1980s an increasingly vocal chorus of observers has taken aim at Hollywood's tastemakers for underwriting productions of films, television shows, and recorded music that convey themes that are hostile to a broad range of "traditional values." The sins of these industries have been catalogued differently, depending in part on the ideology of the source, but there is often agreement from both the political right and the left that too much attention is given to content that is "antisocial." The charges most commonly heard are that films especially are hostile to the traditions of marriage, monogamy, the family, religious convictions and institutions, and the use of peaceful rather than violent means to resolve conflict.

Some of this criticism is simple-minded, missing one of the traditional functions of narrative as an explicator of the consequences that follow from actions. In drama, for example, context is everything. Violence in a film can be graphic, but still moralize us into disliking the act, and perhaps the villain. Such moments in films like *West Side Story*, *Regarding Henry*, or *Forrest Gump* are far different in their effects than revenge films that seem to use such mayhem as an acceptable method of resolving conflicts.

Even so, complaints about the potentially corrosive effects of television and film content—including not only violence but much more—are widespread and pervasive. In 1995 presidential candidate Robert Dole set off an intense week of media scrutiny after a speech in Los Angeles criticizing the media industries for producing "nightmares of depravity." "We must hold Hollywood and the entire entertainment industry accountable for putting profit ahead of common decency," he noted, and then singled out Time Warner for special censure.[40] Its Music Group and film interests had long come under criticism, particularly the music of Madonna and Trent Reznor, and rappers Ice-T and 2 Live Crew. "You have sold your souls," he told Time Warner's executives, "but must you debase our nation and threaten our children as well?"[41] *Time* itself made the speech the basis of its cover story for the week, with thirteen pages of coverage about the charges. Months later the company quietly sold its interests in Interscope, the record label that had created the criticism.

The film critic Michael Medved has captured many of the strands of dissatisfaction with "antisocial" media themes present in much of popular culture. He argues that "popular entertainment seems to go out of its way to challenge conventional notions of decency." He sees Hollywood as largely unable or unwilling to cope with a "crisis of values" that he believes have been created partly by the products of popular culture:

- Our fellow citizens cherish the institution of marriage and consider religion an important priority in life; but the entertainment industry promotes every form of sexual adventurism and regularly ridicules religious believers as crooks or crazies.
- In our private lives, most of us deplore violence and feel little sympathy for the criminals who perpetuate it; but movies, TV, and popular music all revel in graphic brutality, glorifying vicious and sadistic characters who treat killing as a joke.
- Americans are passionately patriotic, and consider themselves enormously lucky to live here; but Hollywood conveys a view of the nation's history, future, and major institutions that is dark, cynical, and often nightmarish.
- Nearly all parents want to convey to their children the importance of self-discipline, hard work, and decent manners; but the entertainment media celebrate vulgar behavior, contempt for all authority, and obscene language—which is inserted even in "family fare" where it is least expected.[42]

Comments like these are not limited to one side of the cultural divide. But there is an enormous divergence in opinion about the causes of media content that is "soulless," "corrosive," and "empty of meaningful values." With some exceptions, the "progressive" side of the culture war sees this content as largely a reflection of its audiences and the society they occupy. In the words of writer Katha Pollitt, "Ultimately, culture reflects society—for a violent nation, violent amusements."[43] For those on the other side, such as the influential conservative writer William Bennett, the issue is ultimately a matter of personal and corporate responsibility. At a meeting of Time Warner stockholders, Bennett, a former Secretary of Education in the Reagan

Administration, asked CEO Gerald Levin and other members of the company's board, "Are you folks morally disabled?"[44]

The irony here is that each side generally abandons its ideological roots in the ongoing debate. Conservatives often attack the media corporations for corrupting output, somewhat at odds with what one would expect to be a baseline faith in the marketplace and corporate freedom. For their part, progressives and liberals tend to define the problem in the society and, presumably, in the tastes and dispositions of the ordinary people they would normally be inclined to champion.

The Imposition of a Bicoastal Liberal Bias

In summarizing the research of two authors on the nation's "media elite," the politically conservative editors of a book described as "a reference guide to media bias" note, "Almost all of the Hollywood elite come from cosmopolitan areas, especially California and the Boston—Washington corridor. Very few . . . have roots in middle America."[45]

It is an old but common complaint that the influential entertainment and news media exist in locations that represent limited geographical regions and "liberal" states of mind. Hollywood and New York, the argument runs, are perhaps the least likely to reflect the true American Zeitgeist, and yet they serve as the decision-making and creative centers for most of our popular media. The programming decisions of the television networks, for example, are made by entertainment division chiefs whose offices look out on what is for many Americans that very foreign location known as midtown Manhattan. And those decisions are executed in an area on the opposite coast that seems equally exotic.

Actors, producers, and other "talent" in the far reaches of Hollywood are sometimes viewed as creatures occupying a very different planet. Not only do the supermarket tabloids remind us of their abnormal appetites and habits, but there is an imprecise yet palpable sense that their backgrounds and their chosen line of work have put them out of touch with America's geographical and ideological heartland.[46] The more liberal milieu of southern California has perhaps made those working there less tolerant of the older virtues that still dominate the vast regions between the two great coasts: that hard work is its own reward, that God still matters, that the family ought to remain at the center of American life.

This argument that middle-American tastes and values has been neglected is intriguing but facile. Perhaps no one would claim that those making management and creative decisions in the film or television business are "just" average Americans, either demographically or in terms of their training or motivations. But the leaders in most industries or occupations would fail the same test. Those who rise to the top in most highly competitive areas of American life carry certain advantages and attitudes. In the entertainment and news businesses, as in others, they are whiter, more male, more educated, more urban, and more Jewish than the population as a whole.[47] And in large numbers they do, indeed, tend to be concentrated on the nation's East and West coasts.

But it is easy to overestimate the effects of this bicoastalism. For example, Atlanta is home to what is arguably the largest American television news organization, CNN. Los Angeles now competes with Florida, South Carolina, and Toronto for many film projects. Faxes and e-mail have contributed to a long-term trend for screenwriters and other media workers to be dispersed throughout the country. Moreover, it takes a special kind of reverse provincialism to claim that residents of Peoria, Illinois—to pick a famous "typical" example—still live in a distinctly a different kind of cultural environment than the citizens of New York or Philadelphia. Residents in each may see slightly different geographical and ethnic environments. But they are apt to listen to the same music and news, use the same internet sources, and see the same films, books, and television shows.

Further, there is no shortage of anecdotal evidence to suggest that where one was raised is a highly unreliable guide to estimating one's access to the popular media or their biases. NBC's Tom Brokaw and CBS's Dan Rather and David Letterman are only a few of many network stars who share rural western and midwestern backgrounds (North Dakota, Texas, and Indiana, respectively, in this example). One of the most ideologically reliable conservatives on television, William F. Buckley, is a product of New York City. And perhaps the greatest liberal thorn in his side, former Harvard economist John Kenneth Galbraith, grew up in rural Ontario. Likewise, for every "New York liberal" like Woody Allen, whose Manhattan-based films and controversial personal life seem alien to many Americans, there are other directors from the same city with more populist impulses. New York City's Garry and Penny Marshall are a brother and sister who have established enviable separate careers as Hollywood directors of commercial successes. His *Beaches, The Flamingo Kid, Nothing in Common*, and *Pretty Woman* are all sturdy vehicles that largely affirm mainstream values regarding family, marriage, and work. Her career as a director is shorter, but *A League of Their Own, Big*, and *Awakenings* pay homage to similar pieties.

In the end, it is difficult to sustain the view that anyone working in the audience-driven mass media can survive if they are isolated culturally, and out of touch with the consumers everywhere they seek to reach.

Hegemony in Prime Time: Focusing on Personal Remedies to Social Problems

If the problem of a "bicoastal liberalism" remains as largely the critique of political conservatives, it can in some ways be paired with a different failure of popular narration alleged by those who might classify themselves as more liberal.

Those who put forward a theory of hegemony, like media writer Michael Parenti, argue that it is in the nature of organizations to protect themselves and to temporize when dealing with change. The organizational impulse for self-preservation is far more potent than the value of exploring rapid or realistic change that could threaten their profitable stake in maintaining attitudes and habits largely as they are. There are far greater risks in thrusting new perspectives or radical proposals on audiences and advertisers who largely want predictable forms of entertainment and nondisruptive versions of news.[48] As Parenti notes:

> *Alternative views are preempted and pushed to the margins of society, rather than censored outright. Censorship is, of course, necessary and useful, but it becomes counterproductive if relied upon too heavily. Hegemony is more effective when oppositional themes are seen as so lacking in validity as to be unworthy of exposure or rebuttal. Thus, the bulk of the public remains unaware and untouched by dissident understandings of past and present political reality.*[49]

In practical terms, the hegemony of television entertainment thus favors dramatic rather than realistic solutions to conflict. Prime time and major films are populated by apolitical figures with little tolerance for social/systemic solutions to problems. A problem is usually resolved through force, or the convenient death of a villain, rather than court injunctions. Characters deal with problems with spouses or families by finding some form of internal courage, rather than help from social service agencies or government programs.

Todd Gitlin documents a similar pattern in his extensive 1993 study of the decision-making processes involved in formulating a prime-time program. Gitlin received permission to follow the decisions of the producers of a family situation comedy under development for ABC. The pilot episode of "American Dream" that Barney Rosenzweig and others were creating was intended to be a generally frank but funny look at a family that moved back to Chicago from the suburbs. His goal was to develop episodes in which the chemistry of the city interacts with the fears and prejudices of the Novak family, an idea that came to him during a football season in which Rosenzweig went from the safety of his home to the tougher Los Angeles neighborhood where USC played its home games. Among other plots, one of the first involved the resentments of Hispanic and African-American neighbors, who fear the gentrification of their working-class neighborhood.

But the producer of "Cagney and Lacey" and other popular hits soon ran into trouble with the network. ABC wanted a host of changes to soften the few hard edges that existed in early scripts. They sought to make the characters of the Novak children more likable, and Donna Novak a less outspoken and self-assured woman. References to birth-control pills would also have to go, as would exterior shots of the graffiti-filled Chicago neighborhood. And the original idea of doing a show about middle Americans dealing with the issues of the inner city was largely abandoned. As one network executive argued, "at least for the first six episodes" the show would have to play it safer.[50]

In general terms, hegemonic theory makes the most sense when media choices within a society are limited, and when the dominant media have a clear stake in the political status quo. Both conditions are true to some extent, as noted in Chapters 1 and 2. It is also relatively easy to see in the 1950s and '60s, when the television industry and publications such as *Time* magazine had especially close ties to congressional leaders and the president.[51] But hegemony theory can easily lead one to miss the diversity that can exist even in media giants such as Disney, General Electric, and the Time Warner empire. These and other conglomerates surely retain aspects of their own corporate cultures.

But there is also a countervailing fragmentation within media industries and organizations. Some of this fragmentation is due to the number of news and information outlets available via print, broadcast, and on-line sources. We are no longer tied to just a few media outlets—such as the traditional broadcast networks—for news or entertainment. And many outlets retain their own voice, either as subsidiaries to much larger corporations, or as contractors to competitors. *Time* magazine's extensive coverage of the problems of its own parent company cited above is one such example. The continued dependence of the entertainment networks on their natural rivals, the film studios, is another. A typical NBC entertainment program is still produced by what is essentially an outside contractor. The very successful NBC comedy "Friends," to cite one instance, is partly owned by Warner Brothers, a Time Warner company. One would have to have a very simplified view of media organizations to assume their divisions and members all conform to the same political, economic, or social assumptions.

Even so, anyone who surveys the film and television industries will often look in vain for realism and a deeper understanding of the social, economic, and political realities that exist in contemporary America. Hegemony theory is a timely reminder that fantasy and melodrama may be more successful in commercial than civil terms. These popular means of escape lack accurate depictions of political, social, religious and economic institutions. As such, they teach little of what Americans may need to know about their society in the difficult years that lie ahead.

SUMMARY

Art—including most forms of popular entertainment—can no longer be ignored when assessing the forms of American political discourse. In this chapter we have touched on a number of themes tied to the general proposition that there is no distinct threshold that separates the political from the merely "artistic." Our starting point was in the basic observation that much of what gives us pleasure in our lives involves portraiture and storytelling. Stories inherently assert values and pass judgments. Films, television programs, music lyrics, and novels function to extend the political into everyday settings. Portraiture presents individuals who represent groups with identifiable political goals. The relatively unusual and sympathetic portrayal of a homosexual HIV-positive man in the 1993 film *Philadelphia*, for example, was widely seen as a breakthrough. Up to that time few commercial films had risked asking the audience to sympathize with such a victim.

Part of the argument of this chapter was that art can be political in three senses. Artists may take it upon themselves to participate in the civil affairs of the nation by using their work to participate in public debate on an issue. In a second sense art is political when it portrays historical events, re-creating words and images that evoke sympathy or anger. And finally, the creators of art and entertainment probably cannot avoid the indirect political commentary that flows from the portrayal of power relationships. The ability of a single individual to stand for a whole class of villains or victims makes art a potent form of public reassurance or social agitation. To be specific, the stature of Native Americans, African Americans, or women in our national life is unavoidably communicated in the ways in which they are portrayed in vehicles of popular entertainment.

The observer of political meaning in the context of art and popular entertainment needs to have a sensitivity for its "latent" or "subtextual" content. The wise analyst looks for levels of messages. Some meanings are manifest, as when a contemporary play or TV sketch demonizes a recent political leader. Other meanings are established in the smaller but important subtextual details of narratives that seem to be far removed from political or social issues. From this perspective we noted that the film *Pretty Woman* is entertainment, but it carries an unmistakable political subtext suggesting female dependency.

Finally, we noted that the arts are sometimes at the center of debates about how they should be financed, and how the political attitudes of their workers should be judged. The "culture war" that has surfaced in the United States over the last several decades has increasingly pitted various segments of society against one another on these and other issues. Sometimes simplified as a debate between "traditionalists" and "progressives," the discussion hinges on a number of differences that yield better questions than answers. Should the arts protect traditional "mainstream" values, or challenge them? Should federal tax money be used for arts activities and, in the process, lend legitimacy to groups such as homosexuals who may use their art to critique the prejudices and values of the larger culture? And what is the responsibility of Hollywood to the rest of society? When films and music contain messages of questionable social value, are their producers showing a "bicoastal" contempt for the rest of the nation? Or does their profit motive trigger a hegemony that keeps them from using their art to expand our understanding of deeper social realities?

However these questions are answered, it is increasingly obvious that future descriptions of political discourse will have to include a place for the diverse products of the arts and entertainment communities.

NOTES

1. George Gerbner, quoted in S. Robert Lichter, Linda S. Lichter, and Stanley Rothman, *Watching America* (New York: Prentice-Hall, 1991), p. 1.

2. H. C. Robbins Landon, *Beethoven: A Documentary Study* (New York: Macmillan, 1974), pp. 93–94.

3. David E. Pitt, "Retracing Diego Rivera's American Odyssey," *New York Times*, August 28, 1988, pp. 29–30.

4. Richard Schickel, *The Disney Version* (New York: Simon and Schuster, 1968), p. 13.

5. For a more traditional definition of art—one that dismisses the popular film—see James B. Twitchell, *Carnival Culture: The Trashing of Taste in America* (New York: Columbia, 1992), pp. 131–140.

6. For a comprehensive survey of many perspectives within this debate, see Richard Bolton, ed., *Culture Wars: Documents from Recent Controversies in the Arts* (New York: New Press, 1992).

7. A contrasting view is offered by the conservative thinker Irving Kristol, who argues that part of what is wrong with America is that it has produced postmodern art that is "politically charged" and "utterly contemptuous of the notion of educating the tastes and refining the aesthetic sensibilities of the citizenry. Its goal, instead, is deliberately to outrage those tastes and to trash the very idea of an 'aesthetic sensibility.' " Quoted in Michael Medved, *Hollywood vs. America: Popular Culture and the War on Traditional Values* (New York: HarperCollins, 1992), p. 26.

8. See Robert Hughes, *Culture of Complaint: The Fraying of America* (New York: Oxford, 1993), pp. 174–182.

9. Ibid., pp. 176–177.

10. Michael Ryan and Douglas Kellner, *Camera Politica: The Politics and Ideology of Contemporary Hollywood Film* (Bloomington: Indiana University, 1988), pp. 11, 157, 159.

11. See Mark Crispin Miller, *Boxed In: The Culture of TV* (Evanston, IL: Northwestern, 1988), pp. 69–75.

12. Beth Austin, "Pretty Worthless," *Washington Monthly*, May 1991, p. 33.

13. Benjamin DeMott, "In Hollywood, Class Doesn't Put Up Much of a Struggle," *New York Times*, January 20, 1991, Sec. 2, pp. 1, 22.

14. Jeff Silverman, "TV's Creators Face a New Caution," *New York Times*, December 8, 1991, Sec. 2, pp. 1, 31.

15. Kenneth Baker, "A Nightmare of an Exhibition that Really Happened," *Smithsonian*, July, 1991, pp. 86–95.

16. Randy Shilts, *Conduct Unbecoming: Lesbians and Gays in the U.S. Military* (New York: St. Martins, 1993). See also Kevin Buckley, "There Was not Much Worse You Could Call a Man," *New York Times Book Review*, May 30, 1993, p. 2.

17. Harold C. Schonberg, "Words and Music under Stalin," *New York Times Book Review*, October 21, 1979, pp. 1, 46, 47.

18. Kenneth Auchincloss, "Twisted History," *Newsweek*, December 23, 1991, pp. 46–49.

19. For a discussion of films judged "political" in this obvious sense, see Terry Christensen, *Reel Politics: American Political Movies from "Birth of a Nation" to "Platoon"* (New York: Blackwell, 1987); and Michael A. Genovese, *Politics and the Cinema: An Introduction to Political Films* (Needham Heights, MA: Ginn Press, 1987).

20. Robert N. Bellah et. al., *The Good Society* (New York: Knopf, 1991), pp. 138–144.

21. These applications of Marx are well developed by Hugh Dalziel Duncan in *Communication and Social Order* (New York: Oxford, 1962), pp. 181–188.

22. Roger Ebert, *Roger Ebert's Movie Home Companion*, 1992 Edition (Kansas City Mo.: Andrews and McNeel, 1991), p. 470.

23. See, for example, Molly Haskill, *From Reverence to Rape: The Treatment of Women in the Movies* (New York: Holt, Reinhart and Winston, 1973), pp. 189–230.

24. Christensen, *Reel Politics*, p. 1.

25. Their stories are brilliantly told by Neal Gabler in *An Empire of Their Own* (New York: Crown, 1988).

26. Ibid., p. 2.

27. Ibid., pp. 6–7.

28. See Gerald Gardner, *The Censorship Papers: Movie Censorship Letters from the Hays Office, 1934 to 1968* (New York: Dodd and Mead, 1987), pp. xv–xxiv.

29. For a brief survey of this period, see Robert Sklar, *Movie Made America* (New York: Vintage, 1975), pp. 249–268.

30. Ronald Reagan, *Where's the Rest of Me?* (New York: Karz, 1981), p. 159.

31. Mark Crispin Miller, "Hollywood the Ad," in *State of the Art: Issues in Contemporary Mass Communication*, ed. David Shimkin, Harold Stolerman, and Helene O'Conner (New York: St. Martin's, 1992), pp. 320–425.

32. For background on some of the research leading to this conclusion see Shearon Lowery and Melvin DeFleur, *Milestones in Mass Communication Research*, 2d ed. (New York: Longman, 1988).

33. James Davison Hunter, *Culture Wars: The Struggle to Define America* (New York: Basic, 1991).

34. Ibid., p. 126.

35. Ibid., p. 226.

36. Hughes, *Culture of Complaint*, p. 156.

37. Philip Brookman and Debra Singer, "Chronology," in Bolton, *Culture Wars*, pp. 342–347.

38. Documemtaries produced by independent filmmakers are often deemed unfit for local broadcast by affiliates fearful of offending viewers and underwriters. For examples, see Pat Aufderheide, "A Funny Thing Is Happening to TV's Public Forum," *Columbia Journalism Review*, December 1991, pp. 60–63.

39. Robert Hughes, "A Loony Parody of Cultural Democracy," in Bolton, *Culture Wars* p. 91.

40. Richard Lacayo, "Violent Reaction," *Time*, June 12, 1995, p. 26.

41. Quoted in Richard Zoglin, "Company under Fire," *Time*, June 12, 1995, p. 37.

42. Medved, *Hollywood*, p. 10.

43. "Tough Talk on Entertainment," *Time*, June 12, 1995, p. 34.

44. Zoglin, "Company," p. 39.

45. L. Brent Bozell III and Brent H. Baker, *And That's the Way It Isn't* (Alexandra VA: Media Research Center, 1990), pp. 271–272.

46. See, for example, Ben Stein, *The View from Sunset Boulevard* (New York: Basic, 1979); and Michael J. Robinson, "Prime Time Chic: Between Newsbreaks and Commercials, the Values are L.A. Liberal," in Robert Atwan, Barry Orton, and William Vesterman, *American Mass Media: Industries and Issues*, 3d ed. (New York: Random House, 1986), pp. 360–368.

47. Bozell and Baker, *And That's the Way*, p. 274.

48. For views on hegemony in news coverage, see Edward S. Herman and Noam Chomsky, *Manufacturing Consent: The Political Economy of the Mass Media* (New York: Pantheon, 1988); W. Lance Bennett, *News: The Politics of Illusion*, 2d ed. (New York: Longman, 1988), pp. 14–18; and Allan Rachlin, *News as Hegemonic Reality* (New York: Praeger, 1988), pp. 5–29.

49. Michael Parenti, *Make Believe Media: The Politics of Entertainment* (New York: St. Martins, 1992), pp. 206–207.

50. See Todd Gitlin, *Inside Prime Time*, (New York: Pantheon, 1983), pp. 86–112.

51. See, for example, David Halberstam's discussion of CBS and *Time* magazine in *The Powers That Be* (New York: Knopf, 1979), pp. 45–93, 225–255, 317–341, 351–365.

SELECTED BIBLIOGRAPHY

Adams, William. "Covering the World in Ten Minutes: Network News and International Affairs," in *Television Coverage of International Affairs*, ed. William Adams. Norwood, NJ: Ablex, 1982, pp. 3–14.

Altheide, David. *Creating Reality: How TV News Distorts Events*. Beverly Hills, CA: Sage, 1976.

Arlen, Michael. *Living Room War*. New York: Viking, 1969.

Aufdeheide, Pat. "A Funny Thing Is Happening to TV's Public Forum." *Columbia Journalism Review*, November–December, 1991, pp. 60–63.

Auletta, Ken. *Three Blind Mice: How the TV Networks Lost Their Way*. New York: Random House, 1991.

Bagdikian, Ben. *The Media Monopoly*, 4th ed. Boston: Beacon, 1992.

Barnouw, Erik. *Tube of Plenty: The Evolution of American Television*. New York: Oxford, 1979.

Bellah, Robert, et al. *The Good Society*. New York: Knopf, 1991.

Bennett, W. Lance. *News: The Politics of Illusion*, 2nd ed. New York: Longman, 1988.

Blumenthal, Sidney. *The Permanent Campaign: Inside the World of Political Operatives*. Boston: Beacon Press, 1980.

Bolton, Richard, ed. *Culture Wars: Documents from Recent Controversies in the Arts*. New York: New Press, 1992.

Boyer, Peter. *Who Killed CBS?*. New York: Random House, 1988.

Braestrup, Peter. *Battle Lines: Report of the Twentieth Century Fund Task Force on the Military and the Media*. New York: Priority Press, 1985.

———. *Big Story*, vol. 1. Boulder, CO: Westview, 1977.

Broder, David. *Behind the Front Page*. New York: Simon and Schuster, 1987.

Brownstein, Ronald. *The Power and the Glitter: The Hollywood Washington Connection*. New York: Pantheon, 1990.

Christensen, Terry. *Reel Politics: American Political Movies from "Birth of a Nation" to "Platoon"* New York: Blackwell, 1987.

Collins, Mary. "News of the Congress and by the Congress." *Washington Journalism Review*, June 1990, pp. 30–34.

Cook, Timothy. *Making Laws and Making News.* Washington, DC: Brookings, 1989.

Cornwell, Elmer. *Presidential Leadership of Public Opinion.* Bloomington: Indiana University Press, 1965.

Cose, Ellis. *The Press.* New York: Murrow, 1989.

Crouse, Tim. *The Boys on the Bus.* New York: Random House, 1972.

Davis, Richard. *The Press and American Politics.* New York: Longman, 1992.

DeFleur, Melvin, and Dennis, Everette. *Understanding Mass Communication,* 5th ed. Boston: Houghton Mifflin, 1994.

Denton, Robert, Jr. *The Prime Time Presidency of Ronald Reagan.* New York: Praeger, 1988.

Denton, Robert, Jr., and Gary Woodward. *Political Communication in America,* 2d ed. New York: Praeger, 1991.

Dionne, E. J., Jr. *Why Americans Hate Politics.* New York: Simon and Schuster, 1991.

Donovan, Robert, and Ray Scherer. *Unsilent Revolution: Television News and American Life.* New York: Cambridge University Press, 1992.

Edelman, Murray. *Constructing the Political Spectacle.* Chicago: University of Chicago, 1988.

———. *The Symbolic Uses of Politics.* Urbana: University of Illinois, 1967.

Entman, Robert. *Democracy Without Citizens.* New York: Oxford, 1989.

Epstein, Edward. *News from Nowhere.* New York: Vintage, 1973.

Fisher, Walter. *Human Communication as Narration: Toward a Philosophy of Reason, Value, and Action.* Columbia: University of South Carolina, 1987.

Fishman, Mark. *Manufacturing the News.* Austin: University of Texas, 1980.

Freedman, Warren. *Press and Media Access to the Criminal Courtroom.* New York: Quorum Books, 1988.

Friendly, Fred. *Due to Circumstances Beyond Our Control.* New York: Vintage, 1967.

Gabler, Neal. *An Empire of Their Own.* New York: Crown, 1988.

Gans, Herbert. *Deciding What's News.* New York: Vintage, 1980.

Germond, Jack, and Jules Witcover. *Whose Broad Stripes and Bright Stars?* New York: Warner, 1989.

Gitlin, Todd. *Inside Prime Time.* New York: Pantheon, 1983.

Glasser, Theodore L., and Charles Salmon. *Public Opinion and the Communication of Consent.* New York: Guilford, 1995.

Goldman, Peter, et al. *Quest for the Presidency, 1992.* College Station: Texas A and M University Press, 1994.

Graber, Doris. *Mass Media and American Politics,* 4th ed. Washington: Congressional Quarterly, 1993.

———. *Processing the News: How People Tame the Information Tide.* New York: Longman, 1984.

Grossman, Michael, and Martha Kumar. *Portraying the President.* Baltimore: Johns Hopkins, 1981.

Hadar, Leon T. "Covering the New World Disorder," *Columbia Journalism Review,* July–August 1994, pp. 26–29.

Halberstam, David. *The Powers That Be.* New York: Knopf, 1979.

Hariman, Robert, ed. *Popular Trials: Rhetoric, Mass Media, and the Law.* Tuscaloosa: University of Alabama, 1990.

Haskill, Molly. *From Reverence to Rape: The Treatment of Women in the Movies*. New York: Holt, Reinhart and Winston, 1973.

Hedges, Chris. "The Unilaterals," *Columbia Journalism Review*, July–August 1988, pp. 48–49.

Herman, Edward, and Noam Chomsky. *Manufacturing Consent: The Political Economy of the Mass Media*. New York: Pantheon, 1988.

Hertsgaard, Mark. *On Bended Knee: The Press and the Reagan Presidency*. New York: Schocken, 1989.

Hess, Stephen. "The Golden Triangle: Press Relations at the White House, State Department and Department of Defense," in Proceedings of the New York Univesity Conference on *War, Peace, and the News Media*, ed. David Rubin and Ann Cunningham. New York: New York University Press, 1983, pp. 134–164.

———. *Live from Capitol Hill!* Washington, DC: Brookings, 1991.

———. *The Government/Press Connection*. Washington, DC: Brookings, 1984.

———. *The Ultimate Insiders: U.S. Senators in the National Media*. Washington, DC: Brookings, 1986.

———. *The Washington Reporters*. Washington, DC: Brookings, 1981.

Hodgson, Godfrey. *All Things to All Men*. New York: Simon and Schuster, 1980.

Holsinger, Ralph. *Media Law*, 2d ed. New York: McGraw Hill, 1991.

Hughes, Robert. *Culture of Complaint*. New York: Oxford, 1993.

Hume, Ellen. "Why the Press Blew the S&L Scandal." *New York Times*, May 24, 1990, p. A25.

Hunter, James. *Culture Wars: the Struggle to Define America*. New York: Basic, 1991.

Iyengar, Shanto. *Is Anyone Responsible?* Chicago: University of Chicago, 1991.

Iyengar Shanto, and Donald Kinder. *News That Matters: Television and American Public Opinion*. Chicago: University of Chicago, 1987.

Jaehing, Walter, et al., "Reporting Crime and Fearing Crime in Three Communities" *Journal of Communication*, Winter 1981, pp. 88–96.

Jamieson, Kathleen. *Eloquence in the Electronic Age*. New York: Oxford, 1988.

———. *Packaging the Presidency*. New York: Oxford, 1984.

Kelman, Stephen. *The Making of Public Policy*. New York: Basic, 1987.

Kerbel, Matthew. *Edited for Television: CNN, ABC and the 1992 Presidential Campaign*. Boulder, CO: Westview, 1994.

Kernell, Samuel. *Going Public: New Strategies of Presidential Leadership*. Washington, DC: Congressional Quarterly, 1986.

Kimball, Penn. *Downsizing the News: Network Cutbacks in the Nation's Capital*. Baltimore: Johns Hopkins/Woodrow Wilson Center, 1994.

Knightley, Phillip. *The First Casualty*. New York: Harcourt, Brace Javanovich, 1975.

Laqueur, Walter. "Foreign News Coverage: From Bad to Worse," *Washington Journalism Review*, June 1983, pp. 32–35.

Larson, James. "International Affairs Coverage on U.S. Evening Network News," in *Television Coverage of International Affairs*, ed. William C. Adams. Norwood, NJ: Ablex, 1982, pp. 15–41.

Lichter, S. Robert, and Daniel Amundson. "Less News Is Worse News: Television News Coverage of Congress, 1972–92" in *Congress, the Press and the Public*, ed. Thomas Mann and Norman Ornstein. Washington, DC: Brookings, 1994, pp. 131–140.

Lippmann, Walter. *The Public and Its Problems*. Chicago: Swallow, 1954.

Lovell, Ronald. *Reporting Public Affairs*. Belmont, CA: Wadsworth, 1983.

McCombs, Maxwell. "The Agenda Setting Approach," *Handbook of Political Communication*, ed. Dan Nimmo and Keith Sanders. Beverly Hills, CA: Sage, 1981, pp. 121–140.

Madison, James, Alexander Hamilton, and John Jay. *The Federalist Papers*, ed. Clinton Rossiter. New York: Mentor, 1961.

Mann, Thomas, and Norman Ornstein, eds. *Congress, the Press and the Public*. Washington, DC: Brookings, 1994.

Markoff, John. "If Medium Is the Message, the Message Is the Web," *New York Times*, November 20, 1995, pp. A1, D5.

Matalin, Mary, and James Carville. *All's Fair: Love, War, and Running for President*. New York: Random House, 1994.

Mathews, Christopher. *Hardball*. New York: Summit, 1988.

Medved, Michael, *Hollywood vs. America: Popular Culture and the War on Traditional Values*. New York: HarperCollins, 1992.

Meyrowitz, Joshua. *No Sense of Place*. New York: Oxford, 1985.

Miller, Mark. *Boxed In: The Culture of TV*. Evanston, IL: Northwestern, 1988.

Murrow, Edward R. "Address to the Radio and Television News Directors." *Reporter*, November 13, 1958, pp. 32–36.

Nelson, Barbara. "Making an Issue of Child Abuse," in *Agenda Setting: Readings on Media, Public Opinion, and Policy Making*, ed. David L. Protess and Maxwell McCombs. Hillside, NJ: Lawrence Erlbaum, 1991, pp. 161–170.

Nimmo, Dan, and James Combs. *Mediated Political Realities*, 2d ed. New York: Longman, 1990.

———. *Nightly Horrors: Crisis Coverage in Television Network News*. Knoxville: University of Tennessee, 1985.

Nimmo, Dan, David Swanson. *New Directions in Political Communication*. Newbury Park, CA: Sage, 1990.

Olsen, Walter. *The Litigation Explosion*. New York: Plume, 1991.

Paletz, David, and Robert Entman. *Media Power Politics*. New York: Free Press, 1981.

Parenti, Michael. *Inventing Reality: The Politics of the Mass Media*. New York: St. Martins, 1986.

Patterson, Thomas. *Out of Order*. New York: Knopf, 1993.

Postman, Neil. *Amusing Ourselves to Death*. New York: Penguin, 1986.

Rachlin, Allan. *News as Hegemonic Reality*. New York: Praeger, 1988.

Rada, S. E. "A Class Action Suit as Public Relations," *Journalism Quarterly*, Spring 1985, pp. 150–154.

Rivers, William. *The Adversaries: Politics and the Press*. Boston: Beacon, 1970.

Robinson, Michael. "American Political Legitimacy in an Era of Electronic Journalism: Reflections on the Evening News." *Television as a Social Force: New Approaches to TV Criticism*, ed. Richard Adler. New York: Praeger, 1975, pp. 97–139.

Robinson, Michael, and Kevin Appel. "Network News Coverage of Congress," *Political Science Quarterly*, Fall 1979, pp. 413–436.

Robinson, Michael, and Margaret Sheehan, *Over the Wire and on TV: CBS and UPI in Campaign '80*. New York: Russell Sage, 1983.

Rogers, Everett, and James Dearing. "Agenda Setting Research: Where Has It Been and Where Is It Going?" in *Communication Yearbook*, vol. 11, ed. J. Anderson. Beverly Hills, CA: Sage, 1988, pp. 555–594.

Roschwalb, Susanne, and Richard Stack. "Litigation Public Relations," *Communications and the Law*, December 1992, pp. 3–23.

Rosenstiel, Tom. *The Beat Goes On: President Clinton's First Year with the Media*. New York: Twentieth Century Fund, 1994.

———. *Strange Bedfellows: How Television and the Presidential Candidates Changed American Politics, 1992*. New York: Hyperion, 1993.

Ryan, Michael, and Douglas Kellner. *Camera Politica: The Politics and Ideology of Contemporary Hollywood Film*. Bloomington: Indiana University Press, 1988.

Sabato, Larry. *Feeding Frenzy: How Attack Journalism Has Transformed American Politics*. New York: Free Press, 1991.

———. *The Rise of the Political Consultants*. New York: Basic, 1981.

Sanit, Tal. "The New Unreality: When TV Reporters Don't Report," *Columbia Journalism Review*, May–June 1992, pp. 17–18.

Schneiders, Greg. "The 90-Second Handicap: Why TV Coverage of Legislation Falls Short." *Washington Journalism Review*, June 1985, pp. 44–46.

Schorr, Daniel. *Clearing the Air*. New York: Houghton Mifflin, 1977.

Schram, Martin. *The Great American Video Game*. New York: Murrow, 1987.

Schuetz, Janice. "Narrative Montage: Press Coverqage of the Jean Harris Trial," *Journal of the American Forensic Association*, Fall 1988, pp. 65–77.

Sennett, Richard. *The Fall of Public Man*. New York: Vintage, 1978.

Shoemaker, Pamela. *Gatekeeping*. Newbury Park, CA: Sage, 1991.

Simon, Roger. *Road Show*. New York: Farrar, Straus, and Giroux, 1990.

Smith, Hedrick. *The Power Game: How Washington Works*. New York: Random House, 1988.

Smith, Sally. *In All His Glory: The Life of William S. Paley*. New York: Simon and Schuster, 1990.

Smolla, Rodney, *Free Speech in an Open Society*. New York: Knopf, 1992.

Sperber, A. M. *Murrow: His Life and Times*. New York: Freunlich, 1986.

Sperry, Sharon. "Television News as Narrative," in *Understanding Television: Essays on Television as a Cultural Force*, ed. Richard Adler. New York: Praeger, 1981, pp. 295–312.

Steel, Ronald. *Walter Lippmann and the American Century*. New York: Vintage, 1981.

Steele, Richard. "News of the 'Good War': World War II News Management," *Journalism Quarterly*, Winter 1985, pp. 707–716.

Stephens, Mitchell. *A History of News: From the Drum to the Satellite*. New York: Viking, 1988.

Stoler, Peter. *The War Against the Press*. New York: Dodd and Mead, 1986.

Taylor, Paul. *See How They Run*. New York: Knopf, 1990.

Tedford, Thomas. *Freedom of Speech in the United States*, 2d ed. New York: McGraw Hill, 1993.

Thaler, Paul, *The Watchful Eye: American Justice in the Age of the Television Trial*. New York: Praeger, 1994.

Thompson, Mark. "With the Press in the Persian Gulf," *Columbia Journalism Review*, November–December 1987, pp. 40–45.

Tidmarch, Charles, and John Pitney, Jr. "Covering Congress," *Polity*, Spring 1985, pp. 463–483.

Trent, Judith, and Robert Friedenberg. *Political Campaign Communication*, 2d ed. New York: Praeger, 1991.

Tuchman, Gaye. *Making News: A Study in the Construction of Reality*. New York: Free Press, 1978.

Tulis, Jeffrey. *The Rhetorical Presidency*. Princeton, NJ: Princeton University Press, 1987.

Turner, Kathleen. *Lyndon Johnson's Dual War*. Chicago: University of Chicago, 1985.

Twitchell, James. *Carnival Culture: The Trashing of America*. New York: Columbia, 1992.

Vatz, Richard, and Lee Weinberg. *Thomas Szasz: Primary Values and Major Contentions*. Buffalo: Prometheus, 1983.

Volk, Patricia. "The Steinberg Trial: Scenes from a Tragedy," *New York Times Magazine*, January 1989, pp. 22–25.

Waite, Teresa. "As Networks Stay Home, Two Agencies Roam the World," *New York Times*, March 8, 1992, p. F5.

Wallis, Roger, and Stanley Baran. *The Known World of Broadcast News*. New York: Routledge, 1990.

Webster, David. "New Communications Technology and the International Political Process," in *The Media and Foreign Policy*, ed. Simon Serfaty. London: Macmillan, 1990, pp. 219–228.

Wicker, Tom. *On Press*. New York: Viking, 1978.

Wilkie, Carol. "The Scapegoating of Bruno Richard Hauptmann: The Rhetorical Process of Prejudicial Publicity," *Central States Speech Journal*, Summer 1981, pp. 101–110.

Woodward, Bob. *The Agenda: Inside the Clinton White House*. New York: Simon and Schuster, 1994.

Woodward, Gary, and Robert Denton, Jr. *Persuasion and Influence in American Life*, 2d ed. Prospect Heights, IL.: Waveland, 1992.

———. "The Rules of the Game: The Military and the Press in the Persian Gulf," in *Mass Media and the Persian Gulf War*, ed. Robert Denton, Jr. New York: Praeger, 1993, pp. 1–26.

Zelizer, Barbie. "CNN, the Gulf War, and Journalistic Practice." *Journal of Communication*, Winter 1992, pp. 66–81.

INDEX